INNOCENT III

THE MEDIEVAL WORLD
Editor: David Bates

Already published

. . . .

INNOCENT III

Leader of Europe 1198–1216

Jane Sayers

LONGMAN
London and New York

Longman Group Limited
Longman House, Burnt Mill,
Harlow, Essex CM20 2JE, England
and Associated Companies throughout the world.

*Published in the United States of America
by Longman Publishing, New York*

First published 1994
Second impression 1995

ISBN 0 582 08342 7 CSD
ISBN 0 582 08341 9 PPR

British Library Cataloguing-in-Publication Data

A catalogue record for this book is
available from the British Library

Library of Congress Cataloguing in Publication Data

Sayers, Jane E.
Innocent III: leader of Europe, 1198–1216 / Jane Sayers.
p. cm. – (The Medieval world)
Includes bibliographical references and index.
ISBN 0-582-08342-7. – ISBN 0-582-08341-9 (pbk.)
1. Innocent III, Pope, 1160 or 61-1216. 2. Popes–Biography.
3. Popes–Temporal power. 4. Church history–12th to 13th century.
5. Europe–Church history–600-1500. I. Title. II. Title: Innocent three. III. Title:
Innocent 3. IV. Series.
BX1236.S38 1993
282' .092–dc20 92-46028
[B] CIP

Set by 77 in 11/12 Baskerville
Produced by Longman Singapore Publishers (Pte) Ltd.
Printed in Singapore

CONTENTS

EDITOR'S PREFACE

Innocent III is undeniably one of the most important popes of the medieval period. His pontificate has long been a subject of interest and fascination. It attracts superficially because so much happens; kings are deposed, crusades are launched, the friars begin their long history, and the Church's attitude to heresy is redefined and pushed in a new, less tolerant direction. At a deeper level, it commands our attention because within it are expressed so many of the problems and paradoxes which typify the institution's complex history; the pope's rule was supposedly above the world, yet in practice it was inextricably entangled in it. Innocent tried to decide the disputed succession to the empire, yet he ended up accepting the candidate whose accession he had tried to prevent, and being criticized for underhand manipulation rather than praised for even-handed mediation. The Fourth Crusade, on which so much time was spent, and so much hope pinned, was diverted against his wishes against Constantinople. Yet his reign ended soon after the triumphant Fourth Lateran Council and his achievements with regard to the Church's pastoral work, its law and its government are obvious and considerable.

Jane Sayers brings her great experience in the study and interpretation of the sources for the history of the twelfth- and thirteenth-century papacy to this new book on Innocent III. Of vital importance is her wide-ranging familiarity with both the papacy's own records and with the sources from Europe's regions, most notably, England. Her treatment is therefore appropriately papally-centred, but it also examines how Innocent's authority was regarded and how his subjects reacted to his rule. The influences which shaped both Innocent personally and the papacy at the time of his pontificate are discussed in depth. An intellectual and psychological formation which gave Innocent an interest and expertise in pastoral work and law is emphasized. The role of tradition at the heart of the exercise of papal authority is made explicit, and it is made clear that, for all his personal dynamism, Innocent was not a free agent because of the intellectual, spiritual and legal characteristics of the office he occupied. Jane Sayers' *Innocent III* eschews the determinist approaches which have seen the medieval papacy as driven inexorably towards autocracy and bureaucracy, or which place his pontificate within a pre-ordained process of decline. The book is a history of a religious institution, but it is also a social history. Theory and practicalities, ideals and opportunism are all given their place. Innocent's pontificate is set firmly within the context of his own times. He is seen again and again seeking to relate theology, law and morality to the vast changes which were taking place within the Christian and non-Christian worlds during his lifetime. A great pope is shown grappling with the immense range of problems which rule over Christendom and responsibility for Christian souls entailed.

David Bates

PREFACE

In writing this book I have had the help of Professor Uta-Renate Blumenthal, who read the complete typescript and made many important suggestions. I hope that I have faithfully incorporated these, but she is in no way responsible for any doubtful views that remain. Dr Diana Greenway gave up valuable time to go through the whole work very carefully, pointing out errors and inconsistencies, and I am deeply grateful to her also for her perception and general interest. I have had the benefit, too, of the constant support, encouragement and wide experience of both Dr David Bates, the editor in charge of the series, and Longman, the publishers. I wish to thank them all.

Behind my interpretation of Innocent and his world hovers the influence of the late Walter Ullmann, one of the great scholars of the medieval papacy and a dynamic controversialist – intent on understanding the modes of thought of a sometimes alien world. This book must mirror the utterly absorbing lectures and the highly illuminating instruction that took place in Cambridge's Mill Lane Lecture Rooms for we are all shaped by influences in our past. It also owes much no doubt to other papal scholars whose works fill the bibliography.

The final touches to the book were completed in Rome in glorious September sunshine and thanks are due to the Augustinian canonesses of the SS. Quattro Coronati for allowing access to the chapel of St Sylvester, and to Signorina Carla Battelli, who made possible a journey to the birthplace and home region of Pope Innocent III – Gavignano, Segni and Anagni – negotiating all the hairpin bends and narrow streets.

J.E.S.
September 1992

LIST OF MAPS

LIST OF ABBREVIATIONS

c	canon, capitulum
col	column
EHR	*English Historical Review*
ep	epistola (letter)
Gesta	*Gesta Innocentii Papae III* in *Patrologia Latina* 214 (Paris 1890) cols 17–227
LC	*Le Liber Censuum de l'Eglise Romaine* ed. P Fabre and L Duchesne, Bibliothèque de l'Ecole française d'Athènes et de Rome 2 sér. vi, 3 vols (Paris 1899–1952) vol 3 is the index
MGH	Monumenta Germaniae Historica
SS	Scriptores
PL	*Patrologia Latina* ed. J P Migne (Paris 1844–64)
Reg. Inn. III	*Die Register Innocenz' III.* ed. O Hageneder, A Haidacher, W Maleczek, A Strnad (Publikationen der Abteilung für Historischen Studien des österreichischen Kulturinstituts in Rom (Graz-Köln, Rom-Wien 1964, 1968, 1979) Yrs 1–2, 2 vols + index to 1: edition continues
RNI	*Das Register Papst Innocenz' III. über den Deutschen Thronstreit* ed. W Holtzmann (Latin text) 2 pts (Bonn 1947–8)
RS	Rolls Series
SCH	*Studies in Church History*

SLI   *Selected Letters of Pope Innocent III concerning England (1198–1216)* ed. C R Cheney and W H Semple (Nelson: London and Edinburgh 1953)

X   'Decretales' (law collection compiled under Pope Gregory IX) in *Corpus Iuris Canonici* ii ed. E Friedberg 2 vols (Leipzig 1881)

Where x is found between two dates it means that the event took place at some precise (but to us unknown) time between those dates.

FOR MY MOTHER

INTRODUCTION

. . .

THE POPE'S REPUTATION AND CHARACTER

Future generations came to look upon Innocent III as one of the greatest of medieval popes; indeed, one of the greatest of all the popes. But on what does this reputation rest? How far can we say that he was individually responsible for some of the massive changes that are apparent at this time – the claim of the papacy to intervene in European affairs, to act as universal arbiter and lawgiver? Were the great challenges that he met new? Was it, perhaps, particular circumstances that made it possible for him to leave his imprint on Europe? Who were his advisers or did he act alone?

This book will try to answer some of these questions and to examine all aspects of the pontificate. This means, in effect, looking at the whole of medieval Europe in the first decades of the thirteenth century and even beyond its frontiers. We must explore the influences on him and how government worked in this period. Clearly a person's outlook is formed by background and training, but there is also the factor of individual personality.

It is not possible, even if it were desirable, to write a full biography of a medieval person. But we need to discover all we can about Innocent. We have some idea of his personal appearance from two well-known portraits, almost contemporary, which may be likenesses, but there is no death mask so there is no certainty. It was customary to portray important figures as it was thought they ought to look, rather than as they actually were, and the portraits may well be idealized and show him in symbolic papal vestments. According to written sources, he was of medium height and good-looking – a conventional description. There is a mosaic portrait of *c.* 1200 from old St Peter's, which was formerly in Poli, a stronghold of his family – the Conti. He has large eyes and a longish nose and a moustache. It is reproduced in C. W. Previté-Orton *The Shorter Cambridge Medieval History* (Cambridge 1952) ii 648. Gerhard Ladner has gone deeply into the whole subject of surviving representations and reproduces them all.[1] There is also a fresco of Innocent III in the church of Sacro Speco, Subiaco, illustrated in Geoffrey Barraclough *The Medieval Papacy* (1968) pl. 48 and in John Godfrey *1204 The Unholy Crusade* (Oxford 1980) pl. 2.[2] In these pictures, and in the famous Giotto scene of the dream (see below pp. 125–6), he is represented in ceremonial mitre, pallium and mantle. After Innocent III's pontificate, representations of popes became more common and the popes were depicted more frequently in mitre, pallium and mantle. We know something, too, about the speech of this most eloquent of popes (described as 'eloquent in both the spoken and the written word') from his letters, and about his behaviour from books and chronicles. Most revealing are the impressions he made on observers.

We also know that he had a sense of humour – though sometimes acid. Much of it was wit, like his remark at the Lateran Council, when he allowed the admission of the ex-emperor Otto's ambassadors with the words, 'Even the devil would have to be given a hearing – if he could repent'. There was a cutting edge, too, to the pope's comment, which became incorporated in canon 10 of the Lateran Council decrees, that the bishops were not able to preach because of heavy burdens, 'not to say for lack of knowledge'. Many of the jokes were what we would

---

1. G B Ladner *Die Papstbildnisse des Altertums und des Mittelalters* 2 vols + plates, Monumenta di Antichita Christiana 2nd ser. 4 (Città del Vaticano 1941–70) ii 53–79 and plates ix–xii.
2. This is also reproduced as the frontispiece to James M Powell *Anatomy of a Crusade 1213–1221* (Philadelphia 1986), but it is wrongly assigned there.

describe as 'in' humour and had to do with verbal play. For this reason, as Stephan Kuttner has said, it is difficult to transmit or reproduce. For example, the popes had long styled themselves in their letters 'servant (or serf) of the servants (or serfs) of God', so when the pope was consulted about the absolution of certain serfs who had attacked clerics in Denmark, he wrote that they might be absolved by the archbishop of Lund unless their crime was so heinous that they should be sent to 'the serf of serfs' for absolution. In another instance, the pope rejected a certain decretal, or letter making a legal decision, on the grounds that it was a forgery, as he put it, a 'concretalis' or fabrication rather than a 'decretalis' or decretal. A similar play was made in another letter on the words 'divinus', divine, and 'divinare', to devine or to prophesy, where Innocent said 'We take the place of the *Divine* on earth but we cannot *divine* what is unknown'.[3] And when the archbishop of Trier, torn in allegiance between the Staufen king and the pope, fell from his horse and was unable to attend the royal court, Innocent declared 'Oh! What a happy fall!' (*casus* meaning both fall and chance).

These humorous outbursts are extremely interesting especially when they occur in letters, because the humour is personal and cannot have been the product of an administrative machine. To my mind this proves the point that the pope did compose some of his own letters. Often, however, it is difficult to disentangle Innocent speaking from the official verbiage of the chancery officers. But there does seem to be a lighter side to his character which is in contrast to the solemnity of some of the great and sonorous papal pronouncements.

We need to examine closely the pope's political role and its basis. Authority in the medieval period meant rulership and this was a rulership that did not come up from the grass roots of the populace or people, but transcended down from supernatural sources – from God. No medieval political theorist thought otherwise. Power came from above. As the pope was its main mouthpiece, we need to try to understand his aims and his opportunities.

3. S Kuttner 'Universal pope or servant of God's servants: the canonists, papal titles and Innocent III' in *Revue de droit canonique* **32** (1981) 134–5, and *X.* V. 39. 37. and *X.* III. 12. 1.

We must not assume that medieval modes of thought were similar to our own. It appears to have been commonly accepted that the position of the pope would be developed and made clear as the historical process continued. The divine will would be unfolded in its own time. Tierney speaks vividly of the 'conception of a "potential" power inherent in the apostolic see that became explicit only through the unfolding of a long historical process in which the popes themselves were involved as active participants'.[4] The idea of the divine will shaping human history, an essential determinism, has to be borne in mind if we are to understand actions and inevitable human inconsistencies. Tierney has pointed out that it seemed quite consistent to medieval people that a king was supreme in his own realm but limited by divine and natural law and that any king who swallowed up the jurisdiction of his inferior lords would be denounced as a tyrant. There was authority, but there were supernatural limits. This may seem like special pleading but it is necessary to keep in mind if we are to get nearer our goal.

The great English historian F. W. Maitland wrote:

Let us change our point of view. The medieval church was a state. Convenience may forbid us to call it a state very often, but we ought to do so from time to time, for we could frame no acceptable definition of a state which would not comprehend the church. What has it not that a state should have? It has laws, lawgivers, lawcourts, lawyers. It uses physical force to compel men to obey its laws. It keeps prisons. In the thirteenth century, though with squeamish phrases, it pronounces sentence of death. It is no voluntary society. If people are not born into it, they are baptized into it when they cannot help themselves. If they attempt to leave it, they are guilty of the *crimen laesae maiestatis* and are likely to be burnt. It is supported by involuntary contributions, by tithe and tax. That men believe it to have a supernatural origin does not alter the case. Kings have reigned by divine right,

4. B Tierney 'The continuity of papal political theory in the thirteenth century. Some methodological considerations' *Mediaeval Studies* **27** (1985) esp. 236–8.

and republics have been founded in the name of God-given liberty.[5]

And the pope was the head of this organization. His government of the Church was through the law, which he made and declared. During the pontificate, Innocent held a great council of the whole Church at his palace of the Lateran in Rome. Lay representatives were present. Kingdoms were subject to the pope and he claimed a right to approve the emperor.

Within the church structure there was some social mobility. Furthermore, churchmen or clerks were necessary to medieval secular rulers because of their writing and communication skills. They became trusted advisers and counsellors. Their social origins were immaterial. They might come from humble backgrounds and rise to prominence through the favour of kings. The non-hereditary nature of all clerical offices allowed for careers open to talents. Although great clerical dynasties grew up in the early twelfth century, when clergy were sometimes married, by the 1150s papal disapproval of clerical marriage and of illegitimate priests began to bite through legislation. Nor was it permissible or acceptable for benefices or churches (providing the income of the priest) to be bought and sold. For a clergyman to obtain a living by purchase was simony, the sin of Simon Magus (Acts 8: 9–24). Many laymen owned churches, that is to say they had the right of appointing to them, but they had to appoint an ordained or licenced priest, and the bishop needed to approve. Likewise lay rulers, emperors and kings, had an enormous say in the appointment of archbishops and bishops. The royal chancellor, who headed the civil service and administration, was frequently a bishop or an archbishop. Some royal administrators and higher ecclesiastics were aristocrats and the relations of kings, but many more were men of reasonably humble background. By the thirteenth century they were unlikely to have families to provide for – other than nephews. They did not have estates or titles to pass on to relatives or sons.

5. F W Maitland *Roman Canon Law in the Church of England* (1898) 100.

5

Unlike most medieval monarchies, the papacy was elective. Most kingships, of England and of France, for example, were hereditary. The German emperorship, however, and the kingship of the Romans, that went with it, was elective. The princes of the empire constituted the electors and chose from among their number. Because the emperorship was closely connected with the papacy from its origins, popes claimed a right of approving emperors. And emperors, in the tenth and early eleventh centuries, claimed the right to take part in the election of a pope. Strong emperors had been able to appoint whom they liked and Charlemagne had even tried a pope. But gradually the right of the emperor and of the people of Rome to participate in papal elections was eroded. Before Innocent's time election had come to be solely by the cardinals, the pope's advisers. Technically they could choose any Catholic, even a layman. Obviously all sorts of influences and pressures were brought to bear, especially from the important Roman families, but popes did not all come from within Rome and Italy and not all of them were born of noble parentage.

It is obvious that we are not dealing with a dynasty in the sense of a royal dynasty or monarch, but with a clerical caste – a distinctive and exclusive group of people to whom it may be difficult to relate.

The Church is often thought, not without reason, to be one of the most conservative of bodies. Certainly, by its very nature, it must have conservative elements if it claims to reveal eternal truth. But there have always been changes in attitudes towards its role and changes in attitude as to how its mission may be best achieved. There is, of course, in all institutions and governments an ongoing process of change, but it is more marked in some periods than in others. There were those who saw the Church as too structured, hierarchical and legalistic, who thought that popular religion was becoming divorced from the religion of Rome and that lay people were being excluded from real and active participation in religion. The new movements desired a return to what they thought was the simple life of the early Church. Followers desired to live in poverty and to explore, explain and listen to the Scriptures. Some claimed certain priestly functions. So it became necessary to define what was heretical, but the problem was not merely a legal one. How far was Innocent III open to new views, influences and pressures? Was he able to see the possibilities and importance of some of the movements in revitalizing the Church and invigorating society?

Very prominent in this pope's mind were the crusades and the crusading ideal. The mission of Christians on earth was, after all, to convert, and the possession of the earthly Jerusalem was of deep symbolic importance to those who desired to travel to the heavenly city. Perhaps appropriately enough this is the subject of the last chapter.

. . .

THE SOURCES FOR THE HISTORY OF THE PONTIFICATE

It may sound a contradiction to say that the sources are limited but rich. As I have suggested above, they are limited in relation to certain questions. They are also obviously limited in that most of them are sources from within the Roman curia itself. But having said that, there is a better run of official registers of correspondence with all parts of Europe than for any previous pope.[6] There is also the extremely interesting Secret Register (*RNI*) of the pope's correspondence during the imperial schism. There are the law collections and the decrees of the Fourth Lateran Council which show us the sources of authority and tell us much about papal administration and aims. Finally, there is the unique *Gesta*, or 'Acts of the Pope', written by someone from within the curia and extremely close to Innocent, for the author had access to the papal correspondence. It is the nearest thing we have to a biography and there is nothing comparable for other medieval popes. It is concerned most of all with the politics within the Papal State and Sicily. But it also covers other topics of the reign – the Crusade, Philip Augustus's marriage, the Canterbury election, the Patarenes of Milan and papal relations with the rulers of Aragon, Armenia, Norway, Constantinople and Bulgaria. The work ends in the year 1208. Opinions differ but it has been suggested that the

6. These are printed in Latin in *PL* 214–17 and some letters for England are printed and translated in *SLI*.

first part was finished before 1203, when the pope's life was despaired of. Further chapters were then added in 1206, 1207 and 1208.[7] The pope himself wrote several short books, including a best-seller 'On Contempt for the World', as cardinal, and preached some influential sermons of which we have the texts. These tell us much about his training and attitudes.[8]

There are also chronicle accounts written by visitors to Rome and the papal curia. Most notable of these for England are the chronicles of Roger of Howden, who was in Rome at the time of the election of Innocent, and Thomas of Marlborough, who went to the papal court on behalf of the convent of Evesham in Worcestershire and wrote an account of his experiences. Burchard of Ursberg, a Premonstratensian canon from the diocese of Ursberg, is informative about the new religious groups, some of whose members he encountered at Rome in 1210. Both he and the chronicler, Richard of San Germano, are well-informed about the empire and the Annals of Marburg is another chronicle interested in imperial affairs during this period. But there are no imperial archives, or for that matter royal archives, to match the papal archives at this time. The nearest are the records of the English kings. Royal registration of records begins in England in 1199, contemporary with Innocent, but there is no specific registration of dealings with the popes until the Roman rolls commence under King John's grandson, Edward I. Odd little bits, sometimes gossip, sometimes personal impressions or stories, are recorded by Gerald of Wales and the chronicler of Melrose abbey in Scotland. Satire is evident from the pens of the German poet, Walter von der Vogelweide, and the unknown author of 'A new Solomon (i.e. Innocent) reigns'. Finally, as a chilling epitaph, there is the account of Jacques de Vitry, who saw the corpse of the great pope

---

7. Printed in *PL* 214: I have not been able to consult David Gress-Wright 'The *Gesta Innocentii III*: text, introduction and commentary' (Ph.D. Bryn Mawr College 1981). For an assessment see W Imkamp *Das Kirchenbild Innocenz' III (1198–1216)* (Stuttgart 1983) 10–20 and B Bolton 'Too important to neglect: The Gesta Innocentii PP III' in *Church and Chronicle in the Middle Ages. Essays presented to John Taylor* ed. I Wood and G A Loud (Hambledon 1991) 87–99.
8. Printed in *PL* 217.

at Perugia, naked and decomposing, and the looted tomb, and who was thus led to contemplate the passing splendours of this world. In the words spoken three times at the papal coronation, with the burning of the flax, 'Sic transit gloria mundi'. But it is to the living pope and his age that we will now turn.

Chapter 1

THE POPE AND THE PAPACY

. . .

THE FORMING OF INNOCENT III'S PERSONALITY:
INFLUENCES AND EDUCATION

Political imagery expressed in pictures, in elaborate ceremonial and in official narrative sources is the public face
of government. From an early date the imperial palaces
at Constantinople incorporated decorative schemes that
emphasized and glorified imperial power and dominion.
According to the historian Eusebius, when the Emperor
Constantine (*c.* 280–337) became a Christian in the early
fourth century, his triumph over the enemies of the
Church, represented as a dragon, was depicted in a scene
at the entrance to the imperial palace which showed him
trampling upon the beast.

The papacy used similar techniques and by the ninth
century, perhaps even before, pictorial schemes were found
in the papal palace and in the basilica at the Lateran.
Round the walls of the palace of St John Lateran in Rome,
the main residence of the medieval popes, and in the great
church or basilica itself, were series of paintings and -
mosaics that depicted the history of the papacy, an institution
that was already very ancient in 1198 when Innocent III
became pope. The twelfth-century papacy was rooted in a
distant and revered past. The papacy had been born in the
ancient world and owed many of its traditions, as well as its
administrative functions, to late imperial Rome. The popes,
as bishops of Rome, had a 'genealogy' going back to the
first pope, the apostle Peter. As in a great Jesse window, the
ancestry of the pope could be portrayed descending from

the apostle to whom Christ had said 'Thou art Peter and upon this rock I will build my Church'. Scenes of triumph in the papacy's long struggle for political and spiritual dominion were presented in pictures that made contemporary and future generations aware of past landmarks in its eventful history.

Among the themes familiar to visitors to the Lateran in the twelfth century were three which were doubtless familiar to Pope Innocent III. The first was the Legend of St Sylvester and the Donation of Constantine,[1] the second the triumph of the legitimate popes over the anti-popes of the early twelfth century, and the third the settlement of the Investiture Contest.[2] All had a marked influence on the papacy's outlook and development. It is not important to be concerned with the historical veracity of these statements (for in any case they were often added to, touched up and re-interpreted) but with the impact that they had. They were a political statement, providing an account of the past and also a programme for the future.

The late fifth-century Legend of St Sylvester was represented in the portico or main entrance of the medieval Lateran basilica which had been the church of the Emperor Constantine. Here were shown Sylvester I (bishop of Rome from 314 to 335) triumphing over the dragon (symbolizing the enemies of the Church), baptizing the Emperor Constantine, and receiving the 'Donation' from him. According to the Legend – the propaganda of a papacy that by this time was endeavouring to assert its independence of the emperor – on the eighth day after his conversion, the Emperor Constantine divested himself of the imperial symbols, prostrated himself before Pope

---

1. On the Legend and Donation, see Walter Ullmann *A History of Political Thought: the Middle Ages* (1965) 59–62 and *The Growth of Papal Government in the Middle Ages* (1955) 74–86.
2. On the pictorial side in general see Christopher Walter 'Papal political imagery in the medieval Lateran palace' *Cahiers Archéologiques* **20** and **21** (Paris 1970–1) pt i 155–76 and pt ii 109–36, and Gerhard Ladner 'I mosaici e gli affreschi ecclesiastico-politico nell'antico palazzo Lateranense' *Rivista di Archeologia Cristiana* anno xii (1935) 265–92. The frescoes in question have not survived but they are known from Panvinio's sixteenth-century drawings in the Vatican Library. Some of them have been illustrated in Geoffrey Barraclough *The Medieval Papacy* (1968).

Sylvester and laid down his crown. Sylvester, however, refused to wear the imperial crown above his clerical tonsure (by this gesture perhaps accentuating the superiority of his priestly office). So Constantine actually placed the imperial crown, the *phrygium*, on the pope's head. The Legend also proclaimed that Constantine had recognized the unique spiritual status of the Roman see, confirming the primacy of Rome and of the see of St Peter over the four patriarchates of Antioch, Constantinople, Alexandria and Jerusalem. The forged document, the so-called 'Donation of Constantine', which was drawn up before the mid-eighth century, when the papacy was anxious to use and control the Frankish leaders, claimed that Constantine had given his imperial palace of the Lateran and dominion over 'the city of Rome and all the places, cities and provinces of Italy and the West' to Pope Sylvester, handing the pope his imperial insignia and symbols – the lance, sceptre, orb, imperial standards, purple-scarlet mantle, imperial pallium and tunic. So began the long history of the temporal power of the pope, of the pope's control of the Western empire, of papal monarchical powers and of the Papal State, the territories of the pope that survived until 1870. The Donation also claimed that the Emperor Constantine on ceremonial occasions had performed the office of *strator* (leading the horse) and *strepa* (holding the stirrup) for the pope, signifying an almost feudal servility. Later the Emperor Frederick I (Barbarossa) was to maintain that this ceremony had gone out of use and he refused to perform the office for the English pope, Adrian IV, at Sutri in 1155. But, after he had been persuaded by the princes, he later performed it. He may well have seen the picture in the great series of paintings in Pope Innocent II's (1130–43) new rooms at the Lateran.[3] Perhaps this is one of the most vivid examples we have of the effect of the pictorial image on the medieval mind. The eighth-century forger of the Donation, doubtless working within the papal circle, and assisted by later papal propagandists and artists, had provided a most effective story.

3.   There is a fresco of the 'strator' scene in the chapel of St Sylvester in the church of SS. Quattro Coronati (not far from the Lateran) in Rome. In sequence it follows the 'Donation' which is illustrated in Barraclough *Medieval Papacy* pl. 13.

The second series of pictures showed the triumph of the true popes over the anti-popes. These pictures were to be found in the Audience Hall of Pope Calixtus II (pope from 1119 to 1124) at the Lateran.[4] They were known to several medieval writers, including the mid-twelfth century Norman bishop and controversialist, Arnulf of Lisieux. Based upon the iconography of the Roman Empire and of the late Byzantine emperors, the scene showed the anti-pope, Gregory VIII (1118–21), under the foot of Pope Calixtus, the victor, who is trampling his victim in a way reminiscent of the victorious emperors of the past. The Emperor Henry V stands to Calixtus's left. A series of anti-popes, usually candidates of the German emperor for the papal throne, had almost threatened the existence of the medieval papacy and had brought the papacy to a low state in the twelfth century. For not only was the papacy's practical influence severely circumscribed by schism, and the development of its governmental powers halted, but no theory of papal power could be developed with two contenders for St Peter's chair. The unseemly scene on the death of Pope Adrian IV in 1159, when, on the election of the chancellor, Roland, as Pope Alexander III, the anti-pope, Octavian (Victor IV) tore the scarlet papal mantle from the shoulders of Alexander and attempted to carry it off, is recorded by Alexander's biographer, Boso. Furthermore, it was Victor IV who drove Alexander from the city of Rome, represented by Boso as the true pope's 'kingdom'.[5] The issues of anti-popes and schisms were still very much alive in the late twelfth century.

The third most momentous event in papal history, which would have meant much to Innocent III and to all visitors to the Lateran, was the great struggle for dominion between the pope and the emperor, known as the Investiture Contest. The big scroll in the frieze between Pope Calixtus II and the Emperor Henry V contained the first words of the text of the Concordat of Worms of 1122, with the rest of the text to be found elsewhere in the hall.[6] Made in the

4. See Christopher Walter 'Papal political imagery' i 162–6 and ii 109–21. Drawing reproduced in Barraclough *Medieval Papacy* pl. 41.
5. *Boso's Life of Alexander III* introduction by Peter Munz, trans. G M Ellis (Oxford 1973) 43–5.
6. The text no longer survives: for the contingent documents see Robert L Benson *The Bishop-Elect* (Princeton 1968) 228 section 2.

reign of Calixtus, it was obviously seen fitting that it should end the series of pictures of the popes involved in the struggle. For the Concordat, in theory at least, brought to a close the Investiture Contest of the twelfth century. To understand the meaning of the Investiture Contest for the men of the early twelfth century, prior to the pontificate of Innocent III and his successors, we have to remember that the issues were not settled in the way which we now know to have been the outcome. The Concordat, described as 'the best negotiated settlement in Western history', confirmed the German emperor's renunciation of investiture of bishops with the ring and the crozier and the pope's concession that episcopal elections should be held in the presence of the king. But the contest between the two rulers or super-powers was of much deeper significance, amounting to a total re-assessment of Christian society and its government. Investiture was the symbolic part of a struggle behind which there were fundamentally different views about the whole ordering of society and about who was the divinely appointed agent for that purpose. It concerned the source of power and its correct agents and was an investigation into the moral justification for the exercise of political authority. It had repercussions throughout Europe.

The message of these pictorial images was reflected in Innocent III's speech or sermons. On the occasion of the feast of St Sylvester, 31 December, the pope preached a sermon in which he chose to point out that Pope Sylvester was 'sublime' because he had both regal (or royal) power and pontifical (or priestly) power. It was the Emperor Constantine who had given Pope Sylvester the whole kingdom of the West and had attempted to give him the crown. As a sign of his imperial power the pope used the *regnum* (the tiara) and as a symbol of his pontifical power he used the mitre. Innocent's views of Sylvester's position reflected his ideas of his own office as a dual one, for which the Old Testament figure of Melchizedek, the priest and the king, was the prototype. He was 'priest ... according to the order of Melchizedek' (Psalm 110: 4), and vicar of Him who was 'king of kings and lord of lords' (Revelation 19: 16).[7] The

---

7. Sermon VII, *PL* 217 cols 481–2C. The year in which it was preached is unknown.

towering figure of Melchizedek, the priest and the king, and therefore the embodiment of power, was much loved by Innocent, who in his writings constantly returned to the dual aspect of Melchizedek's powers, which were combined, he argued, in the person of the pope. The use of the colourful example of Melchizedek fitted well into Innocent's conception of the pope as 'vicar of Christ', for Christ, too, was both king and priest ('rex' and 'sacerdos').[8] Sylvester was also, says Innocent, the vicar of Christ and successor of St Peter.

Innocent was consecrated pope on the feast of St Peter's Chair or Throne (22 February), which was for him deeply symbolic. His sermon on the primacy of Peter (which mirrored exactly what he had said on the subject in a tract written before he became pope, 'De primatu Romani pontificis') explored the authority by which the pope governed, the Petrine commission.[9] Christ had entrusted the government of His Church to St Peter and his successors in the words, 'Thou art Peter and upon this rock I will build my Church' (Matthew 16: 18) and 'I will give to thee the keys of the kingdom of heaven and whatsoever thou shalt bind upon earth, it shall be bound also in heaven' (Matthew 16: 19). Only to St Peter had the plenitude of power thus been given. Christ had constituted the primacy of Peter and of his successors who were 'sublime' in power, constant in the faith, shepherds of the flock. 'I have set thee over the nations', as the prophet Jeremiah says (Jeremiah 1: 10) and as Innocent quotes. The pope was thus successor of St Peter, between God and man, inferior to God but above man, St Peter's vicar, but also, as Innocent now claims, 'vicar of Christ', as St Peter had been, rather than vicar of St Peter. As we have seen, he had applied this conception, too, to his predecessor, Sylvester.[10] The idea of the pope exercising the vicariate of Christ had been expressed by Pope Adrian IV some forty years before:

8. K Pennington 'Pope Innocent's views on Church and State' in *Law, Church and Society. Essays in honor of Stephan Kuttner* ed. K Pennington and R Somerville (Philadelphia 1977) 56–7 summarizes Innocent's views of Melchizedek.
9. Sermo II in *PL* 217 cols 653–60; cf cap. 7 col 778 for his views on this expressed in 'De sacro altaris mysterio'.
10. Pope Gelasius had said that Christ was the last 'rex et sacerdos'.

'we who, although unworthy, act on behalf of Christ on earth'. It originated probably with St Bernard in the late 1140s or early 1150s in his address to the first Cistercian pope, Eugenius III, whom he calls 'vicar' and 'vicar of Christ', but it had only been employed domestically within papal circles before Innocent's time.[11] Innocent was the first pope to proclaim publicly that he was the vicar of Christ – a title that had been used previously of themselves by the Byzantine emperors and by the Emperor Henry III (d. 1056). Under Innocent it was to become commonplace in the official correspondence of the curia. The implications of the vicariate of Christ and Innocent's conception of his office are at the heart of an understanding of both his view of the past and his view of his role. As a Roman, the pictorial imagery of the historic papacy surrounded him. His mental imagery, on the other hand, reflected influences from wider sources and to understand this we need to examine what is known about the relatively young pope – he was 37 or 38 – elected to the chair of St Peter in January 1198, whose reign later generations came to see as 'the apogee of the medieval papacy'.

Fortunately we have the *Gesta* (or 'Acts of the Pope'), composed for posterity by a close contemporary (possibly even, it has been argued, by the pope himself). From this splendid source we know important facts about his parentage, background and education.

He was born Lothar dei Conti of Segni in 1160 or 1161 during the long reign of Pope Alexander III. Maternal influence did not much interest contemporaries usually, unless some obvious connection could be established, or possibly where the connections on the distaff side were more impressive and influential. This was the case with Innocent's mother, Claricia Scotti (Romani de Scotta), from the Roman family to which Pope Clement III (1187–91) belonged. Lothar owed his first promotion to his uncle, Pope Clement III. Claricia Scotti had married into the Contis of Segni, small landowners in the Anagni region to the south-east of Rome. According to a source from Viterbo, Lothar was born at Gavignano near Segni. The

---

11. *PL* 188 col 1383 ep 15; *PL* 182 col 451 ep 251 and *Saint Bernard On Consideration* trans. G Lewis (Oxford 1908) bk ii ch 8.16.

Conti family house still survives at the top of the ridge on which the little hill town is built: it has extensive views across to Segni and also to Anagni. Lothar received his earliest education in Rome, probably at the Benedictine abbey of St Andrea al Celio where his teacher was Peter Ismael. This suggests that he was already intended for a career in the Church. He may have been the second, or a younger, son.[12] He had a brother, Richard, who was later to play an important part in the family's advancement in Rome, being destined to take over the running of the Conti estates in the Romagna. A son who might rise in the Roman priestly hierarchy was essential to family and dynastic interests.

Paris

Paris was the intellectual magnet of the mid-twelfth century – the place where a dynamic and promising young man would wish to be. Sons of the Roman aristocracy, eager to pursue careers in the curia found their way early on to the Paris schools.[13] Between the 1150s and the 1180s connections between the curia and Paris were built up as the *studium*, or university, began to form. Romans, and even some men from southern Italy, were attracted to Paris as the intellectual centre of Europe at this time. Previous popes had been in France, and the teaching of the school of St Victor in Paris and of Peter Abelard was known to them, but Innocent III may have been the first pope to have studied at the Paris schools.[14] (He is certainly the first pope for whom we have direct evidence that he had been at a centre of learning.) Other members of the curia also by the late twelfth century had been nurtured on Parisian ideas and Lothar himself later promoted some of his fellow

12. This is not the commonly held view, see the genealogical tree in M Dykmans 'D'Innocent III à Boniface VIII. Histoire des Conti et des Annibaldi' in *Bulletin de l'Institut historique Belge de Rome* **45** (1975), but it might explain his entry into the Church.
13. See Peter Classen 'Rom und Paris: Kurie und Universität im 12. und 13. Jahrhundert' in *Studium und Gesellschaft im Mittelalter* ed. J Fried (MGH Schriften **29**, 1983) 127–69, esp. 153.
· 14. The future Pope Celestine III defended Abelard against St Bernard and it is likely that he was in France during the crisis; see D Luscombe *The School of Peter Abelard* (Cambridge 1969) 22, but there is nothing to suggest that he was a student at Paris.

scholars to high office in the Church.

By the time that Lothar arrived in Paris, probably in the 1180s, perhaps earlier, the theology taught there was no longer the speculative, probing theology of Peter Abelard (which was perhaps the reputation that had brought him there in the first place), but had become more concerned with practical issues and doctrine. Among his teachers were Peter the Chanter, Peter of Poitiers, who commented on the Sentences of Peter Lombard (as well as producing his own Five Books of Sentences before 1170), Melior of Pisa and Peter of Corbeil.[15] Peter of Corbeil was a theologian who lectured on scripture and was famous as a preacher. He was considered an original thinker, linking the old twelfth-century theological ideas with the new interests of the thirteenth. Lothar remained grateful to him, praising his knowledge and, as pope, conferring benefices on him. Peter of Corbeil was recommended for a prebend in York, given the bishopric of Cambrai in 1199 and then translated to the archbishopric of Sens in 1200.

Traces of Parisian teaching are to be found in some of Innocent's letters, with their biblical quotations and scholastic distinctions. Prior to Theology, he may have pursued an Arts course when he was a young man. He retained an affection for Paris and a gratitude for the intellectual advantages that it had given him to which he later referred as pope. During this period we know no more about him. But more is heard of his colleagues, Stephen Langton and Robert of Courson. The Englishman, Stephen Langton, from Lincolnshire, was to become the foremost biblical scholar of his day and was to stay and teach in Paris. Both he and Robert of Courson, another Englishman, were made cardinals by Innocent. Langton was to be promoted archbishop of Canterbury by Innocent and so began the long quarrel between the Holy See and King John. Courson, whose interests were in moral theology, was, as legate, responsible for the University of Paris's first statutes in 1215. He seems to have been an influence on Innocent and we are almost surely not far from the mark in imagining

---

15. See John W Baldwin *Masters, Princes and Merchants* 2 vols (Princeton 1970) ii esp. chs 1–5 and W Imkamp *Das Kirchenbild Innocenz' III (1198–1216)* (Stuttgart 1983) 31.

long discussions between the three on theology and politics.

It may have been during his time at Paris that the young Lothar, perhaps in the company of these two and other students, visited the shrine of St Thomas Becket at Canterbury. Chance evidence from one chronicle records that he stayed at the Benedictine abbey of Andres in the Pas de Calais on his way before crossing the Channel. Pope Alexander III had canonized Thomas in 1173, while the papal court was at Segni, the home town of Lothar's family, the Conti. The canonization of Becket may have made a lasting impression on the future pope Innocent, at the time a boy of twelve or thirteen. Certainly the Becket conflict had wider repercussions than an insular struggle between English king and archbishop and the principles and arguments in the quarrel were widely discussed, for there were deeper issues relative to the nature of authority.

Whether Innocent was ever tempted to stay in Paris and to teach, like his fellow student Stephen Langton, we do not know. To his time as cardinal we owe some theological treatises. Despite the fame (at least in the medieval world) of Innocent III's 'De miseria conditionis humane' or 'De contemptu mundi', there is nothing very inspiring about it.[16] Plentiful quotations from the Bible and from the Fathers show a competence but nothing more. There are also citations of Peter Lombard's *Sentences*, of Peter of Poitiers' Sentences, and of Ovid's Ars Amatoria (possibly taken from Peter the Chanter's *Verbum Abbreviatum*), perhaps showing the influence of his teachers. He also cites Lucan, Claudian, Horace, Ovid, Josephus, Pope Gregory the Great's *Dialogues* and certain common medieval myths and stories. There is little evident originality. For that we have to look elsewhere. It has recently been called to our attention that Innocent added the notion of the Church of purgatory to the Church militant (the Church on earth) and the Church triumphant (the Church in heaven), championing the idea of three armies that acted through fire, combat and praise. The Church of purgatory was the 'suffering' Church and the dead for Innocent existed only

---

16. No fewer than 672 manuscripts have been noted. For edition and translation, see Lotario dei Segni (Pope Innocent III) *De Miseria Condicionis Humane* ed. and trans. Robert E Lewis (1980).

through and for the living. This he argued in a sermon delivered on All Saints' Day.[17] There are, too, certain other ideas that scholars are now examining. Further research may demonstrate that he had some knowledge of science and of medicine. He was, it seems, interested in the prolongation of life; but the picture of the sheer gloom of human existence expressed in 'De Contemptu' – which apparently so appealed to contemporaries – does little to enthral the modern reader. Rather it takes us a step away from understanding him. The other tracts which were written by Lothar before he became pope show a pastoral concern, an interest in almsgiving, in sin, in penance, in the sacrament of marriage and in the priestly office ('De sacro altaris mysterio'): perhaps what one might expect of a Paris theologian of this period. The 'Misery of the Human Condition' was to have been followed by a treatise on 'The Dignity of the Human Condition', which was never written, presumably because of Lothar's election as pope.

The cardinal bishop of Porto and St Rufina, to whom the 'De miseria' is dedicated, was Peter Gallocia, created cardinal in 1190 by Pope Clement III. He, too, came from a Roman family and perhaps in some way had been the patron of the young cardinal deacon of SS. Sergio and Bacco as Lothar then was. He was a diplomat of standing, carrying out negotiations with the Emperor Henry VI and with the Byzantine emperor in Constantinople. According to the English chronicler, Roger of Howden, he aspired to the papacy on the death of Pope Celestine III in 1198.[18] Was Lothar, perhaps, dedicating his work to the man he saw as the likely next pope? We do not know.

The statement of his biographer (*Gesta* cap. 2) that Lothar shone above his contemporaries in philosophy and theology is symptomatic of the *Gesta's* generally eulogistic approach. It is impossible to know how far Lothar's own personal interests and inclinations determined general policy, but the proceedings of the great general council of

---

17. See J Le Goff *The Birth of Purgatory* trans. A Goldhammer (1984) 174, 209; *PL* 217 cols 578–90.
18. *Chronica Magistri Rogeri de Houedene* 4 vols ed. W Stubbs (RS 51, 1868–71) iv 33 (hereafter cited as Howden). W Maleczek *Papst und Kardinalskolleg von 1191 bis 1216. Die Kardinäle unter Coelestin und Innocenz III.* (Vienna 1984) 95–6 on Peter.

the Lateran which was to be held near the end of the pontificate were well in line with what he and others had
absorbed on pastoral care at Paris in the last quarter of the
twelfth century.

The 'De missarum mysteriis' of *c.* 1195 shows Cardinal
Lothar as something of a biblical scholar, teasing out
meanings from texts that accentuated the pope's particular
primacy as successor to St Peter.[19] Paris had given him the
intellectual edge and the authority to do this. In discussing
the Petrine texts, Innocent showed his indebtedness to
Paris influences – to the school of St Victor, to Robert of
Courson and to Peter Comestor. We do not know how long
he stayed in Paris – it could have been as long as a decade.
Parisian influences remained strong throughout his life.
However, he was also imbued with papal influences that
came to him no doubt from his Roman and 'papal' background, from Pope Gregory VII and from St Bernard in
his tremendously important address to Eugenius III. It was
not that what he said was startlingly new, for it was based
on a long tradition, but his particular talent and novelty
was that he managed to combine biblical exegesis with
growing papal ideology, to induce the texts to mean something of relevance to his leadership of society.

Bologna

Lothar of Segni's legal education remains something of a
puzzle. The *Gesta* clearly states (though very briefly) that
he studied at the great law university of Bologna. This must
have been in the two years between the autumn or summer
of 1187, when he left Paris,[20] and September 1189, by
which time he had been created a cardinal deacon by his
relative, Pope Clement III.[21] Pope Gregory VIII (the

---

19. Matt. 16: 18–19; Luke 22: 32; and John 21: 15–17: the three texts
that gave St Peter authority over the Church as a whole, over the
Eastern Church, and over kings and bishops. See K Froehlich 'St
Peter, papal primacy, and the exegetical tradition, 1150–1300' in
The Religious Roles of the Papacy: Ideals and Realities, 1150–1300 ed. C
Ryan (Toronto 1989).
20. Innocent returned from Paris via Grandmont in the company of
Cardinal Octavian of Ostia, another heavy-weight in the curia at
this time; Maleczek *Kardinalskolleg* 103 n. 357.
21. H Tillmann *Pope Innocent III* trans. W Sax (Amsterdam 1980) 13–14
n. 51.

former chancellor, Albert de Morra, who had contacts with France), who enjoyed only a ten-week pontificate, had already made him a subdeacon between October and December 1187. This appointment, the lowest rung on the Church's ladder, would not, however, have prevented him from undertaking a period of study at Bologna. The sub-deacon's duties were to prepare the bread and wine and the vessels for the mass and to chant the Epistle. It may have been during this period that he was supported by a canonry in St Peter's, to which he later referred as pope.[22]

Until recently,[23] it had been assumed that the greatest of the medieval pope–lawyers was a pupil of the renowned Master Huguccio of Pisa, teaching in Bologna at this time, whose *Summa* on the *Decretum* of Gratian was well-known and whose teaching, linking theology with canonistics, the science of the Church's law, attracted students. Although the evidence for Lothar's having studied under Huguccio is far from conclusive, the overwhelming weight of the pope's own utterances, turn of mind and passionate inter-est in law seem to endorse the statement of the *Gesta* that he did indeed study at Bologna. Moreover the statement which follows this, namely that he was learned in both human and divine law, as his letters, registers and decretals demonstrate, must preclude Pennington's doubts that he studied law and, most especially, his suggestion that a bright young man would have gone to Bologna at this time to study anything other than law. (He makes the half-hearted suggestion of Lothar's having studied notarial arts.) During his pontificate Innocent chose to surround himself with lawyers. Perhaps if he had not been created a cardinal dea-con he would have stayed in Bologna longer. In any case, length of stay does not predetermine his competence. At Bologna in the late 1180s Lothar may have made the acquaintance among his fellow students of Peter Collivaccinus

---

22. *Reg. Inn. III* i no. 296 p. 418: Maleczek *Kardinalskolleg* 102 and n. 356. As pope, he erected a mosaic at St Peter's with the inscription 'the Mother of Churches' – a definite snub to the Lateran.

23. K Pennington 'The Legal Education of Pope Innocent III' *Bulletin of the Institute of Medieval Canon Law* n.s. **4** (1974) 70–7 and again in *Zeitschrift für Rechtsgeschichte* kan. abt. **113** (1986) 417–28. Maleczek *Kardinalskolleg* and W Imkamp *Das Kirchenbiled Innocenz' III* have dis-puted this with Pennington.

of Benevento, and others, who were later to be important in the legal developments of his pontificate, collecting papal legal decisions or decretals. In sum, it remains extremely likely in view of the pope's keen interest in the law that Lothar did study at Bologna. However, it is unlikely that he is to be identified with Lothar, colleague of the great Romanist Pillius, whom the convent of Canterbury sought to enlist in June or July 1187 in the course of their great struggle with the archbishop.[24] Lothar's (and later Innocent's) knowledge of Roman law is uncertain. He does not cite Roman law sources very often,[25] but he had a practical turn of mind and was active in curial business and administration. Contrary to older views – which saw him as out of favour in papal government under Celestine III (from the Boboni family) – he signs most of the papal privileges in the seven years between 1191 and 1197.[26] While his passion for theology seems to have pre-occupied him mainly during his period as a cardinal, he would not have been the first to have changed the direction of his interests when more practical challenges came his way.

. . .

ELECTION

Lothar of Segni was elected pope on 8 January 1198. He succeeded two Roman popes and a long line of Italians. Only Calixtus II, who was French, and Adrian IV, who was English, broke the sequence of Italians during the twelfth century. He also succeeded a pope, Celestine III, who was 85 at the time of his election and therefore over ninety at the time of his death. Celestine had maintained power through an inner caucus of some seven to ten cardinals, a group that did not include the young Lothar, cardinal deacon of SS. Sergio and Bacco.[27] Lothar's biographer in the *Gesta* makes the point that following Celestine's death he did not immediately join the cardinals assembled in the Septizonium, but attended first the exequies, or funeral

---

24. *Epistolae Cantuarienses* ed. W Stubbs (RS 38, 1865) 68.
25. J Michael Rainer 'Innocenz III und das römische Recht' *Römische Historische Mitteilungen* **25** (1983) 15–33; an attempt to evaluate Innocent's knowledge of Roman law.
26. Maleczek *Kardinalskolleg* 364–76.
27. Maleczek *Kardinalskolleg* 351–2.

rites, for the dead pope, which were taking place in the Lateran basilica.

In the Septizonium, an ancient Roman temple at the south-east corner of the Palatine, which had long since been annexed for other uses, safe from outside interference and imperial troops, for it was still possible for emperors to attempt to interfere with elections, the election commenced after each cardinal had celebrated mass and all of them had exchanged the kiss of peace.[28] Examiners were then chosen to scrutinize the sealed votes and note them down. Apparently Lothar received a majority on the first ballot, but not the two-thirds majority made necessary by the constitution 'Licet de vitanda' of the Third Lateran Council of 1179. This constitution, which had its origins in Roman law, made no distinction among the ranks of the cardinals (i.e. whether bishop, priest or deacon) as to voting rights and allowed an election even if only a small number of the whole college were present, provided there was the necessary majority. By this time, too, the citizens of Rome had been excluded from papal elections; they had formed an important pressure group in the past. Even more important, the emperor's participation, which had accounted for the selection of many eleventh-century popes (and anti-popes) had been totally rejected by 1179. With the introduction of the two-thirds rule, the old principle of 'the greater and *saner* [or most weighty] part' disappeared from papal elections. The implementation of the constitution of 1179 saved the Church from the double elections and schisms which had dogged Alexander III's and previous reigns. The new principle of a two-thirds majority of those present, as it were a head count – without discriminating between them as to worth, age and weightiness – was undoubtedly responsible for Lothar's election. He was almost certainly not the candidate of the *saner* part. Their candidate was probably the cardinal

28. In general on election, see P Herde 'Election and abdication of the pope: practice and doctrine in the thirteenth century' *Proceedings of the Sixth International Congress of Medieval Canon Law*, Berkeley California 1980 (Monumenta Iuris Canonici Ser. C Subsidia 7, Città del Vaticano 1985) 411–36, esp. 411.

priest of St Prisca, John of St Paul, one of the previous ruling caucus. The old pope, Celestine III, had attempted to secure his succession before his death, offering to abdicate in John of St Paul's favour. There may have been some support for him among the cardinals, but they were not prepared to act in concert and several now put themselves forward. The two-thirds majority of only those who were present meant that the views of legates and those absent from the curia on business at the time of the death of a pope carried no weight in the election of a successor. (It was not until the 1939 conclave that *all* the cardinals were present at a papal election, due as one observer put it to 'the advance of medicine and transport'.) The views of the absentees were not canvassed or taken into account. Nineteen to twenty cardinals appear to have taken part in the election of Lothar. We know that there were three other nominations but not whom two of them were, assuming the third to have been John of St Paul.[29] The two unknown cardinals may have been the diplomats and curial heavyweights, Peter Gallocia, cardinal bishop of Porto and St Rufina (to whom Lothar had dedicated his book) and Octavian, cardinal bishop of Ostia, a powerful Roman, both of whom had opposed Celestine's favoured candidate.[30] The English chronicler, Roger of Howden, who was in Rome at the time, saw both of them as *papabile* and ambitious for the papal throne. He is not always reliable, but he may well be correct when he mentions that there were other candidates, including John of Salerno, cardinal priest of St Stefano in Celiomonte (who he says withdrew from the second ballot), and possibly Jordan of Fossanova, former abbot of Ceccano, cardinal priest of St Pudenziana, and Gratian, cardinal deacon of SS. Cosmas and Damian, a lawyer and nephew of the earlier pope Eugenius III.[31] The latter two cardinals had considerable experience abroad.

29. On the election see Maleczek *Kardinalskolleg* 354; Herde 'Election and abdication' on the principles and background.
30. Maleczek *Kardinalskolleg* 80–3, 95–6.
31. See Howden iv 33–4, 174–5; and Maleczek *Kardinalskolleg* 71–3, 86–8, and a critique of Howden by Maria L Taylor 'The election of Innocent III' in *The Church and Sovereignty c. 590–1918. Essays in honour of Michael Wilks* ed. Diana Wood (*SCH* **9**, 1991) 97–112.

The discussion that is recorded about Lothar's age suggests that some were at first not too keen to elect a pope in his thirties who, on recent record, might last for half a century. On the other hand, the pressing need for a dynamic pope to exploit the political vacuum left by the unexpected death of the Emperor Henry VI and the advantages of a third Roman pope in a row may have won over the opposition – and there may have been those impressed by his vigorous views on the papacy's role. Or perhaps he was the compromise candidate who got in because neither of the two senior cardinal bishops was acceptable to the other party's supporters.

As soon as the election was completed and announced in the words 'St Peter elects Lothar pope', three doves flew into the place where the cardinals were assembled and when Lothar was singled out from the others the whitest of them settled on his right shoulder. It was also revealed in a vision that the future pope should take the Church as his wife, and more such visions were experienced but, says the biographer, he refrains from recounting them because Lothar did not like such phenomena to be reported. The new pope was given the name Innocent by the archdeacon and invested with the scarlet mantle which signified his pontificate. He was then led to the high altar where he prostrated himself while the chant 'Te Deum laudamus' was sung. After receiving the kiss of peace from the other electors, the new pope was escorted to St John Lateran, the church of the bishop of Rome. There, within the portico of the basilica, the curious ceremony of seating the pope in the marble chair, called the *sedes stercoria*, took place, from which he was lifted to signify being raised from 'the dust and the dung'. Within the Lateran palace itself, a further ceremony with two seats of porphyry (one of St Peter and one of St Paul) signified the double apostolic foundation and the jurisdictional and magisterial power of the pope, demonstrated by his half lying and half sitting across the two. Physical possession was taken of every room in the palace and a straight staff was handed to the new pope as well as the keys of the basilica and of the palace. He had assumed his lordship like any other feudal lord. He received the homage of the members of his household before going to pray at the oratory of St Laurence, which was filled with relics of the saints, and finally retiring to his private apartments.[32]

.   .   .

CORONATION

The height of the symbolism and ritual in the process of making a new pope was reached in the ceremony of consecration, coronation and enthronement. This exhibited in an outward and visible form the power of the papacy as it had developed by the late twelfth century. This ceremony was witnessed by the members of the pope's entourage, his erstwhile colleagues among the cardinals, with their attendants, and the clergy and people of Rome, plus those visiting the Holy City.[33] It must be seen, as it undoubtedly was by contemporaries, as the constituent part in the ultimate making of the pope, the shafting of eternal power down to St Peter's successor. The pope, as St Peter's heir and bishop of Rome, needed episcopal orders – the highest orders of the Church which gave the bishop power to ordain priests, confirm members of the Church and bless the holy oils which were used for ordinations and for the sick. As Lothar was still only in the lower clerical orders, those of the deacon, he had to be ordained priest, which could only take place on the ember days, so accordingly the ceremonies were delayed until Saturday and Sunday 21/22 February, six weeks after the election. On the Saturday he was ordained a priest and on the following morning, appropriately the feast of St Peter's Chair, the full ceremonial began in St Peter's, when Innocent, anointed with the holy oils by Octavian, cardinal bishop of Ostia, was consecrated a bishop. The archdeacon, in traditional role, gave the pope the pallium (the narrow strip of

32. The procedure followed was that of Ordo Romanus 12, see *PL* 78 chs 77–9, where the different arrangements for a pope elected in or outside the city and whether already consecrated or not are stipulated. On the Lateran palace, see P Lauer *Le palais de Latran* (Paris 1911); in particular, the heads of the two apostles, Peter and Paul were here.

33. The *Gesta* (ch 7) says there were present at his consecration, four bishops (presumably the four cardinal bishops), 28 bishops (presumably from the regions or with business in Rome), six priests (? cardinal priests), nine cardinal deacons and ten abbots (presumably mainly from abbeys in or near Rome).

lamb's wool worn over the shoulders), the symbol of the fullness of power of the pontifical office. Thus robed, the pope proceeded to the altar and celebrated mass, during which the *Laudes* were chanted.[34]

The heart of the ceremony – and the singular feature of the splendid but awesome occasion – was the enthronement. The new pope was enthroned in the most sacred place in the basilica of St Peter, in front of the *confessio* or altar of St Peter, close to the mortal remains of the apostle to whom Christ had committed the government of His Church on earth. No medieval emperor – even the greatest and most powerful – was ever enthroned, and this distinguishing feature of papal ceremonial underlined the pope's uniqueness. Now the new pope, Innocent, was escorted to the front of the basilica where on a platform in full view of the people, he was crowned with the tiara, the senior deacon (i.e. the archdeacon) removing the mitre from the pope's head and replacing it with the tiara. The tiara was in essence a white cap, having two bands at the back like a mitre,[35] but it had incorporated in it a coronet round the lower rim to which was added a second coronet under Pope Boniface VIII at the end of the thirteenth century, symbolizing sacerdotal and regal powers. It is first heard of at the coronation of Pope Nicholas II in 1059, when it appears that because the mitre had passed into general use by bishops (and even by princes) the pope's own headgear had to undergo change to become distinctive and exclusive to the pope.[36] Seated on the chair or *cathedra* of St Peter, the pope now received the kiss of peace – the ceremony of proskynesis, where, starting with the youngest, the cardinals advanced to kiss his feet.

Then began the ceremony of circumventing the city. Mounted on a white horse and crowned with the tiara, the pope, accompanied by high-ranking church officials, the cardinals and abbots, the civil officers, the prefect and the senator of Rome, the nobles, and the consuls and rectors

34. *PL* 78, Ordo Romanus 12, chs 81–2.
35. See Barraclough *Medieval Papacy* pl. 48 and *Shorter Cambridge Medieval History* ii 648 for pictures.
36. See W Ullmann *Growth of Papal Government* 314 esp. on the source found for the new headgear – the Donation of Constantine and the *phrygium.*

of the papal cities processed through the whole city from St Peter's to the Lateran so that the new pope might be seen by the people. The procession stopped at various points along the route for the new pope to receive the homage of the people and to distribute alms; the clergy swinging thuribles of incense and the people laden with palms and flowers, singing hymns and canticles. After acclamations before the Lateran Palace, like those that had already taken place in front of St Peter's, the new pope went up to the principal part of the palace, called the Leonine presbyterium, and later celebrated with a banquet.

. . .

THE CITY OF ROME

Rome, unlike Avignon (and, indeed, many other cities) was inconveniently placed for easy relations with most of Europe and cut off from the north-west, where the papacy's influence was strongest, by the great mountain range of the Alps. However, because of its history and position as the see of St Peter and the imperial city, Rome was without challenge or rival. Other cities where papal government might have settled were on important trade routes which might have added to the pope's powers and security: but Rome remained the favoured city of the popes and, in spite of all the difficulties of controlling the city, the senate and the people, the popes were prepared to suffer all sorts of indignities in order to stay in Rome. 'Vanquished by the power of symbolism', as Le Goff puts it,[37] and disposing of all practical considerations, the fourteenth-century popes returned from what they saw as their 'Babylonish captivity' to their impractical papal capital of Rome. They were as obsessed with Rome, its apostle and his shrine, as their twelfth- and thirteenth-century predecessors had been.

The aim of every pope was to control the city of Rome. The popes regarded the city as the capital of their duchy. But in fact many of the twelfth-century popes spent years in exile and between 1162 and 1188 Rome was only possessed by the papacy at intervals. It has been estimated that the pope was compulsorily absent for more than half the

37. J Le Goff *The Medieval Imagination* trans. A Goldhammer (Chicago 1988) 65.

century between 1099 and 1198 and for a total of 67 years in the next century (1198–1304).[38] Although there may have been surviving some notion of the tradition of ordered government from the ancient world, in actuality Rome had no strong, centralized government since classical times. Popes and emperors disputed the city and the citizens attempted to assert the right to rule themselves. There was a remarkable lack of trade, except in antiques. So rich was the legacy of the ancients that the fund of spoil has lasted into our own times. In the 1150s Bishop Henry of Winchester was described as buying up statues all over Rome which he had shipped back to England.[39] And Abbot Suger of St Denis thought of bringing back ancient Roman columns from Diocletian's baths to use in the construction of his new abbey church outside Paris. The Vassaletti family were busy exporting marble columns throughout the century and everywhere in Rome great pieces of marble were put to base uses, such as meat and fish slabs. The Roman *marmorarii* (marble-cutters, sculptors, mosaic workers) next to the *calcarii* (the lime-burners) were the worst enemies of ancient Roman monuments, destroying them for materials, but the fund of material was plentiful and out of their pillaging emerged some of the great works of art of the thirteenth century. There had begun to emerge, too, before the pontificate of Innocent III, a new feeling for preservation and pride in the past. In 1162 the senate of Rome made great efforts to preserve the column of Trajan for the Roman people and visitors to Rome were beginning to admire the great classical monuments of the past – the Arch of Constantine, the Pantheon and the statue of Venus. Guide books from the mid-twelfth century to 'The Wonders of Rome' (*Mirabilia Urbis Rome*) began to pay attention to the pagan monuments and were not just guides to the tombs of the martyrs and the saints. 'The Wonders' or 'Marvels' was the basic guide book, immensely popular, which everybody read and to which they

38. See the fascinating study of A Paravicini Bagliani 'La mobilità della curia Romana nel secolo xiii. riflessi locali' *Societa e Istituzioni dell' Italia Communale: l'Esempio di Perugia (secoli XII–XIV)* (Perugia 1988) with details from 1181.
39. *The 'Historia Pontificalis' of John of Salisbury* ed. and trans. Marjorie Chibnall (Oxford 1986) 79.

added their own impressions. Master Gregorius, in his *Marvels of Rome*, written possibly during Innocent's lifetime, mentions only three churches. His interest is unashamedly antiquarian and he condemns the iconoclasm of the early Christians, proving himself a true product of the twelfth-century Renaissance.[40]

There was virtually no industry in medieval Rome. The first craft guild, the guild of agriculturists, had been formed in the 1030s. By the mid-thirteenth century they were still the leading guild, although the drapers were now also important. It is true that there were bankers but their reputation for unpleasantness encouraged the popes to turn elsewhere for loans. Rome, in short, lived on its past simply by being a capital city. It produced little, but relied on its tourist industry; most of its citizens were shopkeepers and guides. Bankers and tourism may be seen as signs of economic insecurity. Food shortages were not uncommon and Innocent himself provided communal restaurants and founded hospitals. Rome had probably more than the average number of beggars. What economic security there might be depended on a strong overlordship. This, by the very nature of the papacy, was bound to be lacking, for the papacy was not an hereditary dynasty. The nightmare of the lack of a known heir, which brought many feudal dynasties into disastrous situations, was ever present within the papal court.

The uncertain overlordship of Rome, whether of the emperor or of the pope, allowed the senate to develop within certain limits. The senate, however, consisted of more members of the nobility than of the emerging burgher class, for their economic situation was not strong enough to enable them to develop as they did in the cities of northern Italy and elsewhere in Europe. The popes had to come to terms with the nobles and those who came from the noble families of the city naturally built up their

40. In general see Jonathan Sumption *Pilgrimage* (1975) 220–7; J B Ross 'A study of twelfth-century interest in the antiquities of Rome' *Medieval and Historiographical Essays in honor of James Westfall Thompson* ed. J L Cate and E N Anderson (Chicago 1937) 302–21; and *Master Gregorius The Marvels of Rome* trans. J Osborne (Mediaeval Sources in Translation **31**, Pontifical Institute of Mediaeval Studies, Toronto 1987).

own families and factions in order to survive. Most popes also sought to control the senate by making the key officials their liegemen and placing reliable men (often their relatives – but sometimes kith rather than kin) in key positions. Immediately after Innocent's election, the senator, Scottus Paparonis, resigned, which paved the way for the nomination of a successor who swore fealty to the pope. Also one of the new pope's first actions, taken on the day after his consecration, was to extract an oath of obedience from the prefect of Rome. Peter, who was in office, was accepted and confirmed as prefect, but on condition that he would govern according to Innocent's orders. When a new pope was elected it was customary for him to give presents (the *donativum*) to the chief citizens. Pope Adrian IV paid to ensure friendly relations; Pope Lucius III refused. Innocent, however, did this with a difference, using the occasion to ask the chief citizens for an oath of obedience in return. So from the first he attempted to make himself master of the city – a prelude to an active policy not only to control Rome but to restore the Papal State to its old frontiers. Pope Clement III had repossessed the city in 1188 and made the senate his vassals, but Pope Celestine III, an Orsini, had been more or less confined to the city. Surrounded by imperial possessions and troops he had to be content to remain active only within its walls. He was old and somewhat irresolute and indecisive. The death of the Emperor Henry VI in September 1197, leaving a son of two, came too late for the ageing Celestine to reap the benefit, although he immediately began to re-assert papal claims to the Patrimony, the duchy, the March and Tuscany, now fallen into imperial hands. With Innocent the picture changed completely. He was an opportunist and the opportunity presented itself. He leapt into action. Within a year of his accession, the old boundaries of the Papal State from Radicofani in the north to Ceprano in the south were no longer merely theoretical. The Patrimony of St Peter had been restored and even enlarged, and papal control was to be extended even further before Innocent's death.

. . .

THE FAMILY

Rome was a city of warring families who sought to control the senate and the senators and, of course, the pope himself. For this reason (among others) families directed at least one son into the Church. A position at the papal court brought influence within the city and in a two-way process popes created cardinals from among the Roman baronage. The great families of the city were distributed in certain quarters. From the 1200s onwards Lothar's family, the Conti of Segni, occupied the west slope of the Viminal and the area behind the forum of Nerva and they had property and influence in the rione Monti, where the Colonna and the Frangipani were also settled.[41] A family stronghold in Rome was essential. In all probability, as cardinal deacon of SS. Sergio and Bacco, Lothar had begun the process of establishing his control in the diaconate, the area round his church. As was customary, on his appointment as cardinal (and within two years), he rebuilt the cardinalate church which adjoined the Arch of Septimius Severus in the Forum. He restored the crypt and the basilica, constructed a new elevated high altar, for which he provided a baldacchino and furnishings, and renewed the roof. And after his elevation to the papacy, he built a colonnaded portico out of his income as cardinal.[42]

Most important of all his buildings was the Tor' dei Conti, begun for his family immediately after his election as pope in 1198.[43] This great tower loomed over Rome – as indeed it still does although halved by a later earthquake – dominating the Capitol, the Colosseum, the Quirinal and the route from the Lateran to St Peter's, and was described by one chronicler as touching the clouds. The great

41. See R Krautheimer *Rome, Profile of a City, 312–1308* (Princeton 1980) 157.
42. M Bonfioli 'La Diaconia dei SS. Sergio e Bacco nel foro Romano' *Rivista di Archeologia Cristiana* 50 (1974) 55–85, esp. 13 n. 2, mentions his expenditure on the church (from the *Gesta*) and a later inscription which recorded his munificence, and includes prints of drawings which show the arch and the towers. See also Krautheimer *Rome* 203.
43. Krautheimer *Rome* 204.

families of Rome had fortified towers or residences from which they might control the main routes in and out of the city. In 1199 there were two towers on top of the Arch of Septimius Severus, one of which, the southern, belonged to the church of SS. Sergio and Bacco. There was also a tower on top of the aqueduct that dominated the approach to the Lateran palace – in the hands of a great Roman family, the Annibaldi – which Innocent ordered to be removed. The roads to the Lateran from the west and the north were controlled by another family, the Frangipani. Innocent's own construction of a fortified residence at the Vatican, on the Mons Saccorum, must be seen as a conscious effort to build a power base away from the Lateran (sometimes called 'the winter palace' of the pope), where the Conti were vulnerable.[44] The Roman residence of the pope from the time of the Emperor Constantine had always been the Lateran and before Innocent's time there was only a temporary residence at St Peter's. Possibly started very early on by Pope Symmachus, it had been added to by Pope Eugenius III in the twelfth century. It was used when urban disturbances in the centre of Rome forced flight from the Lateran and when a lengthy liturgical occasion demanded it. Innocent's building at the Vatican was fortified with towers and an encircling wall and was meant for longer residence. It looked no doubt much like other fortified noble houses of the period in Rome, although it was perhaps more lavishly decorated. Clustering round the Cortile del Papagallo, were chapel, chamber, bakery, wine cellar, kitchen and smithy, and houses for the chancellor, treasurer and almoner. For the basilica itself, he devised an elaborate apse with a great mosaic that described St Peter's as 'the Mother of Churches'. The tower in the east wing of the ancient palace is Innocent's construction, but the surviving decorations all date from Pope Nicholas III's additions in the late thirteenth century.[45] While most popes spent out for prestige and show, they reserved considerable sums for strategic buildings.

44. Krautheimer *Rome* 319, 203 fol. and fig. 161. For the phrase 'winter palace', see *Master Gregorius*, trans. Osborne, 36.
45. See D Redig de Campos 'Les constructions d'Innocent III et de Nicolas III sur la colline Vaticane' in *Mélanges d'Archéologie et d'Histoire* (Ecole Française de Rome) **71** (1954) 359–76, esp. 359–65.

The pope's brother, Richard, played an important role in Roman and papal politics. He it was who was associated with the Tor' dei Conti – whose construction had depended on funds provided by Innocent – presumably as its castellan. The family's alliance with the Annibaldi through the marriage of the pope's sister with Peter Annibaldi, seneschal of the pope from 1202 and senator of Rome, brought the Conti to the height of their power not only in the city but also in controlling an extensive area of the Campagna, the region to the south and east of Rome.[46] It was part of a carefully constructed plan to give the family an estate beyond the Liris. The Conti family held on to Sora after the election of Innocent's successor, Honorius III, who wished to retain their loyalty and allowed them to keep it in return for payment,[47] but lost the territory back to the Regno after a successful campaign by Frederick II in 1221. The children of Richard included three sons, the third of whom, Stephen, was promoted cardinal deacon of St Adriano by his uncle in 1216. The other two, Paul and John, became respectively lords of Valmontone and Poli in the Campagna.[48]

Piece by piece, the Conti estates, insignificant at first, were added to by purchase. Non-diocesan property was acquired in the Campagna. Valmontone – the castle with its lands, the palace and houses – was purchased in 1207 and ten days later Manases did homage for the fief to the papal chamberlain, Stephen of Fossanova. Valmontone was just within the diocese of Segni. The castle of Poli, which dominated the north of the Campagna, and its fiefs were slowly taken over. Richard himself spent money on fortifying Poli and was always ready with subsidies to support friends and allies.[49] In the year 1208 Sora (in the *Regno* to the east of

---

46. D Waley *The Papal State in the Thirteenth Century* (1961) 55. The Annibaldi marriage produced the Cardinal Richard Annibaldi (important under Gregory IX) and a daughter, Maccalona, who married Landulf of Ceccano; Maleczek *Kardinalskolleg* 102.

47. *LC* X notes 1000 ounces of gold owing to Honorius III by Count Richard for Rocce Artis.

48. F Gregorovius *History of the City of Rome in the Middle Ages* trans. A Hamilton v pt 1 (1897) 62–3 and Dykmans 'D'Innocent III à Boniface VIII' in *Bulletin de l'Institut Historique Belge de Rome* **45** (1975) 19–211, mainly on the family after Innocent. See Map 1.

49. On the acquisition of the estates see Dykmans 'D'Innocent III à Boniface VIII' 23–7.

Rome) and the title of count were conferred on Richard
Conti by the king of Sicily's representative, and on 6 October Richard tendered the oath of vassalage to the pope
at Ferentino for all the territories he had acquired and
investiture was made with the gilded chalice (*per cuppam
deauratam*).[50] The transaction had taken place in the great
Cistercian abbey of Fossanova which, due to its important
position, Innocent was always very careful to treat with
much favour. It has been noted that the only letters in
which the phrase 'de fratrum nostrorum consilio' ('with
the approval of our brothers' i.e. the cardinals) is consist-
ently used under Innocent are those dealing with the
government of the Patrimony of St Peter where the great
cardinalate families had their influence. [51]

Further relatives were enlisted in the service of the pope
in the Papal State. In the Campagna and Marittima, Lando
da Montelungo, a cousin, was made rector from *c.* January
1199.[52] In Tuscany, Stephen de Romano Carzolus, another
relative, served from 30 June 1203, succeeding a cardinal,
aided by the prefect. Another relative and rector of the
Patrimony was James, son of John Odoline, a cousin, and
count of Andria, who had been papal marshal and com-
mander of Innocent's troops in Sicily in 1200–1201, to
whom he granted the fortress of Ninfa on the southern
border.[53]

Among the cardinals, Hugolinus, one of Innocent's
closest confidants and later Pope Gregory IX, is now generally agreed to have been related to him in the third
degree. Octavian, another relative, followed Innocent in
the old Conti church of SS. Sergio and Bacco from 1206:
he had filled the important office of papal chamberlain.
Stephen, the pope's nephew and Richard's son, has already
been mentioned and John, cardinal deacon of St Maria in
Cosmedin from 1200 was related – possibly another
nephew. Thus Innocent made four of his relatives cardinals,

50. Gregorovius v pt 1 63 n. 2: *LC* no. V.
51. Maleczek *Kardinalskolleg* 315 fol.
52. Waley *Papal State* 51 and 307; but Waley wrongly calls him a
    nephew. For correction see P Partner *The Lands of St Peter* (1972)
    234 n. 1 and Maleczek 'consobrinus'.
53. Waley *Papal State* 43, 51 and 309, and see *Gesta* chs. xxxvii and
    cxxxv.

as opposed to Celestine's creation of only one.[54] We need now to look more closely at the central government of the Church.

· · ·

THE PAPAL CURIA

The structure of papal government was broadly comparable with that of some contemporary secular kingdoms. Like them, it was based originally upon the household, and the household continued to have significance even after the formation of other less personal structures. The household institutions of chapel, chancery and chamber formed the *curia* of the early twelfth century. The chapel had important liturgical and ceremonial duties to perform. The chancery dealt with official communications. The chamber ran the papal finances. The pope's court had from very early times exercised judicial powers of extreme significance. The idea of the curia as a supreme court had been considerably developed by the late twelfth century, with developments in Rome, though the pope might still hear cases within the household.

The main offices of government were based at the Lateran by Innocent's time. The chancery, or writing office, was in existence probably almost from the beginning of the papacy, certainly by the third century. It was modelled closely on the old Imperial chancery, using notaries, who were first employed to record the deeds of the early martyrs and the decrees of councils. By the late eighth to early ninth century, there are some original documents, but not many. With the accession of popes from north of the Alps, the chancery began to travel with the pope and was 'freed' from ancient imperial and more especially from Roman influences, adopting the Caroline minuscule in its letters.

The chancery was immensely important to an active pope for it was mainly through its products that people came to know the pope's thoughts and will. It may be that more surviving documents for Innocent's pontificate than for previous pontificates reflects greater activity, but we cannot prove that. However, to understand Innocent's reign we must not lose sight of the chancery and its

54. Maleczek *Kardinalskolleg* 295 and 102 n. 351.

activities. Innocent's chancery – which was to bear quite a heavy weight of governmental responsibility during the pontificate – appears to have been run personally and autocratically by the pope. The services of Cardinal Cencius Savelli, who had run the chancery under Pope Celestine III (and incidentally the chamber) were not retained by Innocent. The chancellor's duties were to oversee the issue of all curial correspondence. He is unlikely to have supervised personally the drawing up of every document – he had staff for that – but he did have the duty of dating the solemn privileges which were issued. These splendid and costly documents began to decline very dramatically in numbers between the late twelfth and early thirteenth century, as more serviceable and cheaper documents came to replace them. They required for authentication the subscriptions or signatures of the cardinals, the token signature of the pope and an elaborate dating clause by the chancellor. Finally, the leaden seal, the *bulla*, was attached to the document by the *bullator* (normally a lay-brother from the abbey of Fossanova). If the document was a letter of grace or a privilege, conferring rights or possessions, the *bulla* was hung on red and yellow plaited silk strings, but if a mandate or order, plain and undyed hemp was used. The chancellor was, by the nature of his office, very close to the reigning pope. There were extremely important secret and confidential documents to be drawn up. They were drafted individually, as opposed to many letters that used common forms, most likely by the chancellor himself or by a very senior notary, and were sent *closed*, which meant that the *bulla* and the cords were used not just to authenticate document but to close and seal it up.

Innocent had only one chancellor so styled, his relative, John, cardinal deacon of St Maria in Cosmedin, who used the title from 1205 until his death in 1213. Presumably he would have continued in the office for the whole of the pontificate, had he not died before it ended. Innocent also had an 'acting chancellor' in his second pontifical year, from 1199 to 1200, Rainald, a papal notary, but he was sent to be archbishop of Acerenza. Otherwise he used notaries. While chancellors were usually cardinals, the notaries were not. Only John of Ferentino, who acted for Innocent as a notary when subdeacon, was made a cardinal but he was not given the title of chancellor.[55]

THE COLLEGE OF CARDINALS

The Reform movement of the eleventh century was behind the building up of the college of cardinals and its privileges. The cardinals from the fifth century, with their Roman titular churches, provided the weekly liturgical ministry for the basilicas with cemeteries. From the eighth century these duties were attended to in the Lateran by seven bishops from the nearby dioceses and in four other basilicas by the priests of the titular churches, now increased to twenty-eight. Cardinal deacons were added to their number; and by Paschal II's reign (1099–1118) there were seven bishops (later reduced in number), twenty-eight priests and eighteen deacons. A strong *esprit de corps* was developing. The cardinals began to think of themselves as the hinges on which the universal Church turned, a comparison that had already been made by Pope Leo IX (1048–54) and by Cardinal Deusdedit in the 1080s. During the thirteenth century their privileges, dignities and revenues increased. They had the revenues from their cardinalate churches in Rome and in the case of the cardinal bishops from their bishoprics. As the papacy's powers increased so did the cardinals' revenues, for they were involved in general administration and often legal duties and would expect gifts and payments for services. The cardinals' households were mini papal curias. Petitioners came to them; careers were sought in them. The cardinals joined in all the rapidly growing administrative and judicial functions of the papal court. They sat to hear cases in the papal consistory which under Innocent III met three times in each week. Many cases were delegated to them to hear on their own. They filled the administrative offices for the pope. Some were sent as legates or ambassadors, others served as papal chancellor, papal chamberlain or papal vicar, administering the Papal State. They were protectors of the religious orders and preachers of the crusade, the

55. Maleczek *Kardinalskolleg* 136–7, 146–7, 348–9 (in general); C R Cheney 'The office and title of papal chancellor 1187–1216', *Archivum Historiae Pontificiae* **22** (1984) 369–76: mainly 371–2.

pope's natural advisers, though he was by no means obliged to listen to their advice or follow their counsel. They
had special status and legal protection and there were pres-
cribed penalties for those attacking or injuring them. They
were not granted their later symbol of dignity, the red hat,
until Innocent IV's reign.

Romans predominated in the college of cardinals under
both Celestine III and Innocent III. One contrast, however,
was that of the thirty-two cardinals created by Innocent
nearly 50 per cent were masters (men who had been at
universities). At his election Celestine III had inherited a
college with only twelve masters out of a college of thirty-
five. Fractionally more monks were favoured by Innocent
(especially Cistercians), and the 'external' cardinals, those
with permanent commissions outside Rome, declined in
number. Innocent had only two 'outsider' cardinals:
Gerard de Sessa, elect of Novara (1210), Albano (1211)
and then Milan, and Anselm, archbishop of Naples. Although Innocent gave his college an international flavour
and outlook with the appointment of such men as Stephen
Langton, Robert of Courson and Peter of Corbeil, the solid
Roman basis, supported by cardinals from the neighbour-
hood of Rome, remained intact from 1198 to 1216. And,
indeed, the number of non-Italians dwindled from possibly
six (two or three French, two English, one Spanish) to
three (one Spanish, one English and one probably southern French). Even the 'outer' Italians were few in number
– one each from Vercelli, Milan, Viterbo, Benevento and
Capua.[56] Maleczek has shown that from Innocent's sixth
year in office, 1203–4, as the reign progressed, the pope
worked more and more with a smaller group of cardinals,
of whom the key members were Hugolinus, Pelagius and
Guala, and there was less consultation of the whole college.
This came to create a rift between insiders and outsiders.

. . .

CONCLUSION

Innocent's view of government was both traditional and
monarchic. By traditional I mean that it was founded on a

---

56. This is based on the deductions of Maleczek. The origins of some
cardinals are unknown. See esp. 292–5.

growing interpretation of the past, not that tradition was swallowed hook, line and sinker – indeed, in some cases it was turned upside down – but always it was referred to, re-explained. It was a re-working of the past that was partly theological. By monarchic I mean that the pope had an authority and duty to rule and to direct as the representative of the ultimate ruler, and that he exercised power in a monarchic way. He had, as had most strong popes, a clear idea of what he thought the past signified. First and foremost, the Donation of Constantine, whereby the emperor had transferred temporal government to the popes, was not forgotten. Its message was all around him. It explained the pope's temporal power over the city of Rome and the surrounding areas. It also explained the primacy of the Western bishopric of St Peter over Constantinople and the eastern Mediterranean sees. However much the Donation had been perfected and refined by the twelfth century to fit into other papal arguments, there still remained the basic problem not so much as to the origin of power as to its descent. To Innocent it seemed that his political power in general came from Christ. He did not use the Donation in his arguments to restore to the papacy command over the Papal State – his policy of *recuperatio* – but the diplomas of Carolingian and later emperors.[57] This can hardly be to deny the emperor's gift but is certainly the action of a realist, to whom arguments from later, and perhaps what was seen to be better, evidence, are important. He was never in any doubt, however, that obedience of lay rulers, including the emperor, was to him. By the Petrine commission the pope had been given the power to rule. Elaborated by his belief in the Vicariate of Christ and in both the priestly and the monarchic powers of Melchizedek, he seemed in no doubt as to the 'plenitude' of the pope's powers.

In terms of active, practical government and politics, however, it was the Investiture Contest that had already begun to change the face of European government.

---

57. This is pointed out by B Tierney 'The continuity of papal political theory in the thirteenth century. Some methodological considerations' *Mediaeval Studies* **27** (1965) 240 and see M Laufs *Politik und Recht bei Innozenz III* (Cologne 1980).

Europe, emerging in the late eleventh century, after an era of wars and invasions during the 'Dark Ages', to a period of relative peace, began to look towards more settled forms of government. In this climate, it was realized that there was a corrupting element in the exercise of power, so the idea that it was the ruler's duty to exercise authority on behalf of God and of the people began to be re-emphasized. The Carolingians had accentuated the importance of rulership as the ministry of God (the *ministerium Dei*). Rulership was a trust – a trust from God. Successful missionizing activities and the extending of the boundaries and powers of states led secular authorities to an examination of the sources of power and to its exercise.

It cannot be doubted that the Western emperors were, like the popes, sincere in their desire to exercise power justly. The Emperor Henry III had been responsible for the appointment of Pope Leo IX (1048–54), the great reforming pope, to whom Pope Gregory VII (Hildebrand, 1073–85) owed so much. The emperors, indeed, had saved the papacy in the period before Hildebrand. The emperor Henry IV was no less sincere in his outlook than Gregory VII and he was no out-and-out secularist. He accepted that emperorship was responsible and that he was answerable to a higher power. But it was theocratic kingship that was the foundation of his policy and his rulership rather than a kingship or emperorship that looked to the pope for sanction and direction. He was king by the grace of God, not of the pope: indeed, the vicar of God. The national church organization had long been accepted in central Europe: bishops were the crown's natural advisers, the crown's civil servants. Bishoprics were in the royal gift and, as sizeable landed endowments, they were like fiefs. It was hardly surprising that kings wanted solemn oaths from their servants, the bishops, that they looked upon bishoprics as income and that, in line with the symbolic ceremonies of society, they expected to 'invest' their appointees and to receive from them solemn oaths of fidelity. The popes accepted that no bishops should be appointed without royal permission. But the national church organization, which the papacy had encouraged, brought with it lay investiture, the giving to the bishop of the ring and staff and the performance of homage to the ruler. Furthermore, the use of powerful and wealthy nobles and kings as missionizers had led to proprietary churches and monasteries, that is to churches which were built and financed or 'owned' by laymen who might make their own appointments.

There was no real victor from the Investiture Contest. The pope died in exile; the emperor had been 'humbled' at Canossa; and other rulers, the Normans, had been brought to prominence by the papacy. But it left a legacy – a positive one. In the long term it committed the papacy to active government. Popes were no longer content to see political leadership taken from them. The pope has control over the kingdom and kingdoms of this world. He can 'bind and make loose'. He also has access to that other kingdom; he can open the doors of heaven. 'My kingdom is not of this world' was not regarded as releasing the pope from an active role in government, though it did express the great moral fervour that fuelled the late eleventh- and early twelfth-century reforms – especially in the attack on clerical marriage and in the drive to rid the Church of unchaste priests and to control the proprietary church system (secular theocracy). Pope Gregory VII had given the Church an undisputed leadership. His claim that all power proceeded from God was made loud and clear. It marked the end of the possibility of an attitude of withdrawal for the papacy. The world was to be converted by the priesthood.

The emphasis on the role of the priest and the claim of the pope to depose an unworthy emperor were two aspects of Gregory's pontificate that had a marked influence on Innocent. The clergy were integral to government at all levels. Their moral probity and reform, if necessary, was, therefore, imperative. The Church must be purified in its new, active role. The question as to whether an unchaste priest might celebrate the mass became important. The Church must be pure, as government must be pure. For Gregory, mass celebrated by an unchaste priest was invalidated. Here Innocent's views diverged from Gregory's. Undoubtedly influenced by the theology taught at Paris by the end of the twelfth century, he maintained that unchaste behaviour by the priest did not invalidate his orders. But both men agreed implicitly on the unique importance of the priesthood and the priestly function.

Gregory's declaration, known as the *Dictatus Pape*, of 1075, enshrined the clause that stated that the pope had power to depose an unworthy emperor. 'It is permitted to the pope to depose emperors'. The pope, too, alone, can depose bishops and move them from see to see. Such tenets involved the papacy in action. Active government was not in doubt by the end of the twelfth century as the papacy's programme.

Canon law was the statement of how society was to be governed and here Innocent's monarchic views are clearly shown. Certain decretals or rulings of Innocent III illustrate the pope's clear conceptions of rulership and his relationship with earthly rulers, emperors and kings. The decretal letter 'Solite', addressed to Alexis, the emperor of Constantinople, outlined the pope's function as an adviser of monarchs. It was, said Innocent, his duty to exhort and advise rulers. Alexis is at fault in ranking imperial power and dignity higher than sacerdotal power, but the power of the priesthood descends from God and not from kings. 'I am writing not to denigrate you but to help you ... It would be as well if you listened to my advice'. In the decretal 'Novit ille', written to the archbishops and bishops of France, Innocent declared how much he has the interests of King Philip Augustus and his kingdom at heart and how wrong it would be to assume that he had any intentions that were harmful to the French king's jurisdictional powers. He has the right not to judge in feudal (or state) matters but in 'matters of sin'. This should not be taken as an affront to Philip's power and prestige. According to the Emperor Valentinian all matters should be submitted to the Holy See, but we only claim the right to judge in disputed matters. The king of France should, therefore, submit to his right to intervene. As pope he may judge in a matter of broken oaths, an imperfectly observed treaty and a breach of the peace. The letter, 'Per venerabilem', was written to William, count of Montpellier. In it, Pope Innocent refused the legitimization of the count's sons. By showing the authority of the apostolic see to judge in such matters the pope therefore showed his authority to decide on rulers. He gave detailed, legal reasons why William's request was refused while Philip Augustus's had been granted, but it was the very act of authority that mattered.

Innocent was claiming, therefore, the right to intervene in kingdoms. A king's marriage and the legitimization of heirs might well be 'reasons of sin' that allowed the pope to intervene. Or it might be the breaking of an oath or the refusal to accept the decrees of Rome, as with King John. He might also, quite obviously, direct the activities of bishops throughout the Church, translate them and control them. The pope's claims to decide on appeal were witnessed most clearly in the Canterbury election. The elections of the monk Reginald and later of the king's candidate, John de Gray, were clearly uncanonical, and the electors being at Rome, the election of Langton was quite correct. Stephen Langton, however, was consecrated by Innocent at Rome without the king's assent, so that, although Innocent had acted within canonical rules, the king felt threatened by this election outside his court, to which he had not given his consent. To John this seemed likely to be a precedent. He had to resist it. It is a perfect illustration of Innocent's monarchic and autocratic instincts. Chance had played into his hands.

Innocent was in no doubt as to the proper roles of kings and emperors. They were there to assist the papacy in its work of extending the Christian religion and maintaining a just society. With the adoption of Christianity by kings and their subjects had come the conception of the 'Christian ruler', for Christ had been the 'King of the Jews' and the society of the Old Testament was a kingly and patriarchal one. The king was not merely a tribal chieftain and warlord, ravaging and conquering, he was a representative of Christ, 'the king', on earth. The Old Testament kings had been warriors and conquerors, smiting their enemies, but they had also been vehicles through whom the law of God was interpreted and enforced. The Christian emperor and king was seen as a man born or elected to duties and obligations towards God and his subjects, as well as a man with rights and privileges. He had power, but he had to be responsible in the exercise of it. The most solemn of his duties were to keep the peace, to spread Christianity and to declare the law.

The sacring of emperors, kings and bishops signified an acceptance that as Christian rulers they governed subject to eternal or divine laws. The crown, the mitre, the sword of justice, the ring, the sceptre, the rod and the bishop's staff symbolized pastoral and judicial powers.[58] Coronation became important in the acceptance of an emperor or a king and coronation or, more importantly, the prior consecration could only be performed by a high ecclesiastic, the pope or certain specified archbishops.

The popes saw the emperors as their lieutenants. From the coronation of Charlemagne, king of the Franks, as emperor, by the pope on Christmas Day 800, the emperorship was removed to the West. The elaborate ceremonial and the oaths of kingship were spreading throughout the Christian West. In 787 the son of Offa, king of Mercia, was consecrated. The coronation oath of Edgar is recorded for 973: he swore first 'that God's Church and all Christian people of my realm shall enjoy true peace; second, that I forbid to all ranks of men robbery and all wrongful deeds; third, that I urge and command justice and mercy in all judgements' – pious words, perhaps, but solemn and binding, and made at the bidding of Archbishop Dunstan and laid on the altar at Bath.[59] It was in essence this same three-fold promise of the Anglo-Saxons that was used for coronations throughout the thirteenth century in England: King Richard I at his first coronation in 1189 swore 'to maintain peace and honour and to reverence the Church, to annul any evil laws, and to make and maintain good laws'.[60] There can be little doubt that such sentiments reinforced the laws or dooms that were proclaimed by early kings in England and reminded the king of his Christian obligations and duties. We cannot be certain of the precise significance of the separate parts of the royal insignia – the

58. See P E Schramm *A History of the English Coronation*, trans. L G Wickham Legg (Oxford 1937) 8–9 on the insignia of dominion, *given* by the church to the monarch; 134–6 on priestly robes.
59. For the text of the 'Ordo' for Edgar's coronation, in which the ring, sword, crown, sceptre and rod were used, see Schramm 'Die Krönung bei den Westfranken und Angelsachsen von 878 bis um 1000' in *Zeitschrift für Rechtsgeschichte* **54** kan. abt. 23 (1934) 221–30. The oath is on 223; also printed in L G Wickham Legg *English Coronation Records* (1901) 15–23 and trans. into English, 23–9; the oath translated on 13.
60. The source for this is *Gesta Regis Henrici Secundi Benedicti Abbatis* ii ed. W Stubbs (RS 49, 1867) 81. The translation is mine.

sword, the ring, the sceptre and the rod. All were used at the time of the Edgar 'Ordo'. The sword appears to have been to defend the Holy Church, the sceptre to signify royal power and the rod to symbolize virtue and equity. Three swords and two sceptres were carried before the English king at his coronation in 1189: the sceptre with the cross probably signifying power and justice, the sceptre with the dove, equity and mercy, while the three swords may have been associated singly with authority, mercy and justice.[61]

The essence of what the popes required of the emperors and how they saw the imperial office is enshrined in the imperial oaths taken at the time of coronation and in the prayer at the conferment of the sword. The imperial oaths were composed in the pope's curia. The first was probably written and used in the ninth century. By the time of the coronation of the Emperor Otto I in 962, when a new order of service had appeared, the chrism (that is, the oil mixed with balm) was no longer applied on the head, to symbolize directive powers, but between the shoulders. It was thus made clear that there was no connection with the consecration of bishops who were anointed on their heads. Anointing the shoulders or arms was to symbolize the emperor's protective and defensive role. By the middle of the twelfth century, a revised order introduced a solemn oath which was taken on the gospels. And when Innocent came to crown the Emperor Otto IV in 1209 he introduced a new oath in which he incorporated a pledge to conserve the pope's possessions and laws. (No doubt the pope had in mind previous imperial aggression in the Papal State.) Otto promised this before God and before St Peter, as his predecessors had done. Even more indicative of Innocent's intentions were the changes made to the prayer at the conferment of the sword. The sword had first been conferred in 823: it was the symbol of the emperor's role as defender of the Church, to maintain justice and wipe out iniquity. Previously, the emperor had received the sword from God; now he received it, after it had rested (like the pallium

---

61. *Gesta Regis Henrici Secundi* ii 81–2. On Richard I's coronation, see Schramm *English Coronation* 67–70 and 135: the whole of his ch. vii (the king, the law and the coronation oath) is useful.

used for the investiture of archbishops) on the body of St Peter, from the hands of the pope ('however unworthy', as Innocent said), not from God but from his vicar. As the pope strapped the sword round the emperor's waist, he reminded the emperor that the saints had conquered kingdoms not by the sword but by faith.[62]

In Innocent's view, too, there was a clear distinction between royal and episcopal rites, between the anointing of the king and of the priest. He tried, though perhaps without much success, to restrict the use of chrism to bishops, and, making a further distinction between royal and episcopal consecration, he ordered that kings, like emperors, were to be anointed only on the arms or shoulders and hands, not on the head.[63] For Innocent, the vicar of Christ, the commission to St Peter to govern meant implementation of the aims of his predecessors as he understood them. He sincerely hoped to be able to establish the rule of Christ on earth with the help of the Christian emperor, an emperor who could be approved and crowned only by the pope.

62. For the ordines A–D (Ordo XVIII), see *Die Ordines für die Weihe und Krönung des Kaisers und der Kaiserin* ed. R Elze (Fontes Iuris Germanici Antiqui, MGH Hanover 1960).
63. See M Bloch *The Royal Touch* trans J E Anderson (1973) 116 and Innocent's letter on the matter to the Bulgarian archbishop of Trnovo which became part of the Church's law (*X.* I. 15. 1); see Schramm *English Coronation* 120, 126–7; and 131–3, 137, for the 'oil of St Thomas Becket', discovered after the English 'Ordo' of 1308 re-introduced anointing on the head and the use of chrism.

Chapter 2

POLITICS, POWER AND PROPAGANDA

. . .

POLITICS

Politically, fate dealt Innocent III an extraordinarily good hand. In September 1197 the Emperor Henry VI had died at the age of 32, leaving an heir who was little more than a baby. Just as Napoleon in 1804, Henry VI might well in time have had Europe at his feet. His dream of uniting Germany and Italy was based in reality from the time of his marriage to Constance, heiress to the kingdom of Sicily, whose kings ruled over both the island and the southern part of Italy known as the *Regno*. Nor was the Staufen plan to incorporate France in this empire – which is outlined in the Annals of Marbach – beyond the realms of possibility. Henry VI had the subjection of the southern kingdom of Aragon within his sights,[1] and King Richard I of England, who dominated more than half of modern France, had become his quasi-vassal. The Staufen claim to imperial suzerainty over England, too, was not entirely unrealistic either at this time.[2] The Imperial chronicler speaks of 'the whole world' as being the emperor's long-term view of his dominion. Dominion over western Europe was far from impossible for such a man as Henry VI. But Henry's sudden death put an end (at least temporarily) to such imperial

---

1. *Otoboni Annales* MGH SS xviii 112.
2. It was revived at the Fourth Lateran Council, at the end of the pontificate of Innocent III, though not very realistically: see S Kuttner and A Garcia y Garcia 'A new eyewitness account of the Fourth Lateran Council' *Traditio* **20** (1964) 128 and 159–60.

aspirations and caused a power vacuum. According to the historian Ranke, the real heir to the Emperor Henry VI was not his son, the future Frederick II, but Pope Innocent III; he, in fact, was echoing the words of a contemporary writer, Gervase of Tilbury, who called Innocent 'the true emperor' (*verus imperator*).

Immediately the rumours of Henry's illness began, rebellion broke out in the Rhineland and as soon as they were confirmed there was plundering of the imperial estates. The obvious trustee of the empire was Henry's younger brother, Philip of Swabia, who was on his way to Sicily to conduct the two-year-old child, Frederick, Henry's heir, back to Germany for his coronation, when news came to the party at Montefiascone, to the north of Rome, that Henry was in fact dead. As early as 1196 Henry, a ruler of very considerable foresight, had prepared for the succession. His constitutional plan had been to secure the election of his son, the young Frederick, as king, but as soon as the emperor was known to be dead the wisdom of upholding the election of so young an heir was questioned. Some of the princes of Germany doubted the validity of the election on the grounds that Frederick had not been baptized at the time and he had only been elected, they said, out of fear for his father. Philip of Swabia acted with the greatest propriety. He proposed a regency council to uphold the validity of Frederick's election until the heir should come of age. He had no intention of assuming the emperorship himself. Powerful forces, however, that disliked the Staufen family influence were now unleashed. Many of the imperial electors wished to be free from Staufen domination, but they had no constructive plans beyond this goal. Some, disregarding their oaths, favoured the election of the king of France, Philip Augustus; others were prepared to support the candidature of King Richard I of England. In their opposition they were united only by one common interest – a desire to bring about the fall of the Staufer. The most powerful feudal lord in Germany, Adolf, archbishop of Cologne – the last to take the oath to the young Frederick and the first to break it – wanted Richard I. The diocese had strong ties with England and there were important commercial considerations.

The archbishop of Trier convoked a meeting at Andernach,

under the presidency of Archbishop Adolf of Cologne, to elect a new king. The obvious choice of the opposition was the Count Palatine Henry, a Welf,[3] but he was on crusade and so Duke Bernard of Saxony was considered and elected. Bernard, however, refused the offer and the assembly invited King Richard I of England. Philip of Swabia, meanwhile, was maintaining the illegality of the meeting on the grounds that there was a legitimate heir, that oaths had been taken to that heir by all the princes and that, furthermore, few of them had been present at Andernach. A Diet was called for March 1198 at Cologne.

At about this point Philip and his advisers decided that the best way to preserve the crown for Frederick – in view of the failure of the regency council to control the princes – was for Philip to take it himself until his nephew came of age.

On 1 March 1198 the Cologne assembly met. Here Richard I's envoys announced that the king would not stand – they had been ordered to vote for the Count Palatine Henry (whose support Richard wanted in his struggle against the French king) but he still had not returned. Meanwhile, at Erfurt, many of the princes and the archbishops of Mecklenburg and Salzburg and the bishops of Merseburg, Worms and Bamberg proceeded to designate Philip as imperial defender until Frederick came of age. They were on weak ground, for there were no precedents for this, and on 8 March the Cologne assembly, now meeting at Mulhouse, divested Philip of this title and denied the validity of his election, saying that it had been carried out in an unusual place and that the count Palatine and the archbishop of Mainz had been absent.

3. Welf (or Guelph) power was centred on Ravensburg in the north of Germany. The Staufer, or Hohenstaufer family, took their name from the castle of Stauf near Göppingen. The supporters of the Staufen Emperor Frederick II became known as Ghibelline from the name of another of their castles, that of Waiblingen (which was also used as a battle cry). From meaning pro-imperialist (Staufen) and anti-imperialist (Welf), the terms came later to mean imperial (Ghibelline) and French (Welf) and to indicate two alignments: imperial or Italian, on the one hand, and papal and Angevin on the other; see D Waley *The Papal State in the Thirteenth Century* (1961) 194; H Fuhrmann *Germany in the High Middle Ages c. 1050–1200* (Cambridge 1986) 101, 138.

Duke Berthold of Zähringen was now put up as the candidate of the Welfs because he appeared a man of means and was well known for his hostility to the Staufer. But Adolf of Cologne and his supporters, who disliked Philip even more than the young Frederick, had made a miscalculation and chosen a thoroughly bad lot. Duke Berthold sent neither the expected money nor the troops for which he had been asked nor the hostages, nor did he turn up. He had changed sides.

The new Welf candidate was Otto, brother of the count Palatine Henry, a man who knew nothing of imperial affairs. Born about 1182 in Normandy, the son of a German father (Henry the Lion) and an Aquitanian mother, he had been much in the company of his uncle, King Richard I, who created him count of Poitou at the age of fourteen. From Poitou he ravaged French territories. He was glib in tongue, lavish in promises, big in size and somewhat stupid. He was elected king at Cologne on 9 June 1198. Just over a week later his forces marched on Aachen (Aix-la-Chapelle) which fell on 12 July and there the archbishop of Cologne, Adolf, anointed and crowned Otto. The strength of the Welf party lay on the lower Rhine and in the Netherlands and especially in the support of Cologne and of its archbishop, for Cologne had strong trading ties with England. (The archbishop of Trier did not attend the coronation.) The imperial schism had begun.

Philip had already shown himself as king at Worms on 5 April 1198. He had the considerable advantage of possessing the imperial insignia and he began to style himself 'Rex Romanorum et semper Augustus' – the imperial designation. In September 1198 his election was repeated at Mainz and on the 8th he was crowned by the archbishop of Tarentaise, Aimo, not as he should have been by the archbishop of Mainz – recognized as the crowning archbishop from the tenth century – who was absent on crusade. Philip had been slow to move and he had gained little by coronation by such a lowly archbishop as Tarentaise – Trier, Salzburg, Bremen and Magdeburg were all unavailable. Furthermore, the coronation church was at Aachen not Mainz.

The imperial schism had already become a question of European concern, sparking off a network of alliances and counter-alliances only to be matched by those of later eighteenth- and nineteenth-century Europe. Richard I and Philip Augustus of France were at war at the time: the connection between Richard and Otto, supported by Count Baldwin of Flanders and Archbishop Adolf of Cologne, pushed Philip Augustus to the support of Philip of Swabia. Negotiations with the papacy by both parties were in train and the bishops and princes changed sides like rich men throwing off old clothes. Already in November 1197 Philip had approached Pope Celestine III to bring to an end his excommunication, and before his consecration, Innocent III had empowered Philip's envoy, the bishop of Sutri, and the abbot of San Anastasio to absolve Philip, provided he released the abbot of Salerno before his absolution and took an oath to obey the mandates of the Church. By the time the legates arrived, however, they were dealing with a king, not a duke, and the bishop of Sutri was satisfied with a general promise from Philip rather than a formal oath and he absolved Philip secretly. Innocent maintained that Philip should have gone to Rome for absolution but for the moment he let the matter rest. He was playing his cards very close to his chest. Monaco de Villa, a Milanese, who had been at Otto's coronation, was employed in a dual role between the two courts and through him Innocent probably conveyed his conditions for accepting Otto. Although Innocent had recognized Philip there were now signs that he had begun to favour Otto. Even Otto knew that without papal support he could not survive. By the spring of 1199, however, Otto's cause had begun to wane. Henry of Colden returned from the Crusade to help Philip, and Richard I, Otto's main supporter, died on 6 April 1199. The archbishop of Cologne had second thoughts on the wisdom of helping Otto, for with Richard's death no more money was coming from England, commercial interests suffered and the Rhine and Lotharingian supporters were hard hit. In the spring and early summer the archbishops of Bremen and of Magdeburg and the bishop of Osnabruck went over to Philip. The Declaration of Speyer of 28 May 1199, the great Staufen protest, was despatched to Innocent. It was an impressive political statement that the electors had elected someone who had the *right* to be emperor. Only a formal act of the pope was seen as necessary to crown him. The pope could not reject him. The Staufen ideology, in which imperial election was purely a formality, is clearly stated. 'We will come to Rome and you will crown our lord Philip'.

At this point in the narrative we need to turn to the remarkable *Register concerning the imperial question (Regestum super negotio Romani imperii* or *RNI)*, a secret register opened by the papal curia between August and September 1199, but containing entries going back to 3 May. This register of letters deals with the transactions over the imperial question and contains copies of some incoming letters (including the above) as well as the highly secret ones being sent out. Meanwhile the curia maintained the general register for all the other business of the pontificate and hands of the same scribes are found in both the main register and the *RNI*.[4] The *RNI* was devised as an *aide-mémoire* probably to serve the needs of the pope himself and his innermost circle of advisers. It is a deliberate selection of letters to illustrate a theme. Texts of letters were reduced and adjusted. There are marginal comments and addresses for quick reference. Most significant of all there is an interruption in registration in 1206 when things were not progressing well for Innocent. Then in August 1208, when Innocent had found his way to the point where he wished to be in the dispute, the significant letters of 1205–6 were entered up.[5]

The register opens some three weeks before the Declaration of Speyer of May 1199 had been drawn up. The Declaration was, however, drafted at the end of January at Nuremberg and the curia may well have had advance knowledge of the text. Certainly by the spring of 1199 the pope realized that a major political affair was developing. His position – the position, indeed, to which he clung throughout the long controversy – is made clear in his reply to the Staufer and in the early letters of the register. The pope should have been called upon to act as arbiter in

4.   See F Kempf *Die Register Innocenz III. Eine paläographisch-diplomatische Untersuchung* (Miscellanea Historiae Pontificiae ix, Rome 1945) 45–65 esp. 49.
5.   There is a facsimile edition with an introduction by W M Peitz *Regestum domini Innocentii super negotio Romani imperii* (Rome 1927).

the dispute, as he alone has regal and sacerdotal powers. He is also vicar of Christ. Kings had been instituted to repress evil-doers and the emperor is the 'protector' of Christendom whom the pope needs to implement Christian aims. It follows that the pope should arbitrate between claimants to the emperorship. But only Otto had in fact approached Innocent (who did not wish to make a judgment in the matter from which there was no return). He also wished to be satisfied on certain counts as to the suitability of the candidates. The Staufer understood the pope's reply as a sharp refusal. Furthermore, they had no intention of requesting arbitration. It appears that Innocent in November to December 1199 was badly informed as to the power of Otto's party. Contrary to the truth, he believed that the parties were equally matched and that Otto, after Richard I's death, was firmly in the saddle. In fact the Welfs could not get their letters through Philip's lines and Philip was much stronger than Otto militarily and as time wore on attracting more of the princes to his cause.

Innocent's main hope at this point was to bring Otto and Philip to a truce and he had, on 3 May 1199, commissioned Archbishop Conrad of Mainz to bring this about. Conrad, who had remained faithful to his oath to Frederick, achieved a six-month truce and the setting up of a tribunal, consisting of eight princes from each side, which was to meet under his presidency between Andernach and Coblenz on 28 July 1200. What was decided there was to be binding on all. Otto's letter to the pope (asking Innocent to influence the sixteen princes in their decision), which is included in the *RNI*, is the only evidence we have of communications between Otto and the pope before 1200.[6] The curia was taken aback by this letter. That the princes should decide the fate of the empire – and that Innocent should bring influence to bear upon them – went right against the pope's ideas. He and his advisers were so dismayed as to misread the letter, for the reply makes it clear that they understood the meeting of the princes to have taken place already. Conrad was accordingly taken to task for not reporting to Rome and was (wrongly) reproved for taking part in the assembly. A special commissary, Egidius,

6.   *RNI* no. 20.

was sent by the pope to keep an eye on Conrad.[7] Innocent's letters of the summer and autumn 1200 (to all the princes of Germany, to Philip Augustus, to King John and to the duke of Brabant and his wife) did not hide his preference for Otto.[8] The Staufen party and Conrad of Mainz, seeing where Innocent's feelings lay, lost interest in further tribunals.

The pope's intention now was for a diet of princes to be convoked – to be chaired by a papal legate. On Christmas Day 1200 one of the most remarkable political statements in the history of medieval papacy and empire was drawn up in a secret consistory of the pope and cardinals. Under the three headings of (1) what is legally admissible (2) what is morally admissible and (3) what is politically right and proper, the three candidates, Otto, Philip and Frederick, are considered. Otto is dealt with in five lines and the fact that a majority of the princes had elected Philip is glossed over. It takes three pages to demolish Philip. The reasons against Philip are later (and probably less honestly) stated to be his own guilt and actions rather than his Staufen ancestry. Innocent's sense of history breaks through in every line. The position of Frederick, the young heir, shows the political sensitivity, realism and acumen of the pope, for he says that when Frederick grows up, if he sees that he has been deprived of the empire by the Roman Church he will attack the Church.[9]

The secret consistory decided to send Guido, cardinal bishop of Preneste, who was to be joined by Octavian, cardinal bishop of Ostia (described as 'holding the first place in the Roman Church after us'), at present acting as legate in France, and the pope's own emissary, Master Philip the notary, to be present at a council to decide the imperial succession. And on 5 January 1201 Innocent addressed all the secular and ecclesiastical princes of Germany to this end. The Roman pontiff's unique powers as mediator are stressed.[10] But by 1 March all semblance of the princes deciding the matter, with the help of the

7. *RNI* no. 22.
8. *RNI* nos 23–5, 28.
9. *RNI* no. 29.
10. *RNI* nos 30–1.

pope's legates, had disappeared, for on this day the papal chancery addressed Otto as 'illustrious king' and announced him emperor elect.[11] What then had happened between 5 January and 1 March 1201 and why had Innocent declared for Otto before the council?

The answer lies in the secret register. The papal envoy, Egidius, began the journey home after the death of Archbishop Conrad of Mainz – and, incidentally, after a double election to the see of Mainz of a Staufen candidate and of a Welf candidate. Egidius arrived in Rome with up-to-date and reliable news on the political situation in Germany, reporting how badly things were going for Otto, after Cardinal Guido and Master Philip had left. Although Innocent had wished the council and the princes to be brought to the point of declaring for Otto, the news, as related by Egidius, was so bad for the Welfs that he felt forced to intervene and declare for Otto at once. Accordingly the full weight of the curial machine was now brought into play. Letters 32 to 49 of the *RNI* were all written on 1 March with the express purpose of pulling out every stop in favour of Otto with the crowned heads of Europe, and especially with the kings of England and of France. Pressure was put upon both John and Philip Augustus. The pope did not hesitate to point out to John the advantages of seeing Otto as emperor and to Philip Augustus, the threat that a Staufen emperor would present to France if Germany was united with Sicily. Before the end of the year, he was also prepared to make a concession to Philip Augustus and legitimize his heirs – Philip's bigamous wife had conveniently died – to encourage Philip towards the support of Otto.[12]

Events proceeded fast. On 8 June 1201 at Neuss Otto took the oath to the pope and the Roman Church. On 3 July 1201 he was crowned at Cologne. The reports of Master Philip and of Cardinal Guido of Preneste were made to the pope. Guido's is more cautious – he sensed that the bishops of the empire were still dazed by the pope's action in recognizing Otto. The solidarity of the ecclesiastical

11. *RNI* no. 32.
12. See John W Baldwin *The Government of Philip Augustus* (Berkeley 1986) 86–7.

princes was essential in view of the fact that the secular princes were still mainly with Philip.

In September 1201 Philip of Swabia's followers gathered at Bamberg. Although Philip was excommunicated all followed his invitation and the assembly had the semblance of an imperial diet. It was reported that an oath of allegiance was taken here to Philip. And it may have been here that a Staufen protest to the pope was drawn up. This questioned the conduct of Guido, the cardinal bishop of Preneste – probably a device not to offend the pope personally – who had, they said, intervened either as elector or as judge, neither of which role was acceptable to them. The Staufer maintained that they accepted the magisterial primacy of the Roman Church – the pope's power to approve and anoint the emperor – but they challenged the jurisdictional primacy, namely the pope's claim to appoint the emperor. Accordingly they petitioned the pope to anoint Philip. The letter reached Innocent early in 1202.[13] At about this time King Philip Augustus of France directed a letter of protest against the promotion of Otto. The king's advisers were shrewd enough to turn the pope's language against him. Whereas Innocent, in his letter of March 1201, had promised that he would guarantee France against any encroachment by Otto, so Philip was prepared to guarantee that Philip of Swabia, if elected, would do no harm to Innocent.[14] Innocent's reply to Philip of Swabia's supporters, addressed to Duke Berthold of Zähringen, declared that Guido of Preneste had acted neither as an elector nor as a judge but merely as a reporter (*denunciator*) on the qualities of Philip as a person unworthy. He repeated that it was the right of the pope to inspect and crown, absolved all from their oaths to Philip and again exhorted all the princes to adhere or go over to the support of Otto. The Staufer were far from satisfied with this reply, which one chronicler reports on as containing many absurd and untrue things, 'multa absurda et quedam falsa'.[15]

13. *RNI* no. 61.
14. *RNI* no. 63.
15. Burchard of Ursberg *Burchardi Praepositi Urspergensis Chronicon* 2 edn ed. O Holder-Egger, B von Simson MGH SS (Hanover/Leipzig 1916) 77.

Innocent began now to concentrate on the imperial bishops and on securing practical support for Otto, who in turn was exhorted to assume a manly attitude and in short 'to live up to' the title to which he had been called. Under the barrage of letters from the curia, few had the courage to remain loyal to Philip. A series of archbishops and bishops were brought to Rome and 'carpeted'.[16] The archbishop of Besançon was summoned through the bishop of Langres (an intentional slight) for allowing papal messengers to be captured; the bishop of Speyer on the same grounds and also for sending one messenger to the gallows; the archbishop of Tarentaise for crowning Philip; and the bishop of Passau, who had probably been the draughtsman of the Staufen protest, had a long series of charges brought against him – he had not delivered two million marks to the king of Hungary, he had not paid back the money given him by Richard I for his release – indeed, his crimes were so great, the letter said, that he could have been punished without trial. The final blow for Philip was the defection of his chancellor, Conrad, bishop of Würzburg. No other bishop could have done so much harm to Philip as Conrad. Worse was to come. Before Conrad had received the pope's letter, following his overtures to him, he was slain on 6 December 1202 and the body severely mutilated. His blood-soaked clothes were shown to Philip who broke down and wept and ordered the erection of a cross, but rumour spread that Philip was implicated in the murder.

Public opinion swung against Philip. Innocent did not associate Philip with the murder, but relentlessly sought the true murderers who were finally brought to justice in Rome in April 1203 and sent to the Holy Land. They could not enter the church, were excommunicated and were never to eat meat. However, the damage to Philip had been done. Less than six months later Philip was confined to his own estates. Philip himself now began to understand Innocent better. He sent a messenger, a monk, Otto of Salem, to Rome to sound out Innocent. Informal negotiations began between the two parties and in May 1203 Philip was prepared to make concessions – not a single

16. *RNI* nos 70–2, 74.

secular prince was to be found among the names of the signatories. The concessions included no word about the overlordship of north Italy, the Papal State and Sicily, whose integrity Innocent wanted assured. In September 1203 the pope was very ill and his life was despaired of. None was more despairing than Otto, for if the pope died Otto's position would be immediately weakened. But Innocent recovered and immediately began to exert control over the bishops. One by one they were brought to Rome and, as opportunity arose, they were required to take an oath of obedience to the Holy See 'super negotio imperii', 'on the matter of the empire'. But doubt remained among them and many of them continued to think that the legitimately elected king was Philip. Although by the end of 1203 Otto controlled an area from the French frontier to the Elbe, his cause was by no means won. Fortune now began to turn in favour of Philip. At the end of 1204 Otto's brother, the Count Palatine Henry, the landgrave of Thuringia, the king of Bohemia, Adolf, archbishop of Cologne, and the duke of Brabant all went over to Philip, mainly inspired by their own self-interests.

In attempting to understand the imperial question we need to bear in mind the complexity of relations between the princes, especially the lay princes. Opportunism had long been a characteristic of princes and alliances and changes of allegiance were connected with the patronage to be gained from the emperor. The princes needed to support the dominant imperial candidate to maintain and enhance their positions. It was these self-interests that a distant pope was to find difficult to overcome. Innocent's role as a great spiritual ruler, arbitrating on the candidates for the title, was a weak one if the favoured candidate did not have the necessary allegiance and military support of the princes. Innocent was beset with problems which he had little chance of solving as the sands constantly shifted and political and economic undercurrents conditioned behaviour. The 'ideal' emperor for the princes and the great cities was one who granted territories and conferred rights and commercial privileges and gave protection.

It was a complicated struggle between Welfs and Staufer and their supporters and also between the rival princes themselves, some of whom were great ecclesiastics as Adolf, archbishop of Cologne. Archbishop of the second great German province, Cologne, his family had combined the secular and the ecclesiastical princedom for some time. He it was who by crowning Otto at Aachen had plunged the papacy into trouble. He was representative of the German bench of bishops as a whole, who were more prepared to be the servants of the emperor than of a distant pope. A great German temporal prince, he had the outlook of a great secular noble. His interests lay in power in the imperial court not in the papal court. So the struggle became to some extent a contest between the German bishops and the pope, and the position of the German bishops in extending the conflict can only be understood if we understand their relationships with the political parties and the rival claimants.

We need now to go back to the death of Archbishop Conrad of Mainz on 20 October 1200. Mainz was a see where Staufen interests were strong and a majority of the princes elected Lupold, bishop of Worms, a strong adherent of Philip, and a man of few scruples. The Welfs could not allow such an election to pass unchallenged and a minority elected their own candidate, Siegfried. The double election brought schism to the diocese of Mainz. Lupold was never acceptable to the pope (to whom he remained the bishop of Worms who had transferred himself to Mainz without papal licence) and when at the end of 1204 Philip saw hope of victory he made a bad move by sending Lupold to Italy. Innocent was adamant that Lupold was unacceptable and he made it clear in June 1205, at first secretly and later publicly, that Philip would have to drop Lupold as negotiator. Meanwhile on 13 March 1205 Innocent ordered Archbishop Siegfried of Mainz and the bishop of Cambrai to excommunicate Adolf, to summon him to Rome and, if he did not start for Rome within four weeks, to depose him. Four weeks after the pronouncement of the excommunication, Adolf was solemnly deposed in the cathedral of Cologne in the presence of Otto. A new election was ordered and Bruno, provost of Bonn, a faithful adherent of Otto (who had, indeed, brought notice of Otto's election to Rome) was elected archbishop of Cologne and his election confirmed by the pope on 22 December 1205. There was now schism in Cologne as well as Mainz. Philip offered the pope peace negotiations and, in an important communication of June 1206, he surveyed the imperial dispute from its beginnings, stressing the anarchy in the empire and the motives which had led him to accept the kingship. He suggested the dismissal of Lupold if Innocent would drop Siegfried. If he had offended against the Church he was ready to give satisfaction. 'If you have offended against us, we leave it to your conscience.' Skilled Staufen drafting (probably following Philip's own sentiments) accentuates the authority of the pope as vicar of Christ and his plenitude of power and petitions for absolution from the sentence of excommunication which Celestine III had imposed. It was almost the language of the papal chancery itself, but it was asked in such a manner that the pope could not concede.[17] Innocent needed to be approached as arbiter and he wanted certain guarantees.

The pope was still trying to conjure up support for Otto. He wrote to King John ordering him to pay money to Otto.[18] John paid because he needed Otto. However, by late 1206, it is likely that Innocent sensed that Otto's cause was lost, for in a letter of probably August 1206 to the patriarch of Aquileia, Philip is called *princeps* and no longer *dux*,[19] but he proceeded cautiously, aiming to arrive at a point where he might arbitrate between the parties. This was achieved in January 1208 after the princes, meeting at Augsburg in the autumn of 1207, prevailed upon Philip to go to the pope as arbiter. A tribunal was decided on in Rome and Philip sent ambassadors to plead his case.[20] Otto's legates were despatched in May.[21] All was set for Innocent's arbitration. But on 21 June 1208 Philip of Swabia was dead, assassinated, apparently for personal reasons, by the count of Bavaria, Otto of Wittelsbach.

Fate had again taken a hand. Otto was crowned by the pope as the Emperor Otto IV in Rome in October 1209. By the end of his reign, he had broken all his promises. While his position had been insecure, in 1201, at Neuss, he had

17. *RNI* no. 136.
18. *RNI* nos 131–32.
19. *RNI* no. 137.
20. *RNI* no. 148.
21. *RNI* no. 150.

sworn that he would accept the new frontiers of Innocent III's Papal State.[22] He had recognized papal rule over the Patrimony (from Radicofani to Ceprano), the duchy of Spoleto, the March of Ancona with the duchy of Ravenna and the Matildine territory, 'with other adjacent lands mentioned in many imperial privileges'. He had, at Neuss, signed the 'birth certificate of the Papal State'. He did not keep his solemn word, renewed at Speyer just before his coronation in 1209, when as a condition of his coronation as emperor he promised to restore Church properties retained by his predecessors. Otto's conduct, following the conferment of the imperial title, was overbearing and ill-considered. He succeeded swiftly in offending both the princes and the pope. He terrified the inhabitants of Staufen Swabia, confiscated fiefs which had been conferred on ecclesiastics and gave them to his Saxon and English supporters. He repudiated the oath by which he had restored to the Holy See the ecclesiastical rights and privileges enjoyed by the emperors and the kings of Sicily and within a few months of his coronation he began to progress down into Italy. Acting much like previous aggressive and anti-papal emperors, he granted privileges in the duchy of Spoleto, the March of Ancona and the Matildine lands. At Pisa in November 1209, he came under the influence of the imperial captains and plans for the invasion of Sicily secured the support of two of the principal north Italian cities, Pisa and Milan. Otto moved into mainland Sicily and in November 1210 Innocent III excommunicated him. He had the same aim as all previous emperors – to control the papacy and to re-establish imperial rule in the new Papal State, in time no doubt aiming to unite Italy and Sicily under his imperial crown.[23]

Growing unrest among the German princes was now used by Innocent who suggested a new election. In September 1210 the archbishop of Mainz, the landgrave of Thuringia, the king of Bohemia, the duke of Austria and the count of Meran had met with king Philip Augustus of France whose interests lay in the defeat of Otto. Serious

22. See Map 2.
23. See T C van Cleve *The Emperor Frederick II of Hohenstaufen* (Oxford 1972) esp. pt ii.

opposition to the new emperor had also begun to emerge in some of the towns of north Italy, especially Cremona. Otto was counselled by his supporters to return to Germany to maintain his position and to marry Beatrice the daughter of Philip of Swabia to whom he had been betrothed. This he did on 22 July 1212. Beatrice died soon after and without producing an heir. Otto outlived Innocent (dying in 1218) but his cause was lost from 1214.

The princes had begun to look towards the young Frederick, king of Sicily and Henry VI's heir. He must have appeared as 'the man of destiny', the young saviour, as he entered Constance and progressed down the Rhine in 1212. As Otto's cause declined, Frederick's star rose, but without the support of the French king, Philip Augustus, and finally Innocent, Frederick might not have triumphed. In December 1212 Frederick was elected king of the Romans and crowned and anointed in Mainz. The old Staufen cause had revived, ironically upheld by a French king. King John of England, desperate for Otto's support during his struggle with the pope and his old natural enemy, the king of France, granted Otto 9000 marks in 1213 but the Welf position was weak. Careful diplomacy and a wiser man than Otto might have avoided the disaster at the battle of Bouvines in July 1214, where Philip Augustus soundly defeated John and Otto, for the Flemish cities with their economic interests had a natural ally in England and the duke of Brabant and the counts of Flanders, Holland and of Boulogne were playing off Philip Augustus.

Frederick's primary aim was the continued expansion of the Staufen house in Germany. In return for victory over Otto he paid the price – granting lands and conferring and confirming rights and privileges to the princes, bishops and cities of north Italy who needed his patronage. At Eger, in 1213, Frederick made the same promises to respect the Papal State as Otto had done. He had thus paid off the princes and the pope.

It is difficult to resist the conclusion that after 1208 Innocent had been outmanoeuvred by certain forces beyond his control. In his search to act as arbiter and to secure for the papacy the *defensor* so needed in his ecclesiastical-political programme for Europe he had (as it seemed) changed sides three times, much as the princes themselves.

He had perhaps allowed hatred of the Hohenstaufer to cloud his vision. Frederick had true imperial blood in his veins as the son of the Emperor Henry VI and the grandson of Barbarossa and he could not allow the narrow strip of fifty miles or so of corridor land to impede his ambitions.

. . .

POWER: THE PAPAL STATE, ROME AND SICILY

Political power depends upon economic strength and the size of armies. It is dependent, too, upon a territorial base. The pope's territory was the Patrimony of St Peter and the Papal State. The Patrimony of St Peter was the rather emotive name for the area subject to the pope in the immediate vicinity of Rome where the pope held sway. The duchy of Rome was the papacy's ancient land to which the popes were deemed to have succeeded as the continuators of Byzantine rule and as a result of the Donation of Constantine. The Papal State, on the other hand, consisted mainly of the 'donations' of lands in central Italy made to the papacy by the Frankish emperors. The donations of Pepin (754) and Charlemagne (774) gave the popes the area of central Italy that had fallen to the Lombards, together with the former exarchate of Ravenna and the provinces of Venice and Istria. For these, no texts survive. But for the donations of Louis the Pious in 817 and of Otto I in 962 we have texts, the *Ludovicianum* and the *Ottonianum*, which have been accepted as genuine. These two documents named places over a very wide area of Italy (the duchy of Rome, Tuscany, the Campagna, the Ravenna exarchate, Pentapolis, Sabina) rather than defined frontiers.[24] The *Ottonianum* was confirmed by the Emperor Henry II in 1020. Later emperors did not regard suzerainty in central Italy as having passed to the popes by these donations. They had their own imperial interests. To these very sizeable territories were added the 'Matildine' lands,

24. See Maps 1 and 2. The Latin text of the *Ludovicianum* is in *LC* i 363–5; and of the *Ottonianum* (which added the duchy of Spoleto and Benevento) in i 368–70. Innocent III's claims were based on these ancient documents. Maps 1–4 in Thomas F X Noble *The Republic of St Peter. The Birth of the Papal State 680–825* (Pennsylvania 1984) are extremely useful.

given to the Roman Church by the Countess Matilda of
Tuscany in 1102. She was the sole heiress to a huge complex of imperial fiefs and lands in Tuscany, Emilia and
Lombardy. Ownership was constantly disputed and borders
were vague and ill-defined, but Tuscany, Spoleto and Ancona
and parts of the Romagna were all in papal sights by the
thirteenth century.

The Patrimony of St Peter differed markedly in its development from other states whose national identity was not
blurred. The elective nature of the papacy slowed the
development of the Papal State – in a way that showed a
marked contrast to the development of hereditary monarchies, in England for example. Not all popes were
interested, as we shall see, in the furtherance of political
power. The need to rely on the local aristocracy – common
to all rulers – was accentuated by the fact that often the
pope was chosen from among their number. The rise of
one family could mean the eclipse of another also eager
for power. At times even Rome itself was dominated by a
great senatorial family whom the popes could not control.
And the struggles and factions in Rome were reflected in
Latium where the Roman families also held land. The imperial interventions in papal affairs and in the city's
government also halted the development of a controlled
state as found elsewhere in Europe at the time. Finally, the
ambiguous powers conceded in the donations left large
areas of doubt that were to make political advancement by
the popes difficult.

The 'idea' of a Papal State had appeared very early, and
definitely by the ninth century, but it was with the reform
movement of the eleventh and early twelfth century that
the notion of an independent Papal State really took
hold.[25] Without a territorial base the papacy could not be
independent of imperial and other influences. If it was not
free from unwelcome intervention the papacy could not be
active in what it saw as its role. By the late eleventh century
the popes began to regard these lands as a conglomerate,
the 'lands of St Peter' (*terre sancti Petri*) while interestingly

25. Noble (*Republic of St Peter*) argues in fact that the pope emanci-
    pated central Italy from the Byzantine empire in the late seventh
    century and that this was the beginning of what he calls 'the repub-
    lic of St Peter'; see esp. introduction and ch. 9.

the emperors write more vaguely of papal *regalia et posses-siones.* These lands were in effect Latium, that is, the Campagna, Maritima, Sabina and the county of Tivoli.[26] The territorial claims of Pope Adrian IV in 1159 were extremely modest, if compared with the Carolingian donations, and much more realistic, for there was a wide gap between nominal overlordship and reality. Basically Pope Adrian confined his idea of a Papal State to a small-ish area, that of the old Byzantine duchy of Rome with the duchy of Spoleto to the east. The true state must have settled frontiers rather than vague notional territories. It is in the light of this changing view of the papal territories that many modern historians (Partner, Waley, Laufs) see Innocent III as the founder of the Papal State as distinct from previous popes who were little more than nominal overlords of disparate and scattered lands which they found very difficult to control without imperial help.[27]

At the theoretical centre of the Papal State was the city of Rome. The maintenance of control over Rome itself was an aspiration of all popes – as old as the history of the papacy. The residence of the pope in an ancient imperial city had from the first been fragile. But the pope could not be divorced from the see of St Peter. As long as he remained bishop of Rome the pope belonged in Rome. Popes might be – and often were – driven from Rome, but they aspired to be back in the city to which they belonged. Even imperialist anti-popes tried to reside in the city – and the emperors strove to keep them there. Roman as well as non-Roman popes, Italian as well as foreigners, all felt that they belonged in Rome. There in Rome were the bones of St Peter, the apostle to whom Christ had committed His Church.

Innocent commenced his papacy in Rome, but he died in Perugia, a papal town, in the summer months when it was customary for the papal curia to leave Rome. During 1203–4 he was forced to leave Rome. Most years he spent some time in Anagni or Segni, his home region; otherwise Rome was his main place of residence. His first major acts

26. See P Toubert's excellent account and setting of the scene and excellent maps, *Les structures du Latium médiévale ... du ixe à la fin du xiie siècle* 2 vols (Rome 1973) 1038–40.
27. Cf Noble *Republic of St Peter* introduction.

to subdue the Romans followed in the tradition of the agreements made between Clement III and the senate in 1188 and Celestine III and the senate in 1191.[28] He exploited a temporary lull in affairs to extract more concessions from the Romans than had hitherto been possible. He took advantage of the situation that resulted following the death of the Emperor Henry VI, whose troops had been threatening Rome. For Henry VI's death released anti-imperialist forces, anxious to ward off the imperial regime in Italy. It was the ancient story of the Romans playing off outside powers, but it was opportune for Innocent.

His second major act was to clear the Papal State of imperial troops and to restore it to its old frontiers. Such had been the aims of his predecessors, in particular the English pope, Adrian IV. Innocent had the opportunity and he took it. He spent from July to October of the first year in the papal towns. Within a year the imperial governors of Tuscany, Spoleto and Sicily had to flee. Nor did Innocent change the previous policy of attempting to bolster certain towns. Of the Tuscan towns, Amelia and Otricoli were the only ones to accept papal domination without a murmur. Perugia and Todi surrendered some of their independence, but retained the right to their own jurisdiction, appointing their own officers. Città del Castello, which had a long rivalry with Arezzo, had reason to want papal protection in order to stave off the ambitions of Arezzo. Viterbo and Orvieto, on the other hand, refused to come to terms with Innocent. Otherwise, the towns were transferred in many cases from imperial to papal overlordship. The new Patrimony of St Peter was built up by threats and the exploitation of rivalries. The imperial governor of the duchy of Spoleto, Conrad of Urslingen, tried to remain governor as vassal of the pope. Apart from three castles and two towns, Foligno and Terni, sentiment was anti-imperial and pro-pope. Finally, after Conrad had offered Innocent £100 annually, the service of 200 knights and a cash payment of 10,000 lbs of silver – which the pope could not accept – the duchy was brought peaceably into the Patrimony. The cities in Ancona came under the

28. *LC* LXXXIV and CXXVII.

imperial governor, Markward of Anweiler, who only approached Innocent when the situation was hopeless for him after the formation of a league of cities against imperial domination. Markward, too, made offer of payment to Innocent, which was not accepted. He succumbed finally to the two-pronged attack of the papacy and the anti-imperialists, but a number of districts of Ancona never came under Innocent.

To the south of the pope's territories lay the *Regno*. The *Regno* consisted in the twelfth century (and for most of the thirteenth) of two parts: the island of Sicily and the southern half of the Italian peninsular, the mainland. The peninsular lands incorporated the modern provinces of Calabria, Basilicata (or Lucania), Apulia, Campania, Molise, and the Abruzzi, and the trading city of Gaeta. Within them was the small papal enclave of Benevento. The rulers of the *Regno* were thus of prime interest to the popes. In 1184 the Emperor Frederick Barbarossa secured the marriage of his son Henry, duke of Swabia, to Constance of Sicily, the heiress of her nephew, King William II, who died childless in 1189. The situation became even more threatening on the death of the Emperor Frederick Barbarossa in 1190 and the succession of his son, the Emperor Henry VI, now asserting his claims to Sicily through his wife. The Papal State lay wedged like a nut within a giant imperial nutcracker – a small insecure state set within the imperial towns and communes to the north and the tightly-governed *Regno* to the south.

Innocent exhibited no change in previous papal policy on Sicily. As in other instances, the removal of a strong emperor from the scene brought popular revolt against the Empress Constance in Sicily and Innocent reaped the benefit. Constance wanted to return to the *status quo* before the illegitimate grandson of Roger II, Tancred, count of Lecce, became king in 1190 (i.e. to the state under King William I and King William II, 1154 to 1189), but her offers concerned only the continental kingdom not the island. Innocent was determined that she should renounce the rights of the Williams in the island as well. This he achieved, securing the right for the curia to receive appeals, summon synods and approve bishops. Again fortune favoured him with the death of the Empress in November

1198 and his wardship of the young Frederick II which allowed him advantages denied to his predecessors, not the least of which was the opportunity to build a stronger Papal State.

By the late twelfth century the Papal State as a separate entity had been long established as a notion even if its boundaries were in a continual state of flux. Had Innocent III wished – and the evidence is to the contrary – there would have been no going back on previous policy. The twelfth-century popes were committed to maintaining their temporalities by the Reform movement which was pre-occupied with temporal as well as moral rehabilitation, but it was Innocent who brought the Papal State nearer a political reality than it had been before. The compelling idea of a 'free' state (free from the emperor, the senate and people of Rome, and the anti-papal towns of north Italy) lay at the heart of papal territorial ambitions and the monarchical position adopted for the popes by Pope Gregory VII. The *regnum* of the pope goes back to the Donation of Constantine and its title deeds to the diplomas of the eighth-, ninth- and tenth-century emperors. The papal coronation dates from Gregory VII. The papal banner, the *vexillum sancti Petri*, goes back to the eleventh century, perhaps to Alexander II (1061–1073).[29] Like the banners of royalty, it flew on papal castles in the thirteenth century. The *insignia* of royalty that had been assumed by the papacy reflected a monarchical form and structure of government. Reforms and development in the administration followed the pattern in other states. The chancery had long been conducted as an 'imperial' chancery – indeed it was the successor of the late imperial Roman chancery. Both it and the *camera*, the financial department, had their origins in the 'sacred Lateran palace' (*sacrum palatium Lateranense*), the palace of a monarch. Again it is to the Gregorian Reform movement that the development both of the papal curia (comparable with the monarchical courts) and of the papal treasury, or chamber, is due. The papal curia acted much as the *curia regis* and the cardinals became primarily officers of state and administrators who

29. See Carl Erdmann *The Origin of the Idea of Crusade* trans. M W Baldwin, W Goffart (Princeton 1977) ch vi.

could be used as ambassadors or legates – a position they had reached by the early years of the twelfth century. The papal *camera* or treasury owed much to Pope Urban II (1088–1099), who, as a former monk of Cluny, had experience of one of the most advanced organizations of Europe and really established the papal chamber. 'An impoverished Church could never be a disciplined Church' and the Reform movement concentrated on territorial and economic security. Once the papacy had taken on board the idea of a territorial state, economic power and independence became all important and along with it its concomitant military power and force.

.   .   .

ECONOMIC STRENGTH

There is no surviving detailed assessment of income for the eleventh-century papacy as there is for the English kings in the great Domesday Book of 1086. Yet from the sixth century, under Pope Gelasius, there was a *polypticus*, a register of financial rights recording the revenues of the Church, which was revised by Gregory the Great. Under Pope Gregory VII, formerly the Archdeacon Hildebrand and as such responsible for the administration of church property, relationships with monarchs and monasteries were developed which bound rulers and institutions to the Holy See. Such 'special relationships' implied payment for protection and support. Rights and revenues were inextricably mixed and this is reflected in the compilations. The Gregorian Cardinal Deusdedit's canonical compilation of 1087, concerned with the rights and traditions of the Roman Church, includes a very short section, chapter 149 of Book III, on its temporal possessions, which most likely comes from an earlier compilation.[30] No further assessment of papal revenues was apparently undertaken until the compilation by Benedict, canon of St Peter's, some half century or so later, which was finished before the death of Innocent II in 1143. In the 1150s the papal chamberlain, Cardinal Boso,[31] elaborated the statement of the papacy's

30. Text and edition by Victor Wolf de Glanvell (Paderborn 1905).
31. He was an Englishman and it is tempting to speculate what knowledge he may have had of the very advanced English exchequer at this time. He certainly believed in strong territorial lordship for the popes.

financial rights and Cardinal Albinus was at work on a compilation in the 1180s under Lucius II. But it is the *Liber Censuum,* compiled in the last quarter of the twelfth century and incorporating many of these earlier texts, by the papal chamberlain, Cencio Savelli – later to follow Innocent III as pope – ˙that provides us with most of what we know about papal finance.[32] It lists the revenues due to the apostolic see from the patrimonial estates and the tributes and payments from various European secular rulers and religious houses.

The revenue from the Patrimony was the first obvious source of income that the papal chamberlain, whose office dates back to Paschal II (1099–1118), received. All the usual revenues received by a temporal ruler were exploited – payments from towns and castles, taxes and procurations, and also the income in the shape of rents and the payments from tenants which came from the lands of which the pope was proprietor. It may be doubted whether these sources were often on the credit side as long as the papacy had to pay out considerable sums to consolidate its position and to enter into compacts and agreements with some of the towns: but a list of revenues and rents from Spoleto in 1198 is not negligible.[33] The revenue paid to the chamber by states and vassals outside the Patrimony, who were in a feudal relationship with the Holy See – the tribute – was probably more profitable. King John, for example, undertook a payment of 1000 marks annually to the Roman see from 1213 onwards, when he became a vassal of the Roman Church. The kings of Aragon and Portugal paid tribute as vassals of the Holy See under Innocent. Peter of Aragon promised Innocent 250 *massenutinae* when he committed his kingdom to the pope in 1204. While the tribute often remained unpaid, as in the case of Sicily, where an annual payment of 30,000 tarims (about £100,000) had been agreed on in Frederick's minority,[34] it

32. *LC* i: the second volume deals with the post 1227 redaction. Paul Fabre *Etude sur le Liber Censuum de l'Eglise Romaine* (Paris 1892) ch 1 is still the best introduction to the whole question of financial rights.
33. W E Lunt *Papal Revenues in the Middle Ages* 2 vols (New York 1934) ii no. 196.
34. *Reg. Inn. III* i nos 557, 563 (also *PL* 214 ep 557 cols 510–13 and ep 563 cols 518–19).

provided a source of income which the political activities of the popes in their dealings with the separate kingdoms suggest was definitely worthwhile. Obviously, if the pope could collect this, his finances were well in the black.

The ancient payments of Peter's Pence, which had been granted to the popes by early monarchs, were received from England, the Scandinavian kingdoms and Poland. Any grant of papal support or protection, as Alexander II's support of William the Conqueror's invasion of England in 1066, was likely to lead to a request for a *quid pro quo* or a reminder of a payment due. However small they were, such payments must have been thought worth collecting. Apparently it was the withholding or delay in the payment of Peter's Pence from England that led Pope Alexander II to approve the Norman expedition in 1066. Soon he asked for payment and William complied. Originally the tax had been on each house (or chimney) and not a lump sum paid by diocese, and in 1205 Innocent III attempted to get the full amount, seeking Peter's Pence 'from each house that smoke comes out of'.[35] King John forbade the clergy to enact any new decree on the subject. Innocent made a second attempt in 1214, but was no more successful. The payment, however, when it was collected, was small – £199 6s 8d per annum according to the *Liber Censuum*. The associated but very different payment of the Census was made by monasteries that had the protection of St Peter's vicar, the pope. Usually they were very ancient foundations and there were only a handful of such in England. Such payments accorded the payers with rights of exemption from the interference of bishops and hence were thought worthwhile from the payers' point of view. They were made all over Europe and yielded the papacy an annual payment (often of an ounce of gold) from each house. This could not be described as a substantial source of income.

Until the thirteenth century income tax was not tried by the popes. Such taxes begin with the levies imposed by lay rulers to raise money for the crusades (as the kings of England and France did for the Second and Third Crusades). Innocent was the first pope to try such a scheme and in

35. *The Metrical Chronicle of Robert of Gloucester* ed. W A Wright 2 vols (RS 86, 1887) ii 700.

1199 he initiated an income tax on the clergy of one-fortieth of their ecclesiastical income for a year in aid of the Holy Land. The Fourth Lateran Council, held at the end of his reign, imposed a triennial twentieth for the same purpose. Customary by the mid-thirteenth century, largely due to Innocent's introduction of such a scheme, such taxes, however, did not bring money into the papal coffers but were granted to the leaders of the crusades, though there was a widespread belief that money collected for the Crusade by Philip the notary was doing exactly that, and in 1202 Innocent ordered an investigation.[36] Similarly the indults to those who commuted their crusading vows were earmarked for crusading purposes. The justiciar, Geoffrey FitzPeter, who had taken the cross, was absolved as he was dying in return for a 2000 marks' subsidy for the Holy Land.[37]

Subsidies might be paid in cases of emergency but could not be accounted normal income. In 1093 Pope Urban II approached the bishops and abbots of Aquitaine, Gascony and Lower Burgundy for financial aid in ejecting an anti-pope from the Lateran. Pope Lucius III sought aid from Henry II and the clergy of England in 1184 – a request that the clergy agreed to if the king wished to pay it. Ten thousand marks were sought from King John as a subsidy for the Holy Land. Innocent made no such requests for direct financial aid in his imperial dealings, but he was tireless in epistolary exhortations to key figures to support his candidate financially and, of course, with military aid. King John, for example, was asked for 5000 marks in the support of Otto of Brunswick.[38] Implicit, too, in Innocent's dealings with the separate kingdoms was the notion that payment was expected as tribute for crowning kings.

Customary gifts to the popes – the hidden income – were made by archbishops, bishops, and abbots on visits to Rome to secure confirmation. Gifts and legacies, which in

---

36. E Siberry *Criticism of Crusading 1085–1274* (Oxford 1985) 146.
37. A Mercati 'La prima relazione del Cardinale Niccolò de Romanis sulla sua legazione in Inghilterra (1213)' in *Essays in History presented to R L Poole* ed. H W C Davis (Oxford 1927) 286–7. It is interesting to note how much of this register is occupied with money matters.
38. *Rogeri de Wendover Liber qui dicitur Flores Historiarum* ed. H G Hewlett 3 vols (RS 84, 1886–9) ii 35.

early times had been very large, cannot be assessed very precisely, but are likely to have been considerable. The papal legate in England in 1213, Nicholas de Romanis, reported that he had not received the 1000 marks left to the pope (nor the 500 left to the cardinals) by the archbishop of York, Geoffrey Plantagenet. He recommended that the pope should write to Stephen Langton, the executor.[39] The offerings made at the altars of papal churches were shared by the pope with the assisting clergy. Innocent III instructed his court not to be importunate over gifts and he attempted to introduce fixed chancery charges, but the gratuities expected by officials were a part of normal life and these the pope could not control. Walter of Châtillon (*fl. c.* 1170), in his 'Propter Sion non tacebo', compares the curial advocates with the hounds of Scylla, the chancery with Charibdis, the cardinals with Sirens, the doorkeepers with rocks. The only protection for the petitioner at the papal court is the Purse. One historian has written that the criticism was not that the charges were too high, but that there were any at all and has explained the opposition to fixed charges as conservative reaction to a money economy in which one paid for services rendered. Gratuities formed part of the old, traditional and accepted way of conducting business: set charges were the innovation.[40]

The profits of jurisdiction may well have been outweighed by the costs of the bureaucracy. The clause among the Fourth Lateran Council decrees that proposed regulated taxes for the churches and provinces of Christendom suggests as much. It is difficult to answer the question as to whether the papacy may be accounted a financial power of importance on a European level. Toubert is doubtless correct in his criticism that Pfaff's estimate of the income of the papacy – made on the basis of the *Liber Censuum* – is in fact inclusive of many 'ghost monies'; because the *Liber Censuum* is a book of expected monies, compiled over many years, rather than an actual account.[41] But this record

---

39. Mercati 'Prima relazione' 288.
40. Walter of Châtillon cited by J A Yunck 'Economic conservatism, papal finance, and the medieval satires on Rome' in *Mediaeval Studies* **23** (1961) 339–40 and for the general argument 341–8.
41. Toubert *Latium* 1065–6.

shows that something like 30,340 imperial shillings was expected in revenue: 3300 from the Patrimony, 5800 from religious institutions, and 21,200, the lion's share, from states and vassals. Innocent III was not slow in exploiting what was possible. But his financial activities have the air of an assiduous fund-raiser rather than the representative of a really wealthy institution. Taxes on clerical livings, sizeable profits from granting indulgences and the taking of income from benefices when they were vacant – all lay in the future as the mainstay of papal finances.

The papacy's reputation for venality may be more closely related to the difficulties of collecting what was due to it than to the actual amounts of money coming in. The satire 'Novus regnat Salomon' attacks Innocent as the mercenary shepherd who abandons his flock to the wolf and sees 'Salomon' as venal, loving not persons but their goods, and the poet Walter von der Vogelweide portrays Innocent as filling his chests with German silver and deplores his efforts to collect money for a crusade against the Albigensians.[42] Criticisms of the purposes for which the money was raised do not say much about the curia's actual wealth. Such accusations may not 'stick'; and the suspicion that money collected in England in 1200 for the Holy Land would get no further than Rome may be groundless.[43] The refrain 'Nummus vincit, nummus regnat, nummus imperat' ('Money conquers, money rules, money governs'), replacing the coronation chant 'Christus vincit, Christus regnat, Christus imperat', comments on a power where money interests were supposed to rule supreme but it does not indicate wealth. The pope's strongest card was the one that allowed him to raise money from the separate states and their princes – most of it not long-term income but exceptional grants. The papacy's moral powers enabled it to look for money throughout the western world.

42. See P G Schmidt 'Novus regnat Salomon in diebus malis. Une satire contre Innocent III' in Festschrift Bernhard Bischoff ed. J Autenrieth and F Brunhölzl (Stuttgart 1971) 372–90 esp 377–8; 'I saw the World'. Sixty poems from Walther von der Vogelweide (1170–1228) trans. Ian G Colvin (1938) no. 28.
43. Lunt Papal Revenues i 120 (The Historical Works of Master Ralph of Diceto ed. W Stubbs 2 vols (RS 68, 1876) ii 168–9): the pope ordered an enquiry.

. . .

PAPAL ARMIES

'Your power is made of words, but our power is real'. This
remark of King Philip the Fair's minister, Flotte, to Pope
Boniface VIII may be compared with the scathing words of
Mussolini, 'The Pope, how many divisions has he?'[44] But
the truth was that the popes employed armies of mercenaries or paid troops and that one of the reasons for
raising money was to pay armies. The importance of a military force was obvious to Pope Gregory VII. He had not
only to take Rome: he had also to retain it. Similarly he
had to secure the papal lands and ensure that the revenues
from them reached the papacy. Without the existence of a
force of this kind there could be no security or economic
stability. Armies were needed, too, by the popes to subject
the Roman factions, to resist the Hohenstaufer, to guard
the papal palaces and to control the ever unruly Papal
State. Normally feudal grants were made within the Patrimony and the Papal State in return for military service.
The establishment of fortified places in Latium, the papal
castles, meant maintaining garrisons in each one. Both
Pope Eugenius III and Pope Adrian IV pursued an active
policy of acquiring castles, fortifying them and giving them
special status. While castles might be obtained by purchase,
and exchanged to make for a more judicious distribution
geographically, they had also to be manned with troops.
During the whole of the thirteenth century the ancient *cas-
tra specialia* of the eleventh to twelfth centuries fulfilled
their functions as military as well as administrative centres
of the Papal State. They could not do this without troops.
By the thirteenth century the right of founding a castle,
repopulating an existing site and fortifying it was the exclusive privilege of the pope in Latium.[45] The barons of the
Papal State owed military service to the pope, as did the
citizens of all the communes. (And the communes might
ask the pope, as they did in 1199, to order out the troops

44. *Willelmi Rishanger ... Chronica et Annales* ed. H T Riley (RS 28, 1865)
   197–8, cited by D P Waley 'Papal armies in the thirteenth century'
   EHR **72** (1957) 1: the whole article 1–30 is invaluable on this subject.
45. Toubert *Latium* 1069–80.

of a neighbouring town in their defence.) The demand, however, was sometimes for money in lieu of troops. The changeover from unpaid feudal armies to professional armies, which was a common phenomenon with secular governments, was also experienced by the papacy in the thirteenth century. Innocent III employed mercenaries in January 1199 and in 1199–1200, as the *Gesta* tells us. They were probably normally Italians. (Gregory IX, 1227–41, employed French mercenaries.) The demand for money instead of military service became more frequent. But already in the early years of his pontificate, before he was master of the enlarged Papal State from Radicofani in the north to Ceprano in the south, mercenaries had been used in the campaign against Markward of Anweiler, who was fighting the imperial cause in Italy between 1199 and 1201; five hundred at one time and possibly as many as 2000. The rising costs of warfare by the late thirteenth century were a reason for fiscal innovations. Under Innocent the *servitium debitum* (feudal military service) played only a small, possibly no part. In peaceful times this levy might be enough for policing the Papal State, but to stave off imperial claims Innocent used paid troops and relied heavily on diplomatic manoeuvres to gain the support of allies.

Behind whatever economic and military strength the papacy possessed, there existed enormous and immeasurable power as a moral force. In the pursuit of their aims, the popes could excommunicate recalcitrant members of Christian society, depose unsatisfactory rulers and put sections of the community, indeed whole nations, under sentence of interdict. Throughout the imperial struggle and in his dealings with the separate kingdoms, Innocent used the weapon of excommunication. Philip of Swabia was already excommunicate at the opening of the contest over the empire – excommunicated by the late Pope Celestine III – and the fact of his excommunication was to act as a severe encumbrance for it meant not only that the excommunicant was without the sacraments of the Church, it also affected dependants and those who had dealings with him. It was thus a stage towards the releasing of vassals from the oaths of loyalty and obedience. The dire result of that was seen with the invasion of England by Prince Louis of France following such a sentence on King John. It could act as a severe political deterrent. Not only were nobles who defected from the support of Otto of Brunswick punished by sentences of excommunication, such as Otto's brother, Henry the count Palatine, and the duke of Brabant in 1204–5, but also the ecclesiastical hierarchy who as temporal as well as spiritual princes might face revolt on their estates as well as censure from ecclesiastics within the diocese or province.[46] In 1202 Innocent threatened the archbishop of Trier with excommunication. Archbishop Adolf of Cologne, who had at first supported Otto, was threatened with excommunication. The logical result of excommunication was deposition, for an excommunicate bishop or king could not rule a diocese or kingdom. The position was made clear to Adolf in 1205. He was to be excommunicated by three papal commissioners in the cathedral of Cologne, summoned to Rome and, if he did not start within four weeks, he was to be deposed.[47] Some of the English chroniclers supposed King John to have been formally deposed by the pope, for the effects were the same. And how could a Christian king rule if he was banned from the Church? The power of the pope to depose an unsatisfactory emperor goes back to the *Dictatus Pape* of Gregory VII – a power which Innocent preferred to see as a right to inspect, approve and crown, but there is little doubt that it was important in the papal moral armoury.

Also coupled with the censure of excommunication was the imposing of an interdict, a sentence that forbade the celebration of the sacraments except to a limited number of religious communities. In acquiring privileges from the papacy this was very frequently one that was given a very significant place. A whole kingdom, a whole community and all Christian people, save for a few exceptions, might be put under such a sentence. Innocent laid an interdict on Norway because of the 'royal' policies of its ruler, Sverre, who was resisting papal influence and the reception of the canon law and he reproved the archbishop, Eric, for removing it in 1204, after Sverre had died and the fugitive

46. *RNI* nos 119–22.
47. *RNI* nos 116–17.

bishops had been recalled.[48] Nearly everybody suffered in such circumstances – not just the ruler. The interdict imposed upon England by Pope Innocent III in March 1208 lasted until July 1214. During this time, such services as there were took place behind locked doors. Babies were not christened, marriages were not properly celebrated, the dead were not buried with the full rites of the Church. Confirmations and ordinations did not take place – most of the bishops and many of the religious communities were in exile. Such was the papacy's power to bring a king to his knees. A similar sentence had been imposed on the King of France, Philip Augustus in 1200, for his failure to comply with the pope's wishes and exile Agnes of Meran and take back Ingeborg as his wife and queen. Nor did such sentences mean that the wrongdoers were allowed to rot in peace. The Church could not allow sinners to perish without seeing the evil of their ways. Censures were pronounced by the pope, sometimes by his legates, who were despatched to bring the curial arm to the spot. The re-instatement of King John in 1212 by the legates, after his submission to the pope, illustrated the enormous moral power of the thirteenth-century papacy. Even at the height of its propagandist messages, the Staufen chancery found it difficult to counteract papal arguments, for they were conducted on a supernal plane.

In the last analysis Christian rulers wanted the Church's approval and support and Innocent had gone one further step in identifying himself as the representative of the final arbiter and judge of man. The emperor, in particular, needed coronation. It was the symbol of all his earthly power. And he also strove to gain acceptance and coronation for his son. What is more it had long been accepted that only the pope could perform this.

. . .

POLICY

The policies of Innocent were not negative – nor were they new. Steeped in the theory of the two powers of the *regnum* and the *sacerdotium*, Innocent, in his world view, saw the

---

48. *The Cambridge Medieval History* ed. J R Tanner, C W Previté-Orton, Z N Brooke (Cambridge 1929) vi 29.

need for a strong emperor. He had an idealized notion of the Christian emperor of the West furthering the Christian message and fighting the enemies of the faith in crusades within Christendom as well as without. This emperor would be the secular arm of the pope following papal policies: in some ways a simplistic interpretation of the Donation of Constantine, perhaps – the return to an ideal that had never existed. In concrete terms, however, it was the fear of encirclement of the papacy, should the crown of imperial Germany be united with that of the kingdom of Sicily, that conditioned papal and curial thinking. Both Celestine III and Innocent and the cardinals (most of whom came from Latium and north and central Italy) were acutely aware of the influence that the emperor could exercise over Rome and the northern Italian cities both from past history and personal experience. The southern borders of the little Papal State now touched on the lands of the same family. What is more, at the nearest point, they were only some thirty miles from Rome. The Emperor Frederick Barbarossa (d. 1190) had established the German monarchy and built up the power of the emperor in the north to a hitherto unparalleled degree. He controlled the 'imperial' towns. The pacts or concordats of the mid-twelfth century exhibited the popes' worries. In 1153 Frederick I, by the pact of Constance, promised not to make a truce with the two other groups that threatened the papacy – the Romans and the ruler, Roger of Sicily. Four years later Pope Adrian IV at the Concordat of Benevento turned the ruler of Sicily, William, into his liegeman. He stopped all isolationist trends in the Sicilian Church and clearly put it under the papacy.[49] Henry VI, by his marriage, had now removed all possibility of a 'checking' alliance with the rulers of the southern Italian lands. Both Henry VI and his father had devastated the Roman Patrimony and made the popes their victims. The provision of a candidate for the imperial throne, who was not identified with previous depredations and who, furthermore, had no territorial claims to the southern Italian lands, was bound to prove attractive to the papacy. It was Innocent's misfortune that the man chosen was Otto of Brunswick. Dislike of the Hohenstaufer

49. For texts *LC* lxxxv–vi.

blinded the pope to Otto's shallow character. After the murder of Philip of Swabia and Otto's coronation as Otto IV, he did precisely what previous Staufen monarchs had done. He attempted to subject the cities and domains of north Italy and Tuscany, asserted his overlordship over Ancona and the Romagna and invaded the Patrimony. Innocent replied by excommunicating Otto.

In considering Germany, Italy and the empire, Innocent's dream was that Henry VI's son, Frederick, should act in the interests of the Church. The young Frederick was made a ward of the papacy. In 1198 Innocent made a concordat with Constance, his mother. The kingdom of Sicily, it was agreed, belonged to the Roman Church. Innocent asserted his paternal protection of Frederick and the position of Sicily as a fief of the papacy. He took advantage of both a feudal and a monarchical position, treating Frederick as a vassal of the papacy as well as emphasizing his papal rights of protecting a minor. Before the death of the Empress Constance on 27 November 1198, scarcely ten months after Innocent's election, Innocent had been made Frederick's guardian. He was satisfied to leave the government of Sicily largely to the chancellor, Gauthier de Paléar, bishop of Troja, who stood for Sicilian rights and was anti-German. More troublesome was the imperial chamberlain, Markward of Anweiler, who wanted to make the southern lands the centre of resistance for the imperialists. Innocent's attitude towards Frederick is seen at its most raw in the *Deliberatio* of 1200. If Frederick, when he comes of age, sees that he has been deprived of the empire by the Roman Church, he will become its implacable enemy. Papal troops in south Italy could be seen as protecting Frederick II's rights. Otto's aggressively imperialist policy, wedging the papacy between the 'two Italies', led to his final downfall.

. . .

THE SEPARATE KINGDOMS

The imperial schism had its repercussions on the separate kingdoms of Europe with whom the pope kept up a ceaseless round of correspondence, despatching legatine missions in his concern for ensuring Christian rulership and furthering his policies. Philip of Swabia had restored the title of king to Ottokar, duke of Bohemia, a fief of the German empire, on his eastern borders, but Ottokar was persuaded by Innocent to desert Philip and declare for Otto of Brunswick. Both Otto and Innocent confirmed his title in 1207. There were also other influences affecting the kingdoms on the borders of the Christian world – the Muslim threat, heathenism and heresy. These we shall need to consider later. The pope's influence was at its greatest in the papal fiefs, where the kings became his vassals.

Portugal was an apostolic fief from 1179 and soon after his accession Innocent wrote to Sancho I about the payment of the papal dues. Since he was already a papal vassal Sancho found the powers of the Church difficult to check. Furthermore, in his policy of building towns and castles, Sancho had encouraged and endowed the religious orders and had rewarded the bishops and monasteries with extensive territories. Sancho now seized the episcopal estates of the bishop of Porto (against whose oppression the citizens of Porto had risen) and exiled the bishop of Coimbra. Complaints were made to the pope, although the archbishop of Braga remained loyal to the crown. The illness of Sancho in 1211 probably accounted for his reconciliation with Rome and with the bishop of Porto and his acceptance of stringent conditions which seriously limited the powers of his successor, Alfonso II, for the Cortes in 1211 had declared all secular law subject to canon law and had freed the clergy from most taxes.

There had been early ties between Aragon (consisting loosely of Aragon, the county of Barcelona and parts of Languedoc and Provence) and the papacy, and in 1204, alarmed by the prospect of the Albigensian Crusade and the effect on his vassals in the Languedoc, Peter II submitted his kingdom to the pope. The *Gesta* describes in some detail the journey of Peter to Rome to receive the belt, the symbol of the Christian warrior, and the diadem or crown, the symbol of kingship. He came by sea with five galleons and established his party, including the archbishop of Arles and the provost of Maguelonne and other clerks and nobles, on an island between Porto and Ostia. The pope sent cardinals, the senator of Rome and other nobles to escort him to St Peter's and at the monastery of St Pancras the king was anointed by the cardinal bishop of

Porto and crowned by the pope, who gave him the royal insignia. Then the king returned with the pope to St Peter's and there placed the sceptre and diadem on the altar and received from the pope the papal banner and offered his kingdom to Peter, the prince of the apostles.[50] In return for his allegiance the king received papal protection for himself and his kingdom, he could be excommunicated only by the pope and any lands conquered from the Muslims were confirmed to the crown. When Peter died in 1213 the pope took over the wardship of his son, James I, chose his councillors and constituted his government, against the ambitions of Simon de Montfort. In 1207 the king had authorized the election of bishops without lay intervention.

Of the other Iberian kingdoms, Léon was not subject to Rome, but the marriage of Alfonso IX of Léon to a daughter of Sancho I of Portugal threatened the security of the king of Castile, who obliged Alfonso to separate and to take a Castilian princess, Berengaria, instead. This allowed Innocent in 1199 to intervene, as he was asked for a dispensation. Innocent's imposition of an interdict was parried by the archbishop of Toledo who argued that such a sentence would only encourage heresy and the Muslims, but Innocent did not stop trying to break the marriage. Berengaria promised to leave Alfonso in 1204 and the pope legitimized the children. The pope's jurisdiction over marriage had allowed his intervention and approval of a king and his heirs. Navarre, squeezed between two great Catholic and papalist neighbours, Aragon and Castile, was a prey to the interference of both. When Alfonso VIII of Castile invaded Navarre in 1200 there was no protest from the papacy, intent on supporting the strongest royal house in the crusade against the Muslims.

The kingdom of Sicily became a fief of the Roman Church during the minority of Frederick. All government came under the supervision of the pope and the wardship of Frederick fell to Innocent. This was fortuitous for Innocent, as was King John's submission to the pope and his surrender of the kingdoms of England and Ireland to Innocent as his feudal lord in 1213. John's long struggle

50. *Gesta* chs CXX–I. Cf *PL* 215 bk 7 ep 229; bk 8 ep 92; bk 9 ep 101.

against Innocent's interference in the appointment of Stephen Langton as archbishop of Canterbury had been superseded by a struggle against the baronage – his own vassals. In his acceptance of the pope's lordship, John ensured the protection of the monarchy and of the succession. John received the support of Innocent against the Magna Carta which the pope annulled in August 1215, suspending Langton and summoning him as a participant to answer at Rome. He also secured the succession of his heir a minor, the young Henry III. Royal government was to be protected by the despatch of legates to England and the strictures of the Church would not harm John. Furthermore, the kingdom would be protected by the pope.[51]

France was virtually the only kingdom of central Europe to hold out against papal influence. The territorial rivalry between the Angevins and the French accounted for the dividing lines between the imperial candidates and the alliances and counter-alliances. Angevin interests lay in the support of the Welfs as the strongest power in north Germany, who might help them to maintain the crumbling Angevin empire. French interests, on the other hand, were to see the break-up of that empire and King Philip Augustus, therefore, supported the Staufen cause and the candidature of Philip of Swabia. Philip Augustus's marriage to Ingeborg of Denmark had been made in the hope that the Danish king, who was pro-Welf would support him against the English. Its failure and Philip's subsequent marriage in 1196 to Agnes daughter of the count of Meran – a Rhinelander and supporter of Philip of Swabia after 1198 – had accounted for the presence of a legate in France at Innocent's accession.[52] Innocent's main aims were to win the support of Philip for Otto and to enforce the marriage law. He brought out all the papal arguments and the curial forces from legates to censures, but while he obtained acknowledgement of his final authority in matrimonial matters, he made little other headway. He needed Philip

---

51. Jane Sayers *Papal Government and England during the Pontificate of Honorius III (1216–1227)* (Cambridge 1984) 162–71.
52. On the whole question see Baldwin *Philip Augustus* 84–7, 178–80, 194, 199, 204–7, 332–5: the *Gesta* shows a great interest in the affair of Philip's marriage.

more than Philip needed him. With the acquisition of Normandy from its Angevin rulers in 1204, Philip's position was strengthened. Innocent unsuccessfully called upon the French king in 1208, after the murder of his legate, Peter of Castelnau, to lead a crusade against the southern French heretics. Then, in 1210, after Otto had revived the old imperial policies in Italy and had begun to oppress the Church, Innocent turned once more to Philip Augustus. At Bouvines in 1214, the French overcame the joint Anglo-Welf forces: the old Angevin empire was never to be restored and Otto died almost landless in 1218. Innocent had not controlled French aspirations but he had made it clear that he saw himself as the arbiter of Europe and John's cession of his kingdom in 1213 considerably strengthened the pope's hand. Not only was the pope desirous of peace in Europe and settlement of the imperial question, but he was also concerned with establishing a truce between the two kings so that a new crusade might be advanced.

In eastern Europe the kingdom of Hungary had early and direct relations with the papacy, for the Arpad, the holy Stephen, had been crowned king with insignia given by the pope in the year 1000. Hungary was particularly important to the papacy and to the development of papal influence. Placed between between East and West, its missionizing role was important in bringing further territories under the Latin Church rather than the Greek. It also commanded the route the crusaders took to the East. The Magyars had expansionist aims and by the thirteenth century they had missionized much territory and brought Croatia within their kingdom. They were the leading power in eastern Europe; Serbia had a client-prince and a marriage alliance had been made between King Imre of Hungary's sister and the Byzantine emperor. They had further expansionist aims towards Serbia, Bosnia and Bulgaria. It was their own particular relationship with the papacy that allowed precisely those territories that they were seeking to control to open negotiations with the pope. The Kulin of the Bosnians, fearful of a Magyar attack, submitted to the pope, and the Serbians looked to Hungary, Bulgaria and the papacy for support. It was Bulgarian policy that greatly threatened Hungary. Johannitsa of Bulgaria, who styled himself emperor of the Bulgarians and Wallachians, wanted support for his regime against both Hungary and the Byzantine empire. He saw an opportunity in negotiation with the curia. The curia, for its part, saw obvious advantages in the possibility of bestowing a crown on Johannitsa and extending its influence towards the Eastern Church at Constantinople, possibly even in time bringing the Byzantine Church under the papacy. Johannitsa threatened the pope with accepting coronation from the patriarch of Constantinople: in 1203 Johannitsa submitted to the Holy See, the legate bestowed the pallium on the archbishop of Trnovo as primate and in November 1204 crowned Johannitsa king of the Bulgars and Wallachians.[53] The Hungarians had good reason to feel aggrieved, particularly when, despite papal guarantees, the crusaders destroyed Zara in 1204, and because they had remained firm in their support, together with the neighbouring king of Bohemia, for Otto of Brunswick. But from the pope's point of view the boundaries of his influence had been extended by the coronation of Johannitsa and the influence of the patriarch of Constantinople and the Greek Church decreased.

. . .

PROPAGANDA, INFORMATION AND DIPLOMACY

In the history of papal propaganda, the reign of Innocent III is important. The chancery was used as a propaganda machine perhaps as never before. Before 1198 we have only very fragmentary papal registers (and hence statements) and so far as is known no forerunner of the very precious *Regestum super negotio Romani imperii*. The chancery was a public relations office, a press office and a private office all in one. Its letters were like official communications combined with television documentaries and newspaper reports. At least some 6,000 letters are likely to have been issued during Innocent III's reign. Potthast gives the figure of 5,316. To this figure may be added further discoveries and letters for the years where the register is lost or imperfect, as in the third and fourth years.

53. See J R Sweeney 'Innocent III, Hungary and the Bulgarian Coronation: a study in medieval papal diplomacy' *Church History* **42** (1973) 320–34.

We cannot know the pope's part in the composition of the letters. Pennington believes that the style and content of some preclude any other authorship. The letters of the first two years form a remarkable 'political' testimony. Though we cannot imagine that Innocent wrote all these, he appears to have had a close relationship with his chancery. I do not think that it can be doubted either that he wrote, i.e. dictated, a fair number of the letters in the *RNI*. The letters contain a plethora of arguments, analogies, syllogisms, symbolic phrases and quotes, mainly from the Bible and from the Old Testament in particular. The *Ecclesia*, meaning the whole Christian world, the 'congregatio fidelium' of Hugh of St Victor, was the body politic for Innocent, the whole Christian people. Most of the arguments were not new. The Petrine commission, the vicariate of Christ (Adrian IV ep. 15 'Christi vices in terris agimus'), the pope as king and priest 'after the order of Melchizedek' – all have their roots in the past. Even the plenitude of power is the natural extension of previous arguments.

If the message was not new, the persistency and urgency with which it was repeated was. Obviously no one recipient could experience the full range of papal arguments. But a random selection of the massive output of the chancery shows all the stops pulled out of the papal organ: the reminder to the papal judge, acting by delegation in a distant province of the Church, that he will need to answer for his actions before the Supreme Judge, the care with which letters seeking advice are answered (Eustace of Ely), the terrible missives which reached King John and other miscreants and recalcitrants. Letters exhorted, corrected and broadcast excommunications. They found their way into all parts of Europe and all were trumpets of power.

The letters alone, however, could only achieve a limited amount. Crucial to the success of diplomatic missions were first the quality of the ambassadors and secondly the political intelligence. The normal process, as seen during Innocent's pontificate, was for messengers, often close confidants of the pope, but in minor offices, to be sent in the first instance – then to be followed by negotiators of the highest rank. For example, in dealing with Bulgaria and Hungary, the pope's chaplain, John of Casamari, who had considerable local knowledge, was sent in the first instance, to be followed by the 'big guns', Cardinal Leo Brancaleone, a legate with full powers. In the imperial affair the first person to act on behalf of the pope was Monaco de Villa, a Milanese, who had been appointed by Otto as plenipotentiary to deal with the pope. Innocent certainly knew the position of Monaco and it was through him probably that the pope made known his conditions for the acceptance of Otto. Monaco also had several demands to make of Otto and was present at his coronation on 12 July 1198, possibly to seek that the Lombard cities should be free from imperial encroachments. Such officials were used so that if anything went wrong the papal see would be entirely free from reproach.[54] The first legate to enter the scene was Cardinal Peter of Capua whose task was to transform the peace between Philip Augustus and Richard I in late 1198.[55]

Shortage of information was apparent in May 1199.[56] In July 1200 Conrad of Mainz was taken to task for not having sent report to Rome about plans for the tribunal to decide on an emperor. About the same time a papal envoy, Egidius, was despatched to gain news, followed by Cardinal Guido of Preneste, the pope's personal representative.[57] On 5 January 1201 Philip, the notary, and Cardinal Guido were sent: they had gone before Egidius returned with the news that things were going very badly for Otto. In August to September 1200 the legate Octavian, a trusted curialist, was empowered to release King John from his obligations and also to deal with Philip Augustus and Ingeborg: he was particularly charged with getting Philip Augustus to Otto's side. On 3 July 1202, Master Philip, the notary, reported on Otto's coronation at Cologne. Early in 1202 secret negotiations had already begun between Otto and Innocent.[58] Later in the year, after the Staufen protest against Guido of Preneste, messengers and letters of the pope

---

54. *RNI* no. 3.
55. For him, see Maleczek *Papst und Kardinalskolleg von 1191 bis 1216. Die Kardinäle unter Coelestin und Innocenz III.* (Vienna 1984) 117–24: he had been at the Paris schools.
56. *RNI* no. 16.
57. *RNI* nos 21 and 51.
58. *RNI* no. 64.

were captured.[59] Conrad of Speyer was charged with executing one messenger and detaining others.

From what we know when the information did come through, it was sometimes partial and often faulty. In Innocent's dealings with Hungary and Bulgaria, Innocent's diplomacy has been found wanting as a result of this. News did not get through to Innocent at the time of the preparations for the Fourth Crusade: sometimes the news might be deliberately withheld. Sometimes, too, information was deliberately falsified, misrepresented, touched up or omitted or withheld from the pope, as by the emissaries of Baldwin IX of Flanders. Baldwin, following the conclusion of certain pacts with Philip Augustus, sought to extricate himself from the possible threat of excommunication and interdict on his lands which he had accepted at the time of the agreement if certain conditions were not fulfilled. Accordingly he took advantage of a new pope to address the curia for favourable letters. These were issued by Innocent's officials without a full investigation of the facts.[60] Much business took place at second hand, and by delegates, and the curia was not anxious to investigate every case on the spot. It was, therefore, open to misrepresentation and special pleading, to accepting what it was told by the party that secured or took the initiative. Maximum use might be made by supplicants and petitioners of the distance between them and Rome.

The success of a diplomatic mission depends as much as anything on the quality of the information. The sources of information were the letters, the legates and the local churchmen – all fragile. The news might well be outdated by the time it reached the curia, messengers and even legates might be seized, as Cardinal Leo was by King Imre of Hungary, and the curial instructions might well be outdated when they reached their target. Unless full powers were given to the pope's ambassadors their success was likely to be qualified – without telephones, 'hotlines', faxes, they could not speedily refer to the centre. Without ciphers and diplomatic bags, espionage and counter-espionage

---

59. *RNI* no. 61.
60. J C Moore 'Count Baldwin IX of Flanders, Philip Augustus, and the Papal Power' in *Speculum* **37** (1962) 79–89 esp. 82–8.

actions were likely to be circumscribed. Much depended in the last resort, too, on the power with which the negotiators went to the negotiating table, what goodwill there was between parties and what the strength of the bargaining power was.

. . .

CONCLUSION

The reasons for Innocent III's political actions lay firmly in the past. 'Higher than man but lower than God', the pope, if judged by his political programme, appears an arch-conservative.[61] The policies are not new but based on previous papal actions and inspirations. In dealing with Rome, the Papal State and the emperors, Innocent appears as a restorer and a continuator, but an extremely aggressive restorer, it must be said.

The traditional view of the emperor as the protector and defender of the Roman Church and of the *regalia* of St Peter, as expressed in the emperor's oath, remained an essential element in Innocent's thought. There was never any question of dispensing with the services of an emperor. Innocent wanted a strong emperor but one who could be controlled. He was an arch-conservative, indeed, striving and planning for an *imperium* that would promote both the papacy and Christianity. Innocent's aims during the imperial schism (which, it must be remembered, that he had in no way engendered) were to decide between rival candidates – to arbitrate between them as equal powers, not to judge. His insistence on arbitration rather than on judgment may be argued to have prolonged the contest but it was in line with past experience. Yet it took ten years for the pope to arrive at the point he had desired in 1199, where he could treat the parties as equals, the one and the other, *alterum et alterum* as he says, and make his decision in Rome.

What then did Innocent gain from the long struggle? First and foremost he had made it clear that the decision in the imperial affair as to who was the 'suitable' (*idoneus*) ruler must rest in his hands. Secondly, he may be said to have challenged and broken the enhanced idea of empire,

61. Sermo II, *PL* 217 col 656.

albeit with the help of circumstances. For Frederick II at Eger in 1213 (as had Otto at Neuss), repudiated the whole imperial programme and the ambitions of his father, Henry VI, renouncing claims to all the land between Radicofani and Ceprano, the March of Ancona, the duchy of Spoleto, the Matildine lands, the county of Bertinoro, the exarchate of Ravenna, Pentapolis and the Massa Trabaria.[62] He had agreed to the separation of the emperorship from the kingdom of Sicily. Who in 1216, when Innocent died, could have predicted that the agreements would be torn up and that the popes would face another onslaught from an unreliable and unprincipled emperor? Innocent had misjudged the character of Otto, as he later admitted in a letter to Philip Augustus: 'If only, dearest son, I had known the character of Otto who now calls himself Emperor, as well as you ... It is with shame that I write this to you who so well prophesied what has come to pass'.[63] An observer at the end of Innocent's reign, from the facts in front of him, could not have pronounced Innocent other than successful. He had created the reality of a Papal State and had laid secure foundations for his successors, barring the breaking of solemn oaths and international agreements. What would happen was by no means certain in 1216. Thirdly, again helped by circumstances, he had to some extent ended the hereditary principle as applying to the emperorship. Henceforth it would revert to an elected emperorship. Peace had been restored between the *Ecclesia* and the *Imperium*. Whether Innocent could have achieved his ends earlier or by better means must in the final analysis be a matter of opinion. His policy was consistent, unwavering, conservative. In the long term the papacy had shown itself a 'Western' power to be reckoned with in diplomatic and monarchical terms – a power, what is more, that claimed to be able to decide between states on their moral actions, *ratione peccati*. Like all other powers the papacy was intent on reducing the rights of its neighbours.

On the other side, what did Innocent or the papacy lose in the long struggle? The notion that the papacy should be above politics would have made no sense to the people of

62. *LC* p. 442.
63. Quoted by van Cleve *Frederick II* 73.

the medieval world. The papacy's purpose and *raison d'être* was to missionize and convert, to spread the Gospel and all that the Church stood for. Attitudes to the crusades, the regaining of the Holy Places, the Eastern Empire of Constantinople and the Greek Orthodox Church were all conditioned by the curia's ancient policy and purpose of missionizing and converting. It remains to look at Innocent's expansionist views towards the Eastern Church and Palestine, but they were grounded in age-old desires to reunite Christendom and secure the Holy Places from the infidel. At times in the prolonged imperial affair the pope may have looked close to losing face but the overall purpose of curial policy was never weakened nor diminished. It has been argued that the spiritual prestige of the papacy was tarnished by its use of temporal strength to achieve its ends, but that is in many ways a modern concept. In the opinion, however, of the contemporary poet, Walter von der Vogelweide, the civil war that engulfed his land was prolonged by the pope in order to weaken the empire. He complains, too, that the church party resorted to excommunication to achieve its temporal goals. But what other censures could it impose? The main criticism is that the papacy should not be concerned with temporal matters at all. It denies the purpose of the Church in *this* world. According to Walter, the angels in heaven cried out 'Alas!' three times when the Donation of Constantine was made.[64] Such an attitude explains the attractions of the Friars and other contemporary groups who embraced poverty in their search for salvation and a return to what was held to be the simplicity of the 'primitive' Church; but it was remote from the active role of the papacy from the eleventh century onwards, committed to achieving its aims through government, diplomacy and the law.

64. *Poems of Walther von der Vogelweide* trans. Colvin nos 13–15, 19, 25.

Chapter 3

LAW AND SOCIETY

. . .

DECLARATION AND FORMATION OF THE LAW

The power of the medieval papacy was upheld by the law. Popes made law from early times. Those popes who are generally considered to have been most influential and powerful had decidedly legal aims: their political theory was developed within the law. Gregory VII's vision was of a society where the pope controlled the emperor, the clergy and the laity. From this pontificate come, not surprisingly, important collections of church, or canon, law. Alexander III has been seen as a great lawyer pope: he made pronouncements, gave judgments and held a council for the whole Church in which the law was defined.[1] He developed the central court as the hub of a widespread system of justice. His decisions were collected and publicized. At this time lawyers became important in key positions within the Church (and within the states and separate kingdoms). Developing bureaucracies needed lawyers as administrators and the developing universities became the power-houses of legal science, providing the intellectual comment, scholarship and informed criticism necessary for the formulation and conduct of policy.

---

1. It has been questioned whether Pope Alexander III (Rolandus Bandinelli) was the same person as the canonist Rolandus: see John T Noonan Jr 'Who was Rolandus?' in *Law, Church and Society: Essays in honor of Stephan Kuttner* ed. K Pennington, R Somerville (Philadelphia 1977) 21–48. Noonan questions not only the identity of Alexander III but also the value of his legal judgments (p. 44).

We must now consider more closely the pope's relationship with the law and where Innocent stands in its development. It was firmly established from the time of Gregory VII that the pope had the exclusive power to issue new law in case of necessity (*Dictatus Pape* c.7) – to put forward new decrees and remedies against new excesses and to dispense from or mitigate the law in some cases.[2] From this grew the notion that the pope had the power not simply to explain and interpret the law, but to make it, whether by word of mouth in councils or by letter. Here the pope had the advantage over the emperor for, with the removal of the empire to the West, Roman law ceased to be declared and the Roman law dried up as a living law. Canon law, on the other hand, was the clay with which the pope could mould society. The power to bind and to loose had been granted to the Prince of the Apostles, St Peter, by Christ Himself. Through St Peter it descended to his successors, the popes.

. . .

COUNCILS: THE FOURTH LATERAN COUNCIL

Papal declaration of the canon law could take place with or without consultation. It could be made by a public declaration in a large meeting, such as a council, or in the comparative privacy of the pope's household, perhaps in the dictation of a letter. Most early law was declared in councils of the Church and notaries were officially charged with the copying down of the decrees or acts. Those popes who have been seen by posterity as the great lawyers held councils and declared the law: Innocent II summoned the Second Lateran Council in 1139, Alexander III held the Third Lateran Council in 1179. Innocent III himself by the bull 'Vineam Domini' of April 1213 summoned a great council to meet at the Lateran in Rome on 1 November 1215 to be known as the Fourth Lateran Council. The letter of summons declared the pope's aims – the calling of a new crusade for the recovery of the Holy Land and the reform of the universal Church.[3] Innocent moved within

2. See Stephan Kuttner 'Urban II and the doctrine of interpretation: a turning point?' in *Studia Gratiana* **15** (1972) 55–86, reprinted in *The History of Ideas and Doctrines of Canon Law in the Middle Ages* (1980).
3. *PL* 216 Reg XVI ep 30 cols 823–7, translation in *SLI* 144–7.

the framework of the old doctrine that only a general council could declare or pronounce on the faith (Isidore of Seville), establish doctrine and condemn heresies. Berengar of Tours (d. 1088) and Peter Abelard had been denounced for their opinions in councils of the Church. Similarly, the Fourth Lateran Council, in its second decree, condemned the teaching of Joachim of Fiore (namely that there were four persons in the Trinity), as expounded in his book against Peter Lombard,[4] and went on to define the duties of secular rulers and of bishops to fight heresy in their kingdoms and dioceses. Innocent's council was to emphasize the importance of the crusade against the infidel and the importance of a new era of evangelization.

This council was the first to summon lay representatives: proctors arrived on behalf of Frederick II of Sicily, the emperor of Constantinople and the kings of France, England, Hungary, Jerusalem, Cyprus and Aragon.[5] King John had not been invited because he was under sentence of excommunication – he did not, therefore, legally exist – but when the council finally took place five proctors represented the king of England, three of whom were clerics, the archbishop of Bordeaux, the archbishop of Dublin and the king's chancellor, Richard Marsh, and two laymen, John Marshal and Geoffrey Lutterel. Baronial proctors were invited because Innocent wished to settle the differences between the king and the barons to clear the way for full-scale support from the English baronage for his crusade but there is no evidence that any were sent. The count of Toulouse was present to answer charges of heresy and so to protect himself and his lands against Simon de Montfort. It was widely rumoured (by Welf sources) that the pope would rally again to the support of the ex-Emperor Otto IV (still excommunicated) against the claims of Frederick II, in spite of the treacherous behaviour of Otto towards the papacy. In fact he declared for Frederick. The treatment of the problems of the emperorship and of the political state of kingdoms, such as England, and *comtés*,

---

4. M Reeves and B Hirsch-Reich *The 'Figurae' of Joachim of Fiore* (Oxford 1972) 218–19.
5. See R Foreville *Latran I, II, III et Latran IV* Histoire des Conciles Oecumeniques vi (Paris 1965) 251.

such as Toulouse, showed the pope as a world leader in a novel way. There may have been little or no discussion of these issues, even among the higher clerics and ecclesiastical advisers, but Innocent was too polished a performer not to realize the public relations advantages of pronouncement in a general council. It is unlikely that there were discussions with laymen. These groups were brought in to witness decisions.

The Fourth Lateran Council was the first oecumenical council of the medieval period where the two orders, clerical and lay, were summoned, but they were there essentially to witness declarations of the faith, not to treat. It would be a misconception to think that the royal persons (or their representatives) or the addition of some lower clergy admitted new groups of people into the discussion. This council, however, served as a model for other papal councils of the thirteenth and fourteenth centuries in its innovatory inclusion of other groups besides the bishops. When the Emperor Frederick II appealed to the cardinals to convoke a general council of prelates and other faithful in Christ to judge him, he must have had in mind Innocent's council of nearly a quarter of a century earlier. Pope Innocent IV's great council at Lyons in 1245 summoned kings as well as prelates. Thus, although Innocent III's Lateran Council with its inclusion of a wider section of the clergy and some lay people appeared nearer to the conciliarist, Conrad of Gelnhauser's, definition of a general council at the time of the Great Schism in 1381, there was no notion of power-sharing. Nor had Innocent any intention of allowing himself the humiliation of Lateran I where the council defeated the pope. While it is true that lay people were involved as well as bishops, they were hardly as yet the necessary representatives of the separate estates which came later to be associated with a wider view of government and representation. The summons of wider groups, because matters affecting the common good were at stake, in no way diluted Innocent's conceptions of the role of the clergy and of the laity, of bishops and of lower clergy, of kings and of lesser laymen, nor of his own position in leading the *Ecclesia* or 'congregation of the faithful'. The pope may deliberate with certain sections of the clergy and laity but he alone decides and these groups are used as 'rubber stamps' to endorse the proceedings. It is this idea of the universal Church which is a seed of the conciliar movement (when the Church sought to rule itself through councils). But it is no more than a seed in 1215. Nothing was further from Innocent's mind than power-sharing. Only on account of sin, amounting to spiritual fornication, or heresy, can the pope be judged by the whole Church, as Innocent stated in a sermon.[6] It is ironic that the conciliarist idea of power-sharing, buttressed during the fourteenth century by arguments taken from Aristotle, turned upside down the papal stance as expressed by Innocent III.

Not much is known about the course of the Council, although there are two surviving eye-witness accounts, one of which describes all the razzmatazz of a great occasion – crowds, the pope on a dais, festivities, the day-long ceremony of the re-dedication of St Maria in Trastevere, the processions with flags, flares and lights.[7] The Council met first on 11 November 1215, following mass celebrated by the pope at dawn with only the cardinals, archbishops and bishops present. After an appropriate opening, it was addressed by the pope, but so great was the crowd that one reporter could not hear the content of the speech and there appear to have been several fatal accidents in the crush. One bishop, perhaps Bishop Matthew of Amalfi, was suffocated, and the pope commissioned a marble tomb for him.[8] There were two further sessions on 20 and 30 November. The particular business can be briefly summarized as filling the vacant patriarchate of Constantinople, hearing the primatial claims of the archbishop of Toledo and dealing with the heresy in the lands of the count of Toulouse. There were also the matters of the recalcitrance of the English baronage, following the condemnation by

6. *PL* 217, Sermo II col 656C, Sermo III cols 664–5, Sermo IV col 670B.
7. See S Kuttner and A Garcia y Garcia 'A new eyewitness account of the Fourth Lateran Council' *Traditio* **20** (1964) 115–78 esp. 123–67. The other source is the chronicler Richard of San Germano.
8. The text of the opening sermon is printed in French in Foreville *Latran* 333–8. Kuttner and Garcia 'Eyewitness account' 130; *The Chronicle of Melrose* facsimile ed. A O Anderson, M O Anderson (1936) 61.

the pope of Magna Carta on 24 August 1215, and the recognition of the Emperor Frederick II to be considered. Only the decrees of the Council are preserved, seventy-one in all, and nearly all of them became incorporated in the Church's authoritative collection of the canon law compiled in 1234. There are no minutes or other official reports and nothing about their drafting. Many issues and proposals must have been discussed: we know of one proposal, that of Cardinal Robert of Courson for compulsory poor relief, which was rejected.[9] There is some evidence of the pope's personal position on several issues – his reluctance to declare the count of Toulouse excommunicate, his care to see that Simon de Montfort was given only the wardship of the count's lands, and his snubbing of Archbishop Siegfried of Mainz for his inopportune intervention, three times ordering him to sit down. Innocent did not want the recognition of Frederick II to turn into a full-scale debate on the imperial title (which Siegfried's interruption threatened), though he was careful to allow Otto's party to be heard in what was rapidly becoming a shouting-match between Otto's supporters and Frederick's representatives. There is also evidence that there was disagreement in the Council on the recognition of certain religious groups. We shall need to consider this matter later when we examine the new religious movements, but decree no. 13 forbade the foundation of further new congregations. In future those seeking a religious life were to enter an already established and approved order. It would seem that there were forces at work that wanted to check Innocent in his recognition of lay orders and new organizations. There can be no doubt that there was disagreement in the Council on this matter of recognition and that the older orders, the Benedictines, Augustinians and Cistercians, put pressure on the pope. But it appears that the pope may have overruled the Council on this, using his plenitude of power. According to some sources, it was at this time that the pope recognized the Franciscans and announced this to the Council. The recognition does not, however, find a place among the decrees. If it did take

---

9. John W Baldwin *The Government of Philip Augustus* (Berkeley 1986) i 317.

place, it would have necessitated direct and personal papal action, because the group of followers of Francis of Assisi did not fulfil the requirements of the canon law. Among other things, they had no fixed income, which was a definite stipulation, and were thus a definite threat to the older orders. It is very unlikely that Francis had been summoned to Rome: much more likely that he brought himself there seeing the opportunity of such a gathering. Almost certainly there would have been lobbying and wheeler-dealing, meetings and get-togethers behind the scenes. Various religious were in Rome for other reasons, such as Thomas of Marlborough, whom we shall meet later, and Richard, prior of Dunstable, a smallish and not very significant Augustinian house. They had their own purposes. Most of them required or sought the help of the pope or his standing officers and courts. Innocent must have been beset with petitions and business from all and sundry. As one example, we know that it was at this time that he took the opportunity to fill the vacant see of York since the canons were present and thus he could postulate and consecrate Walter Gray. Although all the northern sees (York, Durham, and Carlisle) were vacant, most of the English bishops were present – the archbishop of Canterbury, the bishops of Rochester, Lincoln, Coventry, Exeter, Chichester, Worcester and the bishops-elect of Ely and Norwich. Two of the bishops from Wales, the bishops of Llandaff and St Davids, attended. The bishops were, of course, the persons whom the pope intended to carry out and enforce the decrees of the Council. The lesser representatives were there, too, for the same purpose. The pope also probably intended the introduction of a taxation scheme which would have involved contributions from all cathedral chapters and major religious houses. It came to nothing.

It is well to bear in mind the intention behind the summonses of medieval gatherings. To take the example of the English parliaments, they were wider groups, summoned to approve taxation, not to discuss. Only considerably later were the Commons to aspire to comment and participate in any other sense. Those who took the decisions at the Fourth Lateran Council were a very small group of cardinals close to the pope and, on occasion, the pope himself, alone. The pope needed the cooperation of kings and barons for the coming Crusade, and of the bishops for implementation of the decrees concerning the faith and the reform of morals. The wider Church was there to bear witness to what happened. Even the cardinals' corporate powers lay in the future in 1215.

. . .

DECRETALS

Much of the law of the Church was not declared or made in councils but consisted of the statements or utterances of the popes which were known as decretals (later encyclicals). These pronouncements were not necessarily written down and so they might be carried off into oblivion by the winds of time. Even if they were noted, they might not survive for longer than the solution of the particular case or point. But with more declaration of the law by the pope there came to be a demand, particularly among judges and scholars, for compendiums or collections of these. decisions, for the canon law was, like English common law, a case law or law built upon precedent. What the pope had decided on one occasion would be applicable in a similar instance. Decretal letters, in answer to queries about particular legal points, came to be the major source of declaration during the twelfth century, more numerous than the decrees of councils but not so easily disseminated for use. The spread of the papacy's judicial activities made decretals more and more necessary. But, before delegation of cases to local judges could take place on a wide scale, there needed to be a manual of existing canon law as recognized in the West. The first great collection or book to have a widespread circulation was the *Decretum*, which has long gone under the name of Gratian, and which was made in Bologna in the early 1140s. This collection aimed not only at bringing together all earlier decisions and pronouncements of importance by the pope, many of them in early councils, but also at reconciling conflicting judgments. The author or authors wanted to resolve apparent contradictions in order to make the law more usable and accessible. It was thus not just an ordinary collection of laws, as other previous collections had been, such as those of Burchard of Worms (1012)[10] and Ivo of Chartres (1091),[11] but the beginning of the whole critical study of the canon law, the science of canonistics, indeed, of jurisprudence. What made this work possible at this particular time was the wind of change that was sweeping across Europe. Everywhere there was a new spirit of intellectual enquiry, a spirit that was to be associated not with the old monasteries but with new centres of learning and of study in the towns and connected more with secular masters than with monks. The excitement of the intellectual revolution produced some great minds and some important discoveries. New texts were discovered, in particular of the classic Roman law, the Digest. New methods of work were developed, in particular the dialectical method of the 'Sic et non' of the French master, Peter Abelard. Combining the new technique with the scientific system of the Roman law, Gratian and his school were able to provide the Church with what came to be the first part of its corpus of official law. Although this text was in no way officially commissioned, it was to be the fount of the canon law.

The general assumption of Gratian and his collaborators (ironically they may well have been monks working with him in the Camaldolese monastery in Bologna and not the new secular law clerks of the future) was that the contradictions in the early canon law were only superficial or apparent. They could be reconciled by argument. The *Decretum* provided the Church with its basic laws, consisting of 101 distinctions and thirty-six 'causes' (each with their questions and canons, or chapters). They covered the whole range of the law as so far pronounced. Not only did this great book provide the Western Christian world with its 'moral' code, it also introduced canonistic scholarship. From now on popes would be surrounded by men who would comment on their every dictum. The science of the canon law had been born.

10. Burchard's collection in twenty books was made up from material in two ninth-century collections, the sixth-century Dionysian collections, the False Decretals and from the decrees of Merovingian, Carolingian and later councils.
11. Ivo's three collections were the Decretum, Panormia and Tripartita. His decretum used material from Burchard, some Italian collections and Justinian's Novels.

. . .

BOLOGNA: THE LAW SCHOOL AND PRODUCTIONS

Bologna was the greatest of the law 'schools' by the middle of the twelfth century, unrivalled by the older schools of law at Rome, Pavia and Ravenna. At this date schools still meant places where masters of repute might be found, but the masters might well move on to other cities taking their pupils with them. It was rather the reputation of the individual master that brought the students than the particular location or city. But things were changing. At Bologna, it seems that both laws – the Roman or civil law, much used by the emperor, and the canon law, the law of the Church and of the papacy – were being taught by this date.

The Roman law system is historically the most important and influential of all the historic legal systems. Unquestionably it was ancient Rome's greatest legacy to the medieval world, greater probably even than its literature and its poetry. In the years between 300 and 550 there was much work of codification and it began to take shape under Theodosius the Great in the Western Empire in 438. The northern parts of the empire were, however, under customary laws still, and it was in the Eastern Empire under the Emperor Justinian that most of the advances were made. In 534 the emperor codified the law. The new *Corpus Iuris Civilis*, or Body of the Civil Law, as it came to be called by later commentators, consisted of four books. The first, the Digest, was the classical Roman private law of the jurists. The second, the Code, consisted of the imperial constitutions and edicts. The third, the 'Institutes', was an officially commissioned text-book of Roman law, while the fourth book, the Novels, consisted of Justinian's own laws.

It was the Church, and more specifically the papacy, as Ullmann pointed out, that from the mid-eighth century kept the Roman law alive in the West by its own transmission and absorption of Roman law and Roman law principles of government, and in particular in the *imperial idea* which the papacy began to foster from the end of that century. With the transfer of the empire to the West, when the pope crowned the Frankish King Charlemagne as emperor on Christmas Day 800, Roman law's future was assured in those more rural and agrarian parts of Europe within the empire where it had not already penetrated. And the German emperors, the successors of Charlemagne, saw the advantages of Roman law to themselves in spreading their control. This was especially so under the tenth-century Saxon, Otto III, so weakening the customary and native law. What is more, the cultivation of the idea of emperorship brought with it a renewed interest in the rich sources of the Roman law.

While the Roman law had perhaps never died out in the north Italian cities and was studied in the early eleventh century at Pavia, where the great lawyer, Lanfranc, archbishop of Canterbury under William the Conqueror, taught for a while, an interest in the texts of Justinian was not widely aroused until the discovery of a manuscript of the Digest in *c.* 1070. The fiery and provocative pontificate of Pope Gregory VII may well have inspired the search which brought this manuscript to light. Gregory's programme of radical reform depended upon the law and a renewed interest in legal study and declaration provided the impetus which sparked off the legal renaissance of the twelfth century. The emperors, too, and their advisers badly needed legal texts to reinforce their position as rulers. However that may be – and the question of which side made use of them first may well remain unsolved – the Roman law provided the necessary structure for the growing canon law and its study, canonistics; and it also provided the German emperorship with some possible answers to the canonist onslaught. Between 1100 and 1200, when popes and emperors, locked in a power conflict, were both fortified by the lawyers, it was Bologna that provided the think-tank for both the combatants, papalists and imperialists. For in Bologna the study of the canon law and of the Roman law flourished together as nowhere else in medieval Europe.

Bologna owed its prominence mainly to this fact that *both* laws were studied there. It had received an influx of lawyers from Rome when the Normans had taken the city in 1084. Geographically it was placed on the crossroads of Europe, to the north of the Apennines, between emperor and pope, on the main roads from Milan, Verona and Padua and accessible to Ravenna and Venice, and thus linked with the Adriatic. Many entered Rome by way of Bologna. This position put its schools in the forefront and made it the leading school of Europe from the 1140s, until Paris began to take the lead in theology and philosophy (but never in law) in the 1180s. But while the canon lawyers were protected and enjoyed immunities as clerics, the civilians were open to exploitation and their numbers began to show a dramatic fall until the Emperor Frederick I intervened in 1158 to grant them certain immunities from taxes and tolls – much as the clerics already had – and their own jurisdiction. Both emperor and pope protected the law students of Bologna from the avaricious citizens. Bolognese lawyers were so important to both the papal and imperial parties in supplying them with lawyers to staff their governments and administrations that they were given special protection.

Bologna's own position among the great cities of northern Italy also affected the study of the law. Like other cities, it bargained with the emperor and also favoured the pope when it suited. It gained the right from the emperor in 1116 to keep half the fine for infringing imperial rights. The city joined the Lombard leagues in 1167 and in 1185, seeing that to its advantage. It also had an advanced government: podestà, consuls, commune, fighting forces and cavalry. There were many notaries and much business in the city. Bologna was rich and had the usual rivalries with neighbours, most intensively with Modena, its arch-enemy. It extended its powers over smaller towns and communes, such as Nonantola, and allied itself with others. But it could not do without its law students who brought business and fame and brilliance to the town. Most strikingly, in 1213, the five teachers of law were ordered to take an oath of loyalty to the city. They were to swear not to leave Bologna and not to teach the students elsewhere. The city's prestige depended on them.[12]

The schools themselves could never have flourished so significantly without the presence in the town (at roughly the same time as Gratian) of the great father-figure of the Roman law school, Irnerius, and the group of glossators or

12. For Bologna in general as an important city see D Waley *The Italian City-Republics* 2nd edn (1978) esp. 26, 50, 59, 73.

commentators who gathered under him. Nothing was of more significance in the intellectual and institutional development of medieval Europe, indeed of modern Europe, than the rediscovery of the Roman law texts in the eleventh century. Perhaps the reason for the discovery was the increasingly legalistic papacy that had emerged. The desire to 'discover' useful texts sometimes led to forgeries, as the False Decretals. Once discovered, the law led to ceaseless activity and the interchanges between both systems, the cross-fertilization, that brought a renewed vigour to both laws. Power contests were often set in a legal framework. At the heart of this was Bologna, the pope and the emperor.

After the publication of Gratian's *Decretum* and its wide dissemination, which is illustrated by the large number of manuscripts in different medieval libraries and individually owned by various bishops and scholars, not only could more detailed work be undertaken but it initiated a new epoch in interest in the declaration of law by the pope. This was partly induced or caused by the development of courts at a distance from the curia but directly under the pope. More and more decretals were issued and they needed both collecting and sifting. Here the schools and particularly Bologna and its students, as well as the judges scattered throughout Europe, began to take an interest. These additions were first added to working copies of the *Decretum* in the 1150s and 1160s, but by the 1170s they had become far too numerous and had to be placed in separate books. These were doubtless satisfactory for the individuals who had collected them and for a short period of time, until perhaps superseded by rulings that were seen to be more appropriate. But for wider and easier use system was needed and the need was becoming ever more pressing. It was increasingly imperative to have books which brought rulings on the same subject together under one heading, such as marriage. Furthermore, the decretal letter might deal with more than one point. Innocent's reply to an enquiring letter from Bishop Eustace of Ely, who was requesting clarification and help on a number of problems in order to act as a papal judge delegate, did exactly this. The pope answered twelve different legal points. To be useful, therefore, the letter needed dissecting and the different points putting under separate and appropriate headings (as came to be done in this particular instance). Bernard of Pavia's *Compilatio Prima* of 1190 first assembled material in this way for general use, dividing the texts into five main sections: (1) ordination and ecclesiastical offices; (2) judicial organization and civil cases; (3) matters affecting the clergy; (4) marriage; and (5) criminal procedure. It was not a collection so much as a systematized compilation and its arrangement came to influence all further compilations of importance. A continuation of this, the *Collectio Sangermanensis*, took the material up to the beginning of Innocent III's pontificate.

The first collection of Innocent's own decretals, or legal rulings, was that by Rainer of Pomposa. Dedicated to a papal chaplain, John, priest and monk, perhaps of Pomposa, it had not been commissioned by the pope but was a private collection of decisions of the pope's first four years. It had forty titles (different from the classifications of Bernard of Pavia, therefore) and it dissected the letters, by putting the same decretal under different titles according to context. Historically Rainer is very valuable because there are several extremely important legal decisions of Innocent III which would not have survived but for Rainer's collection. These include the famous letter 'Solite' to the Eastern Emperor Alexis of Constantinople and a letter of 1200 addressed to the archbishop of Canterbury and concerning Bishop Mauger, which we shall have occasion to discuss later.

Among the canonist collectors and commentators at Bologna (and probably also in Rome from time to time) were the Englishmen, Gilbert and Alan, whose importance in canon law scholarship has been recognized only in recent years. They had presumably been drawn to Bologna as students and had stayed there to carve themselves out a teaching or professional career. Gilbert, whose collection appeared in 1203–4, based his compilation on the model of Bernard of Pavia's Five Books. His motive was to supplement Bernard with the more recent decretals that had been issued. Ninety-six of the 258 chapters came from Innocent's pronouncements (sixty-four decretals). The pope, however, denied issuing some of the decretals attributed to him by Gilbert, and others in this collection, coming from Innocent's two predecessors, were incorrectly attributed to Innocent. In 1206 came Alan's collection of Six Books. While Gilbert had inserted some new titles, Alan added a completely new book dealing with sacramental law. Alan included a high proportion of Innocent's rulings (345 chapters out of 484) and 314 of his chapters found their way into later collections, being seen as important and useful. Some of these rulings (as in Gilbert's collection) came from sections of the papal registers that no longer survive (particularly from the lost fourth year) and some of the chapters (as with Gilbert's) Innocent denied ever having issued. There were, too, some new titles of significance, such as unfaithfulness in marriage and right of dower. The source of these collections was said to be the papal registers.

These were all private collections, as was that of Bernard of Compostella, the *Compilatio Romana*, covering the first ten years of Innocent's pontificate to February 1208. Bernard, who was staying at the curia at the time, submitted his work to Innocent for approval, but permission was refused by the pope, who again denied having issued some of the decretals. The collection, however, was welcomed in Bologna, and was doubtless used, but its use was short-lived because in 1210 an official collection of Innocent's decretals was published. Peter Beneventanus Collivaccinus' Collection, known as the *Compilatio Tertia*, was both approved and commended by the pope to the masters and scholars of Bologna for use 'as much in judgments as in the schools'. Master Peter was a papal subdeacon and notary and had access to the papal registers so that the pope felt confident that the collection might be used, as he put it, 'without any scruple of doubt'. It is even possible that Innocent commissioned this collection. The worry that the law in text-books for students, which might be unofficial, might be applied in the decision of cases in court is well-expressed in the letter 'Pastoralis' addressed to the bishop of Ely, where the pope gives voice to his concern about the use of forged decretals.[13] The official compilation was of moment because it ensured that certain general claims of the papacy, and the specific reasons for these claims, were not lost sight of in the later history of the papacy.

13. *SLI* 77 and n. 28.

Following Peter's collection, there were two more unofficial collections for the pontificate. Between 1210 and 1215 John of Wales made a new compilation out of Gilbert and Alan's work (which came, therefore, to be called the *Compilatio Secunda*, though in fact it followed the *Compilatio Tertia*) and in 1216 came the last private collection of the reign, the *Compilatio Quarta* of John the Teuton. This included the decretals of the last six years of Innocent, together with the extremely important decrees of the Fourth Lateran Council. For some reason, perhaps because an official collection had already been issued, the work was coolly received in Bologna and it was little 'glossed' or commented on by canonists, and it was said that Innocent had again refused his official *imprimatur*.

The impressive activity of the collectors of legal decisions in Innocent III's eighteen-year pontificate bears witness to the pope's energy in his court and his zest for settling issues. The immediate impact of the decisions and the context in which they were made belong to the realm of government. What is significant, however, is the pope's determination to see that only valid decisions circulated. It is for this reason that approval of collections was refused in some cases. The only source that the pope could unquestionably approve was his own registers. Early collectors had in many cases got decretals wherever they could find them. Frequently judges delegate appended them to their manuals. But this pope was concerned with veracity and uniformity. He was also concerned in the correct teaching of the law at Bologna. The importance for the future of these collections was twofold. Firstly, official collections came to supersede entirely the old private ones and, secondly, from these four collections (together with one of Innocent's successor, Pope Honorius III) the second great compendium of canon law came to be formed. This was the *Decretales*, commissioned by Pope Gregory IX (the former Cardinal Hugolinus), one of Innocent III's most trusted advisers among the cardinals. The work carried out by Raymond of Pennaforte was called the *Liber Extra*, being seen as an extra or additional volume to Gratian's *Decretum*. When it was issued in 1234, with full papal approval, it was addressed to the masters and scholars of Bologna. Although it clearly superseded the Five Compilations (all previous collections now being declared null and void) it obviously included much of the law found there. It became the second great text and was to last as an authoritative collection for all Roman Catholics until the revision of the canon law in 1918 and the publication of the Codex.

. . .

CLERKS AND LAYMEN

If a distinction between laws – the law of the State and the law of the Church – was blurred in most men's minds, the distinction between the clergy and the laity was not. The exclusion of the lay influence from top to bottom had taken place before Innocent III's time. The laity now played no part in papal elections, laymen were excluded from the investiture of bishops and lay ownership of churches had been diminished and changed. Clerks had particular privileges in society and were as a group apart. This is not, of course, to say that an impecunious clerk or curate was of equal status with a great lay lord, duke or count, or that a simple peasant woman had the rights of a noble lady, for medieval society was a stratified, or hierarchical, one, in which power was conceived as coming downwards from God to His spiritual and temporal vicegerents: popes, emperors, kings and bishops. Authority descended from above: it did not arise from the will of the majority of the people below. But the clergy had specific rights that were denied to lay people, even if influential landowners.

The priest dealt with the Lord's body. No lay person ever claimed that dignity. In terms of legal status the clerk had first of all the right to have his case tried only before a church court – the 'privilege of the forum'. This privilege proceeded logically from the bishop's (or other prelate's) power of correction. Beneficed clergy (those who had parishes) were subject to their bishop, monks to their abbots, and bishops to their archbishops, and they, in turn, to the pope. Correction by one's superiors is integral to most forms of organization: in a hierarchical society it is accentuated.

A multiplicity of jurisdictions, dependent in part on where one lived, meant that a man might be subject to different courts for different reasons. A peasant would be

subject to the manorial court, i.e. his landlord, for misde-
meanours within the manor, encroaching on other
people's lands, brawling, fighting – all the usual 'neigh-
bourly' conflicts. (In some cases, the landlord might be an
ecclesiastic of importance, the bishop of Winchester, say, or
the abbot of Bury St Edmunds, and the same applied
here.) For offences against the moral code, the Church in
the person of the parson was the confessor and imposed
the penalty, though if the behaviour was particularly offensive (e.g. adultery) or pernicious (e.g. heresy, witchcraft),
then it would be brought before the archdeacon or the
bishop to hear in his court. Where blood was shed, the
secular courts of the land came more and more to take an
interest. In England, the king's court had come to claim
'pleas of the Crown' – murder, gross felony – from the
shire courts, which, by the end of the twelfth century, were
mainly left to deal with debt and some land disputes within
the county. There was a sharp distinction between the
'free' and the 'unfree'. The unfree did not exist legally and
could not plead in a court. Freemen, on the other hand,
took part in certain decisions, within the manor and
county court, whereas the unfree did not. Only a person of
non-servile status might be ordained a clerk or become a
monk or nun.

Benefit of clergy was the exemption claimed by the
clergy from lay or secular jurisdiction in certain criminal
cases. The issue of 'criminous clerks' began to be discussed
during the early twelfth century, and by the 1150s in England, there was some acceptance that such men could be
tried only by an ecclesiastical tribunal. A spectacular
twelfth-century case was that of Osbert, archdeacon of
York, accused of murdering his archbishop, William, by administering poison to the chalice. It forcibly illustrates the
principles currently at issue. The case began before King
Stephen, in front of whom Osbert denied the charge and
claimed 'benefit of clergy', saying that because of his clerical status he was not subject to the king's jurisdiction but
only to that of the Church. The archbishop of Canterbury,
Theobald, well aware of the claims of the canon law, 'succeeded in recalling the case to the judgment of the Church
with much difficulty and by strong pressure, to the indigna-
tion of the king and all his nobles', as Theobald's secretary

noted.[14] The point had been successfully made that such a case belonged to the Church's jurisdiction, not to the Crown's.

Most difficult to resolve in the struggle for jurisdiction over clerks who were charged with crimes was whether they could be tried twice, as clause three of the royal Constitutions of Clarendon (1164) outlined, first in the king's court and then in the church court, and whether, if found guilty, they should be handed over to a civil court for the passing of the sentence. This was a matter of extreme concern – with its many implications, for both jurisdictions of Church and State. It was the spearhead of the contest between King Henry II and his archbishop of Canterbury, Thomas Becket. In fact the murder of Thomas Becket by four knights of the king of England in his own cathedral in 1170, sealed the fate of the royal position. Though concessions were made to royal justice over the forest laws and in cases concerning land, the church courts' competence over marriage and legitimacy cases and wills was henceforth assured as was the notion of 'benefit of clergy'. The brilliant and enigmatic figure of Becket had brought England and its Church into closer association with Europe and with the papacy.[15] The tragic event of his murder ensured an increased papal influence over England. Becket had, indeed, died for the liberty of the Church, if by that we mean an acceptance of the universal law of the Church and the freedom of the church courts to try certain cases and exercise jurisdiction over the clergy as a separate caste.

If the clergy had privileges, they also had commensurate duties. Very high among Innocent III's ambitions was the improvement of the parish clergy. The parish priest baptized the babies into the Christian faith. He brought the children to the bishop for confirmation. He heard confessions of sins by his parishioners and gave absolution as he saw fit, enjoining a suitable penance. He witnessed the marriages, gave the last rites and buried the dead; and, most important of all, he administered the sacrament of the mass. All these activities are vividly depicted in the

14. *The Letters of John of Salisbury* i ed. W J Millor and H E Butler revised by C N L Brooke (Oxford Medieval Texts 1986) no. 16.
15. See the analysis in F Barlow's final chapter 'From Death unto Life' in his *Thomas Becket* (1986).

great seven-sacrament fonts of East Anglia and in the stained glass of All Saints', North Street, York. The parson's high social standing in the community remained until recent times. Because he was literate, it was he who helped with the drawing up of wills or testaments, and, in more recent times, it was he who wrote references or testimonials and signed applications for passports. But clerks were human and were open to the temptations of life. Some of them hankered after the company of women, had wives in all but name, and found pleasure in fashionable clothing, drink, revelry and hunting.[16] Innocent's ideal was the sober, clean-living clerk, assiduous in his duties of counselling and caring for his flock, bringing it the word and flesh of God. To be a man apart, he must not be distracted by the frivolities of the world and he must be educated. All this the pope had learned in Paris and he believed passionately in his mission of improvement.

Most prejudicial to the reputation of the Church was the sin of simony, the buying of something of spiritual value for money, such as ecclesiastical office or advancement, or charging for ordaining a clerk or for the performance of any other spiritual service. According to the bishop of Worcester, in 1198, it was widespread in his diocese.[17] Examples of simoniacal practices (and numerous mandates to deal with the problem) abound in the papal registers. Councils, too, such as the Paris councils held by the legate Robert of Courson in 1212 and 1213 legislated repeatedly against priests who sold their services.[18] Hardly less damaging for the Church was clerical incontinency, which sometimes led to the son succeeding the father in a benefice or parish, as reported in the diocese of Worcester at this time, 'so dishonouring ecclesiastical dignity and the canon law'.[19] The long struggle by popes and bishops for celibacy among the clergy was not over by Innocent's pontificate. All over Europe it remained the one really

---

16. For the decrees of the Fourth Lateran Council, see (in English) *English Historical Documents 1189–1327* ed. Harry Rothwell (1975), in this case canons 14–17.
17. *SLI* no. 3.
18. C-J Hefele and H Leclercq *Histoire des Conciles* V ii (Paris 1913) 1309.
19. *SLI* no. 26.

insoluble problem and archbishops and bishops from Lund and Tournai in the north to Arles in the south of France and Gniezno in the east were ordered to deprive incontinent priests of their benefices and stop clerical benefices being transferred from father to son.[20] The Second Lateran Council (1139) had declared the marriage of clerks (both priests and deacons) unlawful and invalid. Local councils of the pontificate, such as that held at Dioclea in 1199, to reform the Dalmatian and Serbian Church repeated the condemnation, demanding the celibacy of priests.[21] However, the difficulty of enforcing the regulations in more remote communities and villages can be appreciated. The priest had to be denounced by his parishioners; many with concubines would have escaped challenge. The married priest might be more obvious to the archdeacon on his visitation or inspection and to the rural deans in charge of the groups of parishes; the unmarried concubinist could well escape justice. In the succession of sons to their fathers' benefices, reform would have depended on the bishops and, of course, the clergy themselves. The bishop had the power and duty of examining the clerk before he allowed the candidate to have the benefice and to become a parish priest. Innocent's reforming programme targeted both the bishops and the clergy. The bishops were to look for exactly these deficiencies; synods were to be held; the clergy were to be better educated, responsible and not ignorant. A master in each cathedral was to instruct the clerks, presumably also in the law (Lateran Council can. 11).

In the general improvement of the clergy, canon 18 of the Fourth Lateran Council declared that henceforth clergy were not to take part in the pronouncement of the death penalty, to fight or duel, or to perform surgery which involved cutting or burning. They were not to be concerned in any way with the shedding of blood. Innocent had already shown himself against clergy being involved in the ordeal and the duel – the two survivals of superstitious methods of proof.[22] The ancient method of

---

20. *PL* 214 ep 469 cols 436–7; 215 ep 198 col 223; ep 213 col 528; ep 235 cols 1070–1.
21. Hefele and Leclercq *Conciles* V ii p 1222.
22. In general see Robert Bartlett *Trial by Fire and Water* (Oxford 1986) 53, 98, 127–8.

trial by ordeal demanded that the accused submit himself to the test of fire or of water. Carrying hot metal, or tripping blindfold between red-hot plough shares, or plunging the arm in boiling water were the usual tests, though the accused might be flung into a pond to see whether he sank or not, or forced to eat an ounce of bread or cheese to see if it stuck in the gullet! It was the priest who examined the wound after three days to see whether it had healed. If not, the accused was pronounced guilty and the priest might, therefore, be associated with a sentence of death. The Lateran decree had an immediate and lasting effect on the English Common Law for the king soon ordered his travelling justices to suspend the practice in trials and to use other methods of proof. The long association of the priest with the ordeal, which took place after the accused had communicated or taken part in the eucharist, must have blurred the distinction between earthly and supernatural justice. Ordeals had taken place in or close to churches – the chronicler, Eadmer, writes in the early twelfth century of ordeals being conducted in the baptistery at the east end of Canterbury cathedral where former archbishops were buried[23] – and so confused the ecclesiastical and the secular law, the law of the Church and the law of the State.

· · ·

MARRIAGE

The way in which the canon law affected most people was in the control of marriage. The Church made the law on marriage – who might marry and with whom and what constituted a marriage.[24] Marriage was forbidden to priests and to professed religious. For lay people, until the Fourth Lateran Council, marriage was forbidden within the seventh degree, i.e. of any persons closer in relationship than sixth cousins. The council revised the prohibited degrees to extend as far as third cousins (common great-great-grandparents). The law of affinity, as defined by the popes, most obviously affected the political marriage-makers, the

23. R W Southern *St Anselm. Portrait in a Landscape* (Cambridge 1991) 320.
24. On marriage in general, see Christopher Brooke *The Medieval Idea of Marriage* (Oxford 1989).

aristocracy. Sometimes to claim too close a relationship became the way of getting rid of a wife, particularly if she had
not produced male children. There were also major political reasons that might affect the making and breaking of
alliances. When the first wife of Philip Augustus, king of
France, died in 1193, the king decided to marry Ingeborg,
daughter of the Danish king, hoping for support against
King Richard I of England. The Danish king, however, was
not prepared to furnish this, so Philip exacted a large
dowry and then proceeded to obtain a sentence of divorce.
Consanguinity was alleged and Philip decided to re-marry
quickly to ensure that the clerical sentence of divorce
would be irrevocable. He married Agnes of Meran, from
the Rhineland, whose father was a Staufen supporter. On
Innocent's accession as pope, Philip Augustus was ordered
to take back Ingeborg as his wife, under threat of excommunication. Innocent wanted support in the imperial
crisis. In May 1201 Philip capitulated and formally took
back Ingeborg (though he actually put her in prison and
restored Agnes to the court). Agnes, however, died soon
after and Philip wanted the legitimization of his and
Agnes's two children. The children were duly legitimized
in a bull of August 1201 because the pope wanted the support of Philip Augustus. The unfortunate Ingeborg
remained a pawn in the game of world politics. In 1210
Philip tried to marry the daughter of the landgrave of
Thuringia, but by 1213 he decided to take back Ingeborg
again because of his plan of conquering England. In deciding the case of legitimization, Innocent claimed the
authority of the apostolic see to pass judgment on the legitimacy of heirs and in the decretal 'Per venerabilem' he
outlined this right and duty in rejecting the petition of
count William of Montpellier.[25] Innocent had also made it
plain that he was the final authority in matrimonial affairs.

That legitimacy belonged to the spiritual jurisdiction
could not really be contested by lay powers because no one
could dispute the Church's power over marriage. But it
came very close to affecting lay rights and particularly, of

---

25. *PL* 214 col 1130 ep 128. On Philip Augustus's marital affairs, see
Gesta LIV etc., and Baldwin *Philip Augustus* 82–7.

course, rights of succession and inheritance of land. The canon law held that the subsequent marriage between two parties, if valid, legitimized the children. This position, however, was never accepted by the English baronage.

The lengthy, complicated and interesting case of Richard of Anstey (of some two generations before Innocent III's time) shows how it was already accepted that the Crown could have no jurisdiction over the solemn sacrament of marriage, though at this stage the canon law of marriage and what actually constituted a legal marriage was extremely fluid.[26] Richard of Anstey was the nephew of William de Sackville. The Sackvilles were considerable landowners and so quite an inheritance was at stake – enough at any rate to turn Richard into the classic professional litigant before both lay and ecclesiastical courts. William de Sackville had contracted, or promised, to marry Albreda de Tresgoz, but he had in fact married Adelizia de Vere and they had a daughter, Mabel. For some reason, William sought to get rid of Adelizia and he began a case against her in the church courts which ended in a declaration by Pope Innocent II that his first contractual marriage was binding. It appears that William on his deathbed confessed that he had indulged in a fraud in getting his marriage to Adelizia nullified and at the eleventh hour did all that he could for Mabel's succession as his heir. Mabel, whose mother came from the wealthy de Veres, had by the time of her father's death married into the Francheville family, and she was not the sort of woman to throw away her rightful inheritance without a struggle. Before the king's court, she, her husband and her mother, Adelizia, maintained that the claim of a daughter was greater than that of a nephew. The case came to hinge on the legitimacy of Mabel because of William's first contracted marriage and so to be a matter for the church courts. Richard, as he saw it, tired of being 'cheated of his just claim by the shiftiness of a woman', spared no expense –

26. See P M Barnes 'The Anstey Case' in *A Medieval Miscellany for Doris Mary Stenton* ed. P M Barnes, C F Slade (Pipe Roll Soc. **76** 1962) 1–24, and Brooke *Medieval Idea of Marriage* 148–52 for the details; also Brooke *Letters of John of Salisbury* i App. vi for a lucid appraisal of the various views of the canonists on what constituted a legal marriage.

such was the prize to be gained – and in the end he was successful. As it so happened the decision of Pope Innocent II that Mabel was illegitimate, because of her father's first contractual marriage, was later superseded by the judgment of Pope Alexander III that the children of annulled marriages, which had been made 'in the presence of the church' (i.e. in good faith and in public), were to be regarded as legitimate.[27] Mabel was the unfortunate victim of the changing marriage law, of the greed of her cousin and of Henry II's restoration of law and order. Without those factors her peaceful possession of her father's properties would have continued. Once the Church had decided that Mabel was illegitimate, the king's court granted Richard the inheritance.

. . .

THE POPE AS JUDGE: LAW COURTS

From earliest times the pope's court acted as the centre of justice, the 'seat of justice' as Pope Innocent II had called it. The centralization of papal government, which was a feature from Gregory VII's pontificate onwards, depended on the building up of the curia and the use of the cardinals in the administration and as advisers. This was household government and justice could be dispensed wherever the pope was. Important cases concerning metropolitans and bishops came before the pope and justice was administered by him in person. Innocent III spent some months outside Rome, but this did not stop him doing justice. But the really significant judicial development that had taken place in the twelfth century was the staggering innovation of papal judges delegate. The pope's tribunal was the highest tribunal for all, but why should this tribunal not be extended in practice by the delegation of cases that came to it from all over Europe to judges, acting on behalf of the pope, in the countries from which the appeals came? The advantages were that local judges could be used, first of all to enquire on the pope's behalf, but

27. X. IV. 17. 2; confirmed by Celestine III and Innocent III (cc 11, 14); modified by the Fourth Lateran Council c 51, which pronounced that the offspring of a marriage, where there was known to be an impediment, were illegitimate, and introduced what was basically the system of banns.

quite soon to decide the case as well. In this way recourse to the papal courts was encouraged, the pope was seen as the final judge and the delegate judges could be kept in touch with the latest legal developments by the terms of the mandate or letter of instruction. The whole system forged bonds between the churches, made for stand-ardization and improvement in the hearing of cases and increased the importance of the pope at the centre.

The author of the *Gesta* of Pope Innocent sets the scene (XLIC–XLII):

In public, three times a week, he held a solemn consis-tory – which had previously fallen into disuse – in which he deputed the examination of lesser cases to others, while the major ones he dealt with himself so subtly and wisely that all wondered at his precision and skill and many educated and legally-learned men came to the Roman Church to hear him and they learnt more in his consistories than they had learnt in the schools, espe-cially when they heard him give sentence. He argued so acutely and convincingly that each party hoped for vic-tory when it heard him arguing on its behalf and there was no advocate who appeared before him who did not greatly fear his cross-examination and interventions. But he was just in passing sentence so that he would not ac-cept money nor shrink from the right way; and these sentences he gave after careful deliberation with much maturity of judgment. On account of this, very many cases from all over the world began to be brought to his audience so that he concluded several major cases in his time which were started long before. Immediately after his promotion, the archbishops of Compostella and Braga came personally into his presence in a case which had been going on between them concerning seven bishoprics. This case was so complex and difficult that it filled many books of written record and there was so much opposing evidence that it was difficult to get at the truth, but he at last clarified everything and settled it with such skill and wisdom that all commended his ex-treme cleverness. At this time, too, he carefully exam-ined and brilliantly settled the old quarrel concerning the metropolitan church of Britanny between Tours and

Dol, which although it had been judged many times by his predecessors would never have been brought to a final settlement but for him. He also brought to an end, but not without difficulty, the suit which had begun between the archbishop and the chapter of Canterbury over the church of Lambeth, which the same archbishop, against the will of the chapter, had built and endowed with many and substantial rents, instituting canons regular in it – noble men, powerful and educated. The king and the archbishop, indeed, had agreed upon this between themselves. But the chapter, having no protector after God unless it be the Roman pontiff, asserted that for a certainty unless he had that church demolished the metropolitical dignity would, for the most part, be transferred to it. Indeed, after the lord pope had heard sufficient arguments from both parties, he decreed with the authority of the apostolic see that the same archbishop should demolish the church at his own expense, revoking completely everything that had been done in this matter. When the archbishop heard this he pretended that the king would not allow it to be done; the pope, fired with the zeal of justice, ordered the archbishop in virtue of the obedience owed to him, not to delay longer in carrying this out or he would find himself suspended from his priestly office and his suffragans released from obedience to him. And so, at length, how ever much the king and the archbishop grumbled and complained, what he ordered was implemented completely.

Innocent played an important part in many of the legal *causes célèbres* of his pontificate. We have detailed accounts of the hearing of some of these cases and they, as much as anything, reinforce the opinion that Innocent himself was a very considerable lawyer. An unusually detailed account survives of the fortunes of the ancient and revered Benedictine abbey of Evesham in Worcestershire in a case against their local bishop, the bishop of Worcester, as to his jurisdictional rights over them and whether he had the right to inspect them. At first some of the monks were loath to enter on a long and expensive case before the pope, but they had among their number a man of mature years, called Thomas of Marlborough, who had been at the schools of Paris and who had taught at Oxford. He was an outspoken opponent of episcopal pretensions and a staunch upholder of what he believed to be the ancient rights of the monastery of Evesham. Accordingly when Bishop Mauger attempted to visit them in 1202, both parties, bishop and monks, believing in the rightness of their positions, appealed to the pope, and the abbey also appealed to the archbishop of Canterbury for tuition, or protection of this appeal, while matters were pending. Only in Rome did both parties feel they could get a final judgment that would be respected. In the first rounds, judges delegate were appointed by the pope to examine the immediate question – who possessed the jurisdiction at the moment – and to make a temporary decision. The main case as to the long-term or lawful ownership was to be sent for the pope to decide when the judges had examined witnesses and collected the evidence. When these details arrived in Rome the task of going over them was assigned to a senior lawyer or papal auditor, Benedict cardinal priest of St Susanna. The two papal judgments issued in the course of this famous suit concerning the exemption of the abbey from the jurisdiction of the diocesan and the position of the abbey's churches in the Vale of Evesham between 1202 and 1206 attracted the attention of the decretal collectors. The sentence over the exemption of the abbey was given by the pope himself in his consistory and Thomas of Marlborough, who had appeared as proctor for the abbey, fainted for joy. His case had rested in part on forged documents, though what these documents contained was not without authority, and the pope's arguments concerned prescription or the power conferred by ancient right. For the hearing a posse of lawyers appeared for both sides, but Thomas, at the time of his deepest depression over the outcome of the suit, comforted himself that he had secured the best lawyers that money could buy before his opponents had managed to secure them. He had also taken the precaution of seeking legal advice in Bologna, where he remained for six months, attending lectures daily in canon and Roman law. On returning to Rome, Thomas went again to the curia and the pope informed him that the case would begin in three days' time. Thomas, as he himself reports, was known as 'the Evesham proctor' by the pope and the whole curia, and there is a hint here of his familiarity with the curia. The case opened with very long and complicated arguments by Master Robert of Clipstone, proctor of the bishop, and Thomas was quick to note that the pope soon became bored by the lengthy statement of the facts by Robert, and told him roundly 'to get to the point'. The supplementary case concerning the jurisdiction over the churches of the Vale brought also a quick retort from the pope when poor Master Robert attempted to argue that prescription had no power against episcopal rights. 'When you learned that', said Innocent, 'you and your masters must have drunk too much English beer'.[28] Thomas's view of the pope as the dispenser of justice and of the cardinals as influential advisers within the papal circle accords with other accounts of the period. The pope's comment that one could never lack for advocates in Rome, his advice to Thomas to go to Bologna and his own interest and concern in the details of hearings present a picture of Rome and a papal court alive with lawyers and those interested in the law.

· · ·

CONCLUSION

During Innocent's pontificate great strides were made in the development of the delegated judicial system. Clearly the availability of judgments and recent canons and books on procedure made a difference to the judges. The pope's ardent desire for clarification and decision made it possible for judges to be used who were not always the bishops, in close contact with Rome, but abbots and other ecclesiastical officials. Many of Innocent's decretals concerned the administration of this system and some of the clauses of the Fourth Lateran Council bore witness to the growing precision and influence of these courts. To begin a case the petitioner needed to go to the curia to get a mandate to judges at home or he could send a proctor. Thomas of Marlborough took about forty days to get himself to Rome, riding fast and wearing out horses on the way. His hurried

28. *Chronicon Abbatiae de Evesham* ed. W D Macray (RS 29, 1863) quotes on 152, 189.

journey allows us to estimate a more usual journey as taking about six to eight weeks. Once the mandate was procured the petitioner, or the proctor, left for home or the letter was entrusted to a messenger. Sealed with the papal leaden seal, the *bulla* or bull, it was the authority for the judges' actions, outlining any specific points which needed to be brought to their attention, informing them in some cases of the law and declaring their actual powers. Many mandates were, like the English royal judicial writs, of a stock type. Once the messenger reached his destination he delivered the mandate to the judges who then proceeded to summon the parties to appear on a stated day at a stated place. As the benches were composed of various judges there were no settled places for their courts. The judges usually used the church of one of their number for the place of hearing and they often chose places that were towns or centres. The parties might be represented by proctors. The judges examined both the evidence of witnesses and written documentation, the procedure being based on the Roman civil procedure. The plaintiff or petitioner drew up a series of charges for the defendant to answer and refute, but the burden of proof was on the plaintiff. Very frequently judges sought to bring the parties to an amicable settlement (which was more likely to be observed) rather than to pass an outright sentence. The advantages of a settlement by a delegated court were an up-to-date judgment and enforcement. But it would be idle to pretend that there were not frivolous appeals and attempts by parties to delay and frustrate justice and to be obstructive if it suited them, when litigants learned how to 'play' the courts to their advantage. However, for the most part it was a civilized system which got to the truth and settled many cases fairly and without chicanery. We cannot know how many cases concerned ordinary people and their marriages, wills and so forth, rather than the ceaseless disputes concerning monastic income and the well-documented cases about elections and jurisdictional powers. The surviving evidence is weighted very heavily towards the property cases (as one would expect), but delegated courts impinged on many people's lives in one way or another. At the heart of the system was the pope, industrious in clarification and in civilizing procedure. He accentuated the importance of evidence and, in particular, the depositions of sworn witnesses (and he introduced the same stringency in canonization cases).[29] Many of Innocent's pronouncements on written record, on the appeal procedure (the case to be returned to the former judges if the objection proved unreasonable and the appellant to be condemned to pay the costs), and on intermediary judgments jostled with other decisions among the decrees of the Lateran Council.[30] Others, on the judge delegate courts, found their way through the Five Compilations into the *Decretales* of 1234. Innocent, by his actions and definitions, had extended and improved the work of the courts. He had held a great council which, in turn, encouraged the holding of local synods, and he had sent out legates and nuncios on the Church's mission. He had extended earlier papal ambitions as the means arose. Above all, in his role as final judge and lawgiver, he had shown himself to be an exponent of definition and codification. The authority of the law was his guiding principle. Upholding the law was an active, not a passive, activity. The banning of the ordeal symbolized a triumph for rational argument over the old magical formulas. The Church might have magical powers but for Innocent they had no part in the legal process. Law meant the right ordering of society on earth and it reflected Divine Law.

29. See below p. 135.
30. e.g. cc 35–8, 40.

Chapter 4

AUTHORITY AND PROTEST: THE CHRISTIAN LIFE

. . .

THE CRISIS OF THE CHURCH

Historically the two personalities of Pope Innocent III and St Francis of Assisi may be seen as in marked contrast – Innocent representing an authoritative papacy, Francis searching for the roots of the simple apostolic life of the early Church. We have, on the one hand, the career ecclesiastic, the planner and man of an essentially legalistic mind, and, on the other, the religious enthusiast who takes no thought for the morrow, preferring to trust in divine power and provision.[1]

Was it possible that the desire to return to the *Vita Apostolica*, the simple life of prayer, personal austerity and poverty was reconcilable with the Petrine commission and all the pomp and authority that suggested? In the upper church of the great friary at Assisi is a fresco by Giotto (Ambrogio Bordone 1267–1337), showing Innocent's dream. A sleeping pope, in an elaborately curtained bedchamber, attired in the red mantle and the tiara, witnesses the bare-footed Francis, clad in a rough brown garment, holding up the tremendous weight of a marble-pillared church, decorated with a Cosmati frieze and surmounted

---

1. One example of Francis's strict interpretation of trusting in divine providence was to be found in the refusal to soak dried peas and beans the night before for the meal of the next day, which must have made life somewhat difficult and infuriating for more ordinary mortals; see R Brooke 'Recent work on St Francis of Assisi' *Analecta Bollandiana* **100** (1982) 672.

by a tower of five storeys. The church is leaning dangerously. The painting is based on the story recounted in Brother Thomas of Celano's *Second Life* of St Francis completed in 1247.[2] Franciscan legend thus presented the faithful a generation later with Francis as the allegorical saviour of the universal Church. To understand the challenge to the papacy that this scene represents, we need to look at the structure of the traditional Church and also at popular religion at the beginning of the thirteenth century.

The Roman Church under the papacy was the established Church of most of western Europe and parts of eastern Europe. Long before Innocent III it had asserted its primacy over the patriarchates of Constantinople, Alexandria, Antioch and Jerusalem. The Petrine commission had given Rome its authority, and although there was resistance and limitation to its eastern aspirations, Rome as the see of St Peter dominated the West. In structure the Western Church was hierarchical, with the pope at the apex, assisted in the Church at large by the archbishops of the provinces and the bishops of their dioceses. By the thirteenth century archdeacons acted as lieutenants of the bishops within the separate dioceses or sees. In 1198 the established central 'Church' at Rome was well on the way to becoming a vast, governmental machine. In Rome itself the cardinals administered their own churches according to their orders of bishop, priest or deacon and they acted also within the pope's household as officers such as chancellor and chamberlain. They had become increasingly important, too, as legates and representatives or envoys of the pope, sent to deal with the problems of local churches and to hold councils. The pope's household was fast developing into defined administrative and judicial offices.

2.   Thomas of Celano 'Vita Secunda S. Francisci' in *Analecta Franciscana* **10** fasc. 2 (Quaracchi/Firenze 1927) 141. The 'dream' scene is also depicted in mosaic in the church of Santa Maria in Aracoeli in Rome (the centre of the Franciscan Order) and is associated with the Franciscan pope, Nicholas IV (1288–92), and, in a long mosaic inscription in the Lateran, Nicholas explicitly connected his restoration of that basilica with Pope Innocent III's dream of Francis sustaining the Roman Church. It was propaganda that suited both the papacy and the Franciscans, see J Gardner 'Patterns of papal patronage' in *Religious Roles* ed. C Ryan 442–4, 449. It is also associated with St Dominic.

Although the 'offices' might be peripatetic, going outside Rome with the pope, and although the pope might still play a dominant personal part, only a total reversal of policy – an annihilation of the authority the papacy had set itself to achieve during the previous 150 years – could have stemmed the march towards authority and central administrative offices.

Innocent had been brought up within the structure of the Roman Church. As a cardinal deacon, he became part of the papal 'civil' service, acting on occasion as auditor of lawsuits and witnessing administrative acts of the curia. He was a 'pastor' within the established framework, devoting his attention to his cardinalate church and writing his theological works. He was not a great spiritual leader, as was Francis. He had not, however, lost sight of the Church's Christian mission to evangelize and declare the faith and his early pre-occupation with pastoral duties and the care of souls did not leave him. This is the programmatic message of many of his letters and of his summons to the Council. While his approach was one of conservative conformity on the whole, in line with previous papal policy, he was not a man to overlook an opportunity to extend the Roman Church's influence. The simple and almost revolutionary message of Francis had the fortune to reach the ears and attention of a pope of spiritual vision who, while not able to fill that role himself, recognized the strength and power that might be harnessed to both the papal curia and the Church as a whole.

It is difficult to speak of popular religion or to define it in a satisfactory way, because it included an amalgam of magic and superstition, belief and doubt, the pagan and the Christian. The Church had struggled against the continuation of certain pagan practices. But it had by no means won on every point.

Our knowledge of the persistence of paganism and the practice of magic is limited. It depends on chronicles, on the evidence of laws, and on the decrees of councils that are mainly later than the Fourth Lateran. Until the detailed investigative sources and court records that begin to appear in the reformed diocesan administration of the fourteenth century, we are almost totally in the dark. But it is certain that superstitious practices and pagan activities had not died out. Laws of Canute of 1020x1022 state: 'It is heathen practice if one worships idols, namely if one worships heathen gods and the sun or the moon, fire or flood, wells or stones or any kind of forest trees, or if one practises witchcraft or encompasses death by any means, either by sacrifice or divination, or takes any part in such delusions.'[3] The London Council of 1074x1075 decreed excommunication for magic and the statutes of Canterbury I 1213x1214 decreed penalties for priests who sacrificed to demons and practised magic.[4] Councils of the mid-thirteenth century in England continued legislating against the worship of wells and springs, stones and trees, spells and superstitions, and penalties were provided. Offenders were to be denied the sacrament by the local priest.[5]

The chroniclers entered the world of witches and spirits and handed on the sort of stories that circulated. William of Malmesbury is our source for the tale of the witch of Berkeley who served the Devil as a sorceress and who was carried off by him from her tomb in spite of the efforts of her family and the priest. Her body had been sewn in a stag's skin and the stone coffin sealed with lead and iron and bound with a heavy chain. Demons broke their way into the locked church, where priests were incanting psalms round her body and the Devil called her up from her coffin and bore her away.[6] The chronicler William of Newburgh was disposed to believe that King Sverre of Norway had brought about the destruction of King Magnus's fleet in 1186 by invoking the Devil.[7] Gervase of Tilbury, writing about 1214, has stories of people who fly at night, of witches who enter houses and have intercourse with sleeping men, who steal infants, and who take the form of animals, especially cats and wolves, at will.[8]

3. *Councils and Synods* ed. D Whitelock, M Brett, C N L Brooke (Oxford 1981) I i 489.
4. *Councils and Synods* I ii 614 c 8 and II i ed. F M Powicke, C R Cheney (Oxford 1964) 25 c 1.
5. *Councils and Synods* II i 303 c 30 (1240) and 622 (1258).
6. William of Malmesbury *De Gestis Regum Anglorum* ed. W Stubbs 2 vols (RS 90, 1887) i 253–5.
7. William of Newburgh in *Chronicles of the reigns of Stephen, Henry II and Richard I* i ed. R Howlett (RS 82, 1884) 231.
8. See J B Russell *A History of Witchcraft, Sorcerers, Heretics and Pagans* (1980) 64.

Thirteenth-century sermons illustrate the mixture of cre-
dulity, ignorance and superstition that permeated popular
belief. Magic was close to miracles and some magic was not
harmful. Whether it was a pagan god, or a Christian saint,
or some superstitious ceremony that brought rain, did not
matter to most people provided the rain came. The primitive instincts described in the extraordinary ceremonies of
'beating' the saints, undertaken in some monasteries in
order to 'encourage' them to provide what was required,
show the psychological difficulties of dealing with saints.[9]
They were there to be beseeched and entreated for their
protection and aid in adversity, but what if they failed? If
monks could act in such a way, tormenting relics, it was
hardly surprising that ordinary people resorted to spells
and superstitious practices. Chinks of light into medieval
beliefs are sometimes provided in accounts of miracles.
Fairies appear in the account of the sanctity of Wulfstan of
Worcester.[10] When the sources improve there is evidence
of pagan practices persisting. Bishop Buckingham in the
fourteenth century tried to stamp out old superstitious
usages and pagan practices in his diocese of Lincoln,
according to entries in his register.[11]

There were local differences between the practice of the
different churches long after there was a semblance of conformity and orthodoxy. Differences between the practice of
Rome and the practice of separate, national churches
could never be entirely removed. There was always a diver-
sity of practice – as there still is – in religious attitudes,
customs and modes of worship. Popular devotion tended
to be non-conformist – in contrast to the liturgy (official
devotion).[12] However, as kingdoms became settled and the
Gregorian reform began to give greater prominence to
centralization, councils and legates – in short to uniformity
and a unifying law – so there were more difficulties in

9.   Patrick Geary 'L'humiliation des saints' *Annales* **34** (1979) 27–42.
10. *The Vita Wulfstani of William of Malmesbury ... and the Miracles and
     Translation of St Wulfstan* ed. R R Darlington (Camden Soc. 3rd ser.
     40 1928) 129.
11. D M Owen *Church and Society in Medieval Lincolnshire* (History of
     Lincs **5** 1971) 25, 32.
12. E Delaruelle 'Dévotion populaire et hérésie au môyen âge' in
     Hérésies et sociétés dans l'Europe pré-industrielle 11e–18e siècles ed. Jac-
     ques Le Goff (Paris 1968) 147.

incorporating a wide variety of practices within a centralized system. While outer differences did not matter much, deeper causes of conflict might exist and already there had been the disastrous schism on doctrinal grounds between the Church of the East and the Church of the West. How in general, then, did the separate churches, at a distance from Rome, and the majority of people, know what accepted belief was?

The answer lies in the provision of a structured Church and in the definition of what constituted heretical belief. First and foremost in importance to the structure were the bishops. Over four hundred bishops from all the dioceses of the Western Church were present at the Lateran for the Council of 1215.[13] Most, if not all of them, would have visited the papal curia before this, on business, on pilgrimage or for confirmation of their appointments. The burden of implementing papal decisions and the decisions of councils fell directly upon the bishops. The pope as the premier bishop was there to settle their differences and to support and encourage. Through the bishops, with their lands, wealth, and judicial tribunals, the whole system of a centralized Church was made to work. They had influence in the imperial and royal courts: they were the pope's permanent delegates. Their attitudes and reactions were just as important to the papacy as those of archbishops and monarchs. During the Becket quarrel, when their support was split between king and archbishop, their crucial and ambivalent position was shown. In the final analysis the majority accepted the authority of the pope. Similarly in the imperial crisis the dual allegiance of the bishops was tested up to (and in some cases beyond) breaking point.

Innocent sought definite controls over the episcopacy: for if in theory bishops were the pope's natural supporters, in practice their allegiance to the Crown might be more pressing. Elections of bishops took place in the royal court in England with the king deciding the number of electors. Free election was a fiction and the king's candidate very rarely failed to win. Innocent's chances of intervention

13. The Fourth Lateran was probably the best attended council up to that date; see Sophia Menache *The Vox Dei. Communication in the Middle Ages* (Oxford 1990) 56, who estimates a total attendance of 1200.

rested on his insistence on confirmation of the elected candidate, on the right of appeal to him if misconduct of the
election was alleged and on election in his own papal court
if both parties brought the case before him. Papal confirmation seems rarely to have been sought before 1198.
Under Richard I only two new bishops from the province
of Canterbury sought papal approval, Savaric of Bath in
1192 and Philip of Poitou, elected to Durham in 1197.
Innocent insisted on upholding the canon law on election –
if an election went against canon law it was *ipso facto* invalid
– and he used every possible opportunity to exercise his
right of approval. The right of appeal depended on reference being made to the pope. Such was the case of
Mauger, bishop-elect of Worcester, the royal candidate and
physician, who was illegitimate. Innocent 'postulated'
Mauger, i.e. using his plenitude of power, he personally
nominated him as bishop, dispensing him from his impediment. He had thus made the point, while accepting the
royal candidate, that the power of confirmation (which was
increasingly insisted upon) lay with the pope alone.

These were the men who formed the main links between the papal curia and the Church at large and who
were charged with the maintenance of orthodoxy in their
dioceses. It was their duty to stamp out unacceptable practices – witchcraft, magic, and pagan superstitions. St Hugh,
bishop of Lincoln from 1185 to 1200, put an end to offerings at streams at Berkhampstead, Wycombe and
elsewhere.[14] The bishops' pre-occupation, too, was with
structured administration, which the registers of their activities begin to record from the thirteenth century. They
gave licences for religious foundations in their dioceses,
for private chapels for the nobility and for clergy from elsewhere to preach. They held their own diocesan synods,
ordained clergy, confirmed children and heard certain
cases in their courts. By visitation of the monastic and parish churches within their dioceses, the bishops heard what
was going on. St Hugh, making a visitation of the religious
houses in his diocese, came to the nunnery of Godstow,
and seeing the tomb of Henry II's mistress, Fair Rosamund,

---

14. *The Life of St Hugh of Lincoln* ed. D L Douie, D H Farmer 2 vols
    (Oxford Medieval Texts 1985) ii 201.

before the high altar, ordered its removal outside the church.[15]

While the bishops were very much at the heart of Innocent's system of church government there were papal expedients that Innocent used quite extensively that minimized their power. By the sending out of legates, papal representatives with very exalted powers, and by the appointment of judges delegate and the encouraging of litigants and petitioners to bring their cases to the papal curia, the bishops' powers were kept firmly to the pastoral side. Centralization acted against permanent devolution to the diocesans. Also, the pope might claim the settlement of certain cases, the dispensations and the final decisions. He could overrule, as it were, by sending 'public' preachers, for example to preach a crusade and, most important, he could build up the power of the monasteries by granting or confirming exemption from the diocesan. The relationship between the popes and the religious houses could be used to papal advantage.

The religious houses fitted neatly into the papal hierarchical structure. Some of the ancient abbeys, such as St Albans and Bury St Edmunds in England, were exempt from the visitation of the local bishop and answerable only to the pope. Others had particular, more limited, exemptions granted to them by the pope. All Cluniac abbeys and priories were directly subject to the abbot of Cluny and to the pope and did not come under the supervision of the diocesan. With the Cistercians (reformed Benedictines) the diocesans were restricted in influence. Exemptions from paying tithes and from visitation were granted to the Order, for the Cistercians had their own developed machinery of the general chapter which met annually at Cîteaux to ensure the maintenance of the rule. There was a supra-national network. Cistercian houses were related in filiations and were subject to visitation by the abbot of the mother house.

A further indication of the hierarchical structure of the monastic order of monks and nuns is the growth of rules. The Rule of St Benedict of the sixth century was a code

---

15. Howden *Chronicle* iii 167–8.

written by Benedict for the use of his own monks. It is patriarchal and envisaged no links between the separate
monasteries. The *Carta Caritatis* ('Charter of Charity') of
the Cistercians on the other hand, was not a rule in the
sense of a code of conduct (as was St Benedict's Rule) but
a fundamental redaction of monastic law which was approved by the pope. The future pattern for a new religious
order was to be papal approval and a definite rule.

The first Cistercians were men who sought to return to
the simplicity of Benedict's Rule and to its strict observance which they argued had been altered out of all
recognition by the Cluniacs who spent much of the day in
a long and elaborate round of services in choir. The
monk's daily routine was to be restored to one of manual
labour, study and prayer in equal parts. His obedience to
the abbot was paramount. But such was the success of the
Cistercians in attracting recruits that, according to one
chronicler, 'The world threatened to become one vast
Cîteaux'. And in escaping from the world to remote places
and using lay brothers to find a vocation in tilling the soil,
the Order was soon transformed into a wealthy economic
organization. Ironically, too, the towering figure of Bernard, abbot of the Cistercian house at Clairvaux, radically
changed the role of the Cistercians. Largely due to
Bernard, they were to come to the forefront of politics and to
find a place within the papal court. There were Cistercian
bishops and by 1145 there was a Cistercian pope, Eugenius
III. It was for him that St Bernard wrote his famous tract
on papal power. Bernard, indeed, does not envisage a renunciation of power, rather he counsels a careful exercise
of it. Bernard paints a picture of a pope harassed by worldly affairs and commends the example of Pope Gregory the
Great, who, while the city was besieged by the barbarians,
found time to sit down and write a commentary on Eze-
kiel. He counsels leisure and reflection. And, in one of the
most remarkable pieces of writing on papal power, he ex-
tols the unique authority of Peter and his successors, who
are entrusted with 'the government of the whole world'.[16]
It seemed impossible to reconcile the ideal of the simple

16. *Saint Bernard On Consideration* trans. G Lewis (Oxford 1908) bk II
    ch 8.

monastic life with a great religious order, just as it seemed impossible for the papacy to exercise leadership without becoming an autocratic bureaucracy. In the halls of power Cistercians became papal confessors and were used by the popes as legates and preachers. The Cistercians were the papacy's missionary storm-troops of the twelfth to thirteenth century as the Jesuits were to become at the time of the counter-Reformation. There were Cistercian cardinals at the curia directing and Cistercians on all the fringes of Europe converting and preaching. Critical of the establishment at the beginning, though never of the episcopacy as such, the Cistercians had a system that was as hierarchical as the papacy.

Criticisms of the excessive organizational structure of the Church and of its wealth were both anti-hierarchical and anti-clerical. The curia was often denounced for its venality and appetite for money, as the 'Gospel according to the marks of silver' of the twelfth-century *Carmina Burana* shows. Nor was the pope immune from criticism and the new pope, Innocent, is described by one writer as caring only for worldly goods. According to the extremely anti-clerical and anti-papal poet, Walter von der Vogelweide, while priests ate chicken and drank wine, laymen fasted and went hungry.[17] Such opinions were not of themselves particularly harmful. They were expressions sometimes of pique and envy and sometimes of an essential regenerative process that caused a return to a stricter and more austere way of life and observance. Provided the role of the priest was not disputed – as the essential and sole provider of the sacrament of the holy communion at the mass – the essence of the Church was not threatened. What part the laity could play in the Church and how far they felt alienated is for discussion later. But the anti-clerical and anti-hierarchical sentiments, unless they undermined the faith and declared doctrine (so far as it was understood), were not in themselves heretical. The heretic was someone who quarrelled with the fundamental teaching of the

17. Schmidt '*Novus regnat Salomon in diebus malis.* Une satire contre Innocent III' in *Festschrift Bernhard Bischoff* ed. J Autenrieth and F Brunhölzl (Stuttgart 1971) 375, 378 – the new pope cares only for worldly goods – and *'I saw the World'. Sixty poems of Walther von der Vogelweide (1170–1228)* trans. Ian G Colvin (1938) no. 28.

Christian Church, not someone who criticized the trappings of religion.

There is absolutely no doubt that the Church was becoming more authoritative, autocratic and legalistic in the twelfth century, and this continued under Innocent. The process of canonization, which in early times had been very informal and by acclamation, became regulated under the Church's supervision and Innocent stressed that only the pope had the authority to declare a saint, 'for the confirmation of the Catholic faith and the confusion of heresy', as he said. There were four canonizations during his pontificate.[18] The process for Cunegunda, the wife of the emperor Henry II (who himself had been canonized by Eugenius III), had begun under Celestine III. Innocent declared her a saint in April 1200, acting out of 'the plenitude of his power', after a fresh application was made. This bull was to serve as a model for the letters canonizing Gilbert of Sempringham and Wulfstan of Worcester in January 1202 and in May 1203. For both these canonizations there survive the evidence of witnesses. Innocent had insisted that the application should be accompanied by the depositions of sworn witnesses and that some of the witnesses should appear in person at the curia.[19] Gone was the old public acclamation. Now, instead, a careful and legalistic 'process' had been introduced.

Another example of the tightening of papal authority concerned relics. It was decreed that no new relics were to be venerated unless approved by the pope and the sale of relics was forbidden.[20] Many flooded on to the market after the Sack of Constantinople in 1204. This authority of

18. The first canonization was that of Homobonus, an honest merchant of Cremona, struck dead during mass, who was declared a saint in January 1199 and of whom the pope said 'like a lily among thorns, sternly holding himself aloof from the heretics whose poison infected those parts': see Diana M Webb 'The pope and the cities: anticlericalism and heresy in Innocent III's Italy' in *SCH* Subsidia **9** (1991) 145.
19. See E W Kemp *Canonization and Authority in the Western Church* (Oxford 1948) 104–5; *The Book of St Gilbert* ed. R Foreville, G Keir (Oxford 1987) esp. pp. xcix–c and 235–7, and *Vita Wulfstani* 148.
20. Kemp *Canonization* 105–6 and c 62 of the Fourth Lateran Council and Statute of Wells (? 1258) *Councils and Synods* II ii 622 – new relics not to be venerated without papal permission.

the pope was matched by high-lighting the role of the clergy and minimizing that of the laity, especially in the administration of the sacraments. While baptism was the main sacrament that could be performed by lay persons, the Church counselled the clergy to check that it had been properly performed.[21] By the thirteenth century, as far as marriage was concerned, church authorities were insisting on the importance of marriage taking place before witnesses in public. Although the priest played no essential part in the contract, he was increasingly present. As for confession, which had been allowed to laymen, this was to be undertaken only when the penitent was in mortal danger: the emphasis now was not on contrition but on absolution which could only be given by a priest. So what had been licit and reasonably commonplace practices were now forbidden and became exceptional. After the Lateran Council all men over fifteen and women over twelve were to confess annually to their own priest (permission was needed for confession to another) and were to take communion each Easter.[22] The increasing exclusion of the laity from an active role within the Church gave them a feeling of alienation and doubtless accounted for the rise in popularity of sects in which lay persons could play a more positive and meaningful part.[23]

There was growing dissatisfaction with the Church and in particular with the way it was developing in the late twelfth century. The monastic and papal revival from about the year 1000 had moved the Church away from the laity. Lay influence was under threat and the laity's rights as patrons were being questioned. The Catholic clergy became more exclusive as the Gregorian Reform was accomplished. The up-grading of the priest meant the down-grading of the layman and, as status declined, so criticism began to be voiced against the ecclesiastical hierarchy and against exclusive administration of sacraments by priests as the sole

21. Cf Statutes of Canterbury I 1213x1214 c 29 in *Councils and Synods* II i 31.
22. c 21 (Fourth Lateran). Cf Statutes of Canterbury I c 43 (i32).
23. *PL* 214 col 526 (*X*. I. 4. 3) – Innocent condemned the custom in Passau whereby in ecclesiastical cases the whole of the assembly, literate and illiterate, declared the decision rather than just the ecclesiastical judges.

means of salvation. Christianity seemed more and more to mean clericalism and once the Second Crusade of 1147 was over the popular religious fervour that had been channelled into it needed a new outlet. [24]

Some groups of the dissatisfied were influenced by the Manichaean teachings which came from the east of Europe after the Second Crusade (1147) and were transmitted along the trade routes to the towns of north Germany and Lombardy. The Manichaeans, described also as Bogomils, Cathars and Patarenes, believed in equal forces of good and evil. Hence they were also called Dualists and the Church condemned them accordingly as heretical in their beliefs. They were less concerned with what was wrong with Christianity: they were totally opposed to it. But while it would be wrong to minimize the hold of this movement, particularly in the south of France and in the Balkans, and especially between Bulgaria and Constantinople, the major threat to the future of the Church was not from the heretics but from the popular movements that sought to restore the laity's role in the life of the Church.

There were many well-meaning groups, who were not totally at odds with Catholic teaching, but merely wished to follow a different fashion of Christian life and observance. In particular the lay movement, seeing the ill-life of some priests and the increasing grandeur of the Church, sought to insist on chastity, abstention from luxury and avoidance of meat-eating, and aspired to renounce property, or at least to hold goods in common. Few of these people – at least at first – questioned the importance of the sacraments, but the quality of the life that was led was very important to them. Great emphasis was put on preaching, and this preaching advocated in particular a return to what was conceived to have been the 'apostolic' way of life. Followers were prepared to live a life of poverty. In the climate of the time anyone who appeared strange was suspect of heresy, especially those who voluntarily embraced poverty and wandered about. They seemed a threat because they looked odd and acted in an odd way. Reports

24. Delaruelle 'Dévotion populaire' 147–55 esp. 152; and see also C Thouzellier 'Tradition et résurgence dans l'hérésie médiévale' in *Hérésies* 105–12.

from the clergy in some of the affected dioceses show that they were perplexed by the variety and number of the movements emerging at this time.

But what did the Church define as heresy? Gratian (following the great Father of the Church, St Jerome) in his *Decretum*, the first widely-used manual of canon law, says that heresy is 'perverse dogma' (C xxiv q.3 c.26), i.e. a false and new opinion at variance with established dogma. But such a definition was in effect very vague and blunt and was notoriously difficult for the Church to apply: it followed that many harmless groups were confused with heretical ones by the authorities in their attempts to control what was going on. In 1184, fourteen years before Innocent's accession, Lucius III had issued the first curial pronouncement on heresy in the decree 'Ad abolendam heresam'. This defined heresy as any opposition to the Catholic doctrine of the sacraments, but it also specified that any preaching which took place without licence was to be deemed heretical. It was clear that the curia wished to keep the growing hierocratic structure intact. Frequent episcopal visitation was ordered in areas where there were suspected heretics, and secular rulers were called upon to assist in this process. This ruling had been made at a meeting with the Emperor Frederick Barbarossa. From early times the papacy had allied with the imperial power to condemn the unorthodox. Heresy provided a threat to civil as well as ecclesiastical order, to political settlement and to peace. It was also in the interest of secular rulers that Catholic orthodoxy was maintained. For the Catholic Church, the emperor's role was to persecute and eliminate those whom it defined as heretics. Innocent decreed in 1200 in the decretal 'Vergentis' that heretics were to receive punishment from the lay authorities. Their goods were to be confiscated and all who protected them were to be pronounced excommunicate.[25] The response of the secular rulers depended on a wide variety of factors, but mostly it was conditioned by political considerations.

At the beginning of his reign Innocent III bunched together the Cathars, the Patarenes, the Waldensians and 'other heretics of different names', as his predecessor

25. *X. V. 7. 10.*

Alexander III had done. He grew, however, to see that many of the new movements were not seriously deviationist or dissident. They wanted quite simply 'a return to the Apostolic Life', a more simple Church and a Church that they could understand. In some ways one might say that they wanted a life more like that of early monks – embracing poverty, chastity, even obedience. Their increasing interest in the New Testament and the Life of Christ led them to concentrate on poverty and preaching – which previous authorities had seen to be dangerous. Before we look at the separate groups and the new pope's treatment of them, more needs to be said about poverty and preaching.

. . .

POVERTY

There was very considerable variation in the approach to poverty.[26] Most of the groups saw riches as associated with power – the *dives potens* (the rich, powerful person), as opposed to the *pauper humilis* (the humble beggar). Was it not 'easier for a camel to go through the eye of a needle than for a rich man to enter the kingdom of heaven'; and were the poor not 'blessed for theirs is the kingdom of heaven'? Surely riches were a definite hindrance to the Christian and opposed to the teaching of Christ? The Arnaldists of Lombardy (followers of Arnold of Brescia, who died in 1155) argued against the Holy See having property. The Waldensians (followers of Peter Waldo of Lyons) believed that the authority of the Roman Church was annulled when Pope Sylvester had accepted temporal possessions from the Emperor Constantine. They wished to make poverty their way of life, to follow the 'Lady Poverty' as the Franciscans were to do. This was total poverty. Nobody should own gold or silver or take thought for the morrow. Many of them went further and maintained that the priest could not celebrate a valid mass unless he lived in poverty, too. They wanted, furthermore, to preach

26. Much of this section is based on Menache *Vox Dei* 213–21; C Violante 'La pauvreté dans les hérésies du xie siècle en occident' 347–69, and C Thouzellier 'Hérésie et pauvreté à la fin du xiie et au début du xiiie siècle' 371–88 in *Etudes sur l'histoire de la pauvreté* ed. Michel Mollat (Paris 1974).

poverty. Other groups, such as the 'Poor Catholics', believed that if property or goods were held at all, they should be in common. Certain heretics round Arras in the early eleventh century thought manual labour important for salvation. Some, like the Humiliati, practised manual labour to earn a living. They thus avoided begging and came nearest to the monastic conception of poverty. In a world where poverty was all around – and there were severe famines in Europe in the 1180s and 1190s from a series of bad harvests – men could not help but ask whether the religious message was right. Many aimed to assist the poor by living like them and the motivation of the 'Poor Catholics' was not so remote from that of Mother Teresa and her fellow-workers in present-day Calcutta. The Church accepted the voluntary poverty of individuals, but it could not accept it for the Church as an institution. At first Innocent III reinforced the traditional church view that absolute poverty was contrary to the Church's structure and hesitated to sanction it. Poverty was only acceptable in religious terms if practised within monasteries. It was thus 'structuralized poverty'. Nothing could more swiftly bring religion into disrepute than begging and the curia had always insisted on adequate financial support for religious ventures. Equally a poor clergy was not acceptable to Innocent.

Other groups put chastity and a simple way of life – abstinence from meat, non-violence and mutual trust (they were opposed to oath-taking) – above or on a par with poverty. To the Monforte group, and among the Poor Catholics, chastity was the most important virtue; for the Arras sect poverty was part of a programme, not the whole, while the Patarenes of Milan saw an immoderate desire for money and power, above what was necessary, as evil, and considered this to be the source of simony. Brotherly love, non-violence and personal abstinence of various kinds – not eating more than twice a day and dressing soberly, as the Humiliati, or never sleeping in a bed like the Poor Catholics – could scarcely threaten the established order.[27] However, a denial of the principle of oath-taking might, and so, like poverty and preaching, was seen to be a threat.

27. *PL* 216 col 601C.

. . .

PREACHING

Lucius's legislation to forbid preaching without licence widened the gap between the curia and the new groups. Though preaching was not common in the twelfth century – even by its last years – it was commonly accepted that it was the clergy's role to preach and interpret the teachings of Christ, as part of the duty to care for souls. It was the curial view that only clergy – bishops, priests, and other appointed ecclesiastics – might preach. Not only did many of the members of the new groups desire a life of poverty for themselves, they also wanted to preach, and this was seen as a definite threat by the authorities who viewed with growing alarm the rise in the number of these poor preachers. The enthusiasm to preach the gospel came very close to the desire to follow the *vita apostolica*. Had not the life of Christ been one of poverty and preaching? Both the desire for poverty and the desire to preach might be seen as no more than comments on Christian practice. They did not express doubts about doctrine; nevertheless the Church wanted such manifestations bridled. In the early twelfth century St Norbert, founder of the Premonstratensian Order of white canons, who had been given papal permission to be a wandering preacher, was finally persuaded by the church authorities to settle down and found an Order. The enthusiasm to preach the gospel by non-priests, by laymen (and even by women) might lead to and, indeed, spread heresy. The Church was right to have fears here because it was not possible to control what was being said and many of these new groups, both heretical and non-heretical, produced fine preachers. One Cathar heretical preacher was described as having 'the mouth of the angel', while the sermons of the papal legate sent to combat the heresy were likened to 'the drone of the bee'.[28] The new preachers, with exciting new things to say, attracted crowds. As in nineteenth-century England, the preaching heard in the meeting places and open spaces

28. Cited E le Roy Ladurie *Montaillou. Cathars and Catholics in a French Village 1294–1324* trans. B Bray (1978) 240, and Jonathan Sumption *The Albigensian Crusade* (1978) 226.

was heady stuff compared with what was delivered in the established Church.

To preach effectively, of course, it was necessary to be able both to move about and to read and discuss the Bible. By the late twelfth century translations began to appear. The official fear of the dangers is well set out in the following account.

> He (Peter Waldo) caused to be translated into the French tongue, for his use, the Gospels, and some other books of the Bible, and also some authoritative sayings of Saints Augustine, Jerome, Ambrose and Gregory, arranged under titles, which he and his followers called 'sentences'. They read these very often and hardly understood them, since they were quite unlettered but, infatuated with their own interpretation, they usurped the office of the Apostles, and presumed to preach the Gospel in the streets and public places. And the said Waldes or Waldo converted many people, both men and women, to a like presumption, and sent them out to preach as his disciples. Since these people were ignorant and illiterate, they, both men and women, ran about through the towns, and entered the houses. Preaching in public places and also in the churches, they, especially the men, spread many errors ...[29]

While many of the new movements were against the hierarchy, they were not, at least at first, opposed to the priesthood as such or to the sacraments. Most accepted baptism. Some, like those of Arras, felt that baptism was of such importance that it should be given only to adults. Most again accepted marriage as indissoluble, as the Waldenses, but they preferred people to live as celibates. Bernard Prim's followers were conformist enough to pay, and exhort others to pay, tithes and offerings to the clergy. Only when the role of the priest was questioned did they really begin to challenge orthodoxy. The priesthood had long been seen as worldly by some, and chroniclers harped constantly on the degeneracy of the clergy, sometimes

29. Quoted Menache *Vox Dei* 239, citing Bernard Gui *Manuel* ed. G Mollat i (1926) 35–7.

attributing all ills to this factor. During the Gregorian reform period the mass had been greatly stressed as the
central sacrament of the Church. It could only be administered by the priest and the question as to whether the
character and moral life of the particular priest could influence the validity of the sacrament began to be discussed.
By the time of Innocent III, the Waldenses in Lombardy
were of the opinion that the sacrament was valid only if the
celebrant was in a state of grace. Those in France were
more radical and believed that the sacrament could be administered by anyone of pure life and action, even by
laymen. Some sects, therefore, took matters into their own
hands and administered the sacraments themselves, maintaining that the worthiness of the administrator was what
mattered, not the fact of ordination to the priesthood.
'The priesthood of all believers' was born.

.   .   .

THE WALDENSES AND THE HUMILIATI

Most prominent among the sects at the end of the twelfth
century were the Waldenses and the Humiliati.[30] The
Waldenses took their name from their founder, Peter Valdès
(variously called Waldes or Waldo) of Lyons, a wealthy
merchant and former usurer, who had made a dramatic
renunciation of his property and wealth to live as the
apostles had done. His followers, known sometimes as the
'Poor Men of Lyons', presented a major challenge to the
towering majesty of the Church. Valdès emphatically did
not wish to part from the official hierarchy. He wished
solely to preach and give an example within the Church.
He sincerely tried to get advice from theologians in Rome
and he asked clerics to translate the Bible for him. The
local bishop forbade their preaching, but Valdès thought
of himself and his followers as still within the Church and
he arrived at Rome during the Third Lateran Council of
1179 seeking some authorization and approval. Pope Alexander III and the curia apparently applauded Valdès'

---

30. In general see R I Moore *The Origins of European Dissent* (1977) esp.
    125, 227–8, 230, and on the Humiliati the articles of B Bolton
    'Innocent III's treatment of the *Humiliati*' in *SCH* **8** (1971) 73–82,
    and 'Sources for the early history of the *Humiliati*' in *SCH* **11**
    (1975) 125–33.

enthusiasm and vision, but repeated the prohibition on preaching and set up an investigative tribunal. This tribunal decided against Valdès and his followers. It saw curial schemes threatened, and many curialists, proud of their theological training and exalted position viewed these lay people with contempt.

The Humiliati, from Lombardy, had also been to Rome seeking recognition. These were people who did not give up their social positions but desired to live the apostolic life within the community. There were early communities in the north of Italy: in Como, Pavia, Piacenza, Brescia, Bergamo, Verona and Milan. For the most part, they were literate – some of them were of high birth – and they pursued an austere personal life, dressing simply and eating little, while working and living with their families. They wanted recognition in case they were accused of heresy, but they, too, were disappointed. No encouragement was forthcoming and preaching was forbidden to them. The stumbling block for both groups had been preaching – 'How shall they preach unless they be sent?' (Rom. 10: 15) was the curial attitude – and they were included among the heretical sects named in Lucius III's 'Ad abolendam'.[31] They had wanted to work within the established framework, but they had been refused. A natural consequence was that they drifted further towards heresy and heretical beliefs.

The situation facing Innocent after his accession was tense. There were growing divisions between the Catholic hierarchy and lay people and between priests and lay people. In or soon after 1198 it appears that there must have been a papal decree exhorting the new religious movements to come to terms with the curia. Certainly a letter to the bishop of Verona makes a clear-cut distinction between the outright heretical and harmful and those whose way of life and belief did not seriously threaten the Church and were therefore harmless.[32] Innocent declared himself prepared to accept the desire of the sects to follow the life of apostolic poverty within the Church and to

---

31. The others were the Arnaldists, the Pasagini, the Josephini, the Cathars and the Patarenes.
32. D M Webb in *SCH* Subsidia **9** deals with the problem of anti-clericalism and heresy in Italy under Innocent (135–52).

preach, provided that they did not discuss doctrine and that the position of the clergy was not attacked. The sects were either to come within the established, official Church, or they would be declared heretical and as such persecuted relentlessly. In short, new 'Orders' were to receive recognition if they kept within the guidelines; heretical groups were to be wiped out using the full force available to him. The message left the bishop of Verona in no doubt. He was to stop indiscriminate persecution, establish precisely what were the beliefs of certain suspected persons and enquire whether some groups wished to return to the Church. If so, they were to be sent to the curia.[33] In late 1199 or early 1200, following these negotiations, the leaders of the Humiliati in northern Italy approached Innocent for direction.

The *Propositum* (or Statement of Intent) that the Humiliati brought with them was approved by the pope in 1201, following examination by a papal commission.[34] Two separate enclosed orders for men and for women religious were instituted and a third order, the so-called Tertiaries, of lay people living under vows in the world, was introduced. For them, a code of life, incorporating principles based on patience, humility and love, was confirmed. They were to avoid luxury in clothing, earn their living by manual labour only, give surplus income to the poor and observe the strictest matrimonial relations. They were permitted to say the seven canonical hours, but they had to swear obedience to their ecclesiastical superior and pay tithes. The Humiliati had forbidden their people to take oaths and on this matter a compromise was reached. The Humiliati were allowed to avoid oath-taking in all but the most pressing cases. Most important of all they were given permission to assemble on Sundays with preachers from their own ranks, provided they were qualified and approved by the local bishop. While Alexander III had insisted that the initiative for preaching must come from the bishop, Innocent declared that the Humiliati might themselves approach the

---

33. *PL* 214 ch 228 cols 788–9.
34. For the text of this and the other 'rules' discussed below see 'Dossier de l'ordre de la pénitence au xiiie siècle' ed. G G Meerssemann in *Spicilegium Friburgense* 7 (1961): 276–82 for the Humiliati.

bishop who should not reasonably withhold permission. They might preach on moral matters but never on theology, dogma and the sacraments. These concessions (for that is what they undoubtedly were) succeeded in incorporating many Humiliati within the traditional Church. There had thus been formed an important lay congregation with ramifications that were good and positive. By 1216, in Milan alone, long regarded as the 'capital of heresy', there were at least 150 convents and more family groups than could be counted, according to the writer, Jacques of Vitry.[35]

There was some reason to suppose that Innocent would also succeed in bringing the Waldenses within the framework of the established Church. The Waldenses, however, presented more intractable problems. They never lived in communities but were a loose group of preachers, mostly without homes and possessions. Their rebuff at the Third Lateran Council had made them more radical and aggressive. The Gospel to them was more important than the law and the Gospel made it clear that all were entitled to preach. Nor was ordination necessary to administer the sacraments. Lay persons might give them, since, according to the Waldenses, the efficacy of the sacrament depended on the worthiness (the *merita*) of the administrator, not on the fact of ordination (the *officium*) as the Church maintained. Here there was a progression towards radicalism in their views which had not been there at first.

The first move in Innocent's dealings with the Waldenses appears to have been prompted by the bishop of Metz (perhaps in answer to the curia's opening initiative) who, in 1199, consulted the pope about certain secret meetings of lay men and women in his city, at which they read aloud French translations of the Bible and preached. They refused obedience to their ecclesiastical superiors and said that it was more important to implement the teaching of the Bible than to obey the bishop. Innocent's reply declared the secret meetings and preaching to be inadmissible, but requested a detailed report from the bishop, especially on the Bible translations and who made them and on whether these people were obedient to the

35. Jacques of Vitry cited by Moore *Origins of European Dissent* 228.

Roman Church. It is not known what the bishop of Metz reported back but, the pope's next step was to commission three Cistercian abbots (of Cîteaux, Morimond and La Crête) to go as legates to Metz and investigate all the points with the bishop. Innocent wanted to know what the people believed, who they were, and how they lived. Again we do not know what the abbots reported, but we do know from a chronicle source that they took repressive action – they burned the translations and attempted to stamp out the sect.[36]

The Waldenses had a firmer hold in the south of France than north-east of the Loire. In late 1207 a discussion took place at Pamiers between the Spaniard, Durandus of Huesca, spokesman for the Waldenses (and a convert from the heretical Cathars) and the zealous bishop of the Spanish see of Osma, Diego. Following this, Durandus, according to two southern French chroniclers, went to Rome, gave Innocent certain promises, was reconciled to the Catholic Church and received papal permission in 1208 for the group to live as 'poor Catholics'. Durandus 'put his hands between the pope's' and swore to observe the agreed 'rule'.[37] The group was not an Order in any sense for they had no common life. Most of them were educated men and clerics who were intent on spreading the faith by living and moving within the community, not owning property, accepting the efficacy of the sacrament even from unworthy priests and acknowledging that military service was not sinful, as they had previously held.

The success of Diego, bishop of Osma, in bringing this group within the Church, seems to have been due to a new approach in dealing with the so-called heretics. This was the adoption of 'bare-foot evangelization', meeting the 'heretics' on their own terms, wandering among them, dressed in much the same way, living simply and arguing

36. *PL* 214 ep 141–2 cols 695–9, ep 235 cols 793–5, and Chronicle of Aubry des Trois-Fontaines MGH SS **23** (1874) 878, lines 13–15. The papal legate, Bishop Guy of Palestrina, ordered the condemnation of books in French and German in Liège in 1203; C Thouzellier *Catharisme et Valdéisme en Languedoc* (Louvain/Paris 1969) 161 n. 1.
37. 'Dossier' ed. Meersseman 282–4, and for the Penitents' (who came under the Poor Catholics) 'rule' of 1212, 286–8; *PL* 216 ep 78 col 274D and *PL* 215 ep 196 cols 1510–13.

the Church's case. While the bishops and the papal legates and the papacy's traditional missionaries, the Cistercians, were seeing to the burning of offending books, the exhumation of heretics and other repressive measures, the pope's views were veering towards persuasion and argument, at least as a first approach. In 1204 the pope wrote to the Cistercian legates round Montpellier, counselling them to take care that there should be nothing in their speech and acts that the heretics could find fault with, and two years later Innocent commissioned the legate, Raoul of Castelnau, to send suitable people among the suspected heretics who 'by imitating the poverty of Christ' will win them back to the faith.[38]

The evidence from the pope's letters shows that many of the bishops prickled at the new developments. They were alarmed at what they saw as a challenge to their authority.[39] Some, like the bishop of Carcassonne, became almost paranoid in denouncing secret meetings, unauthorized services, runaway monks; no doubt they echoed the feelings of many of the lower clergy. The condition of the bishops themselves in the south of France was a serious cause for alarm.[40] Unlike the bishops of the north, who as Crown appointees had an important notion of responsibility, those of the south in the ferment of heresy, without a strong royal power to control them, were often irresponsible and lawless. Not only were the bishops feeling challenged in their vested interests, but also the Cistercians were apparently aggrieved at the pope's new methods which he justified in the terms of 'it is more acceptable that some "perverse" ones survive than "just" ones perish'.[41]

Innocent remained adamant in his injunction that any preaching undertaken should be restricted to exhortation and should not stray into explanation of the faith which was the preserve of the clergy alone. He also insisted on approved 'rules' or 'ways of life'. In 1210 Bernard Prim, the leader of the Lombard Waldenses, made his way to the pope to seek permission for wander–preaching. Bernard

---

38. *PL* 215 ep 76 col 358, ep 79 cols 361–2, and ep 185 cols 1024–5.
39. *PL* 215 ep 198 col 1514.
40. Thouzellier *Catharisme* 191; Steven Runciman *The Medieval Manichee* (Cambridge 1955) 134–6.
41. *PL* 216 ep 67 col 74 end C.

had in fact been active against the heretics, though he and his followers had been treated as heretics by a hostile clergy. Bernard admitted to Innocent that they had administered the sacraments, but promised that they would not do so in future, accepting that only ordained men could do this and that the sacrament administered by an unworthy priest was equally valid. The *Confession of Faith* was on the lines of the Society of the Catholic Poor. Innocent, thereupon, approved the Society and declared that it had proved its innocence and had wrongly been accused of Waldensian heresy. In 1210 the Society of Bernard was recognized and given a 'rule', permitting the study of the Bible and manual labour, and, two years later in 1212, Prim and two companions returned to Rome to seek approval for a Third Order of Poor Catholics which was set up at Elne in southern France.[42]

It was in the summer of 1210 that the chronicler, Burchard of Ursberg, visited Rome and heard something (though not all and not correctly) of what was going on. He knew of the charges against Prim and his followers, but he was apparently unaware of the fact that the pope recognized them, believing that he had in effect confirmed the Franciscans:

At a time when the world was ageing, two 'orders' appeared in the Church, whose youthfulness was renewed like the eagle's and these 'orders', the Friars Minor and the Friars Preacher, were confirmed by the apostolic see. Perhaps they were approved at this time because two sects called the Humiliati and the Poor of Lyons, originating in Italy sometime back, continued to flourish. Pope Lucius had previously included them among the heretics on account of their superstitious doctrines and observances. Moreover in their private addresses which they generally delivered in secret places, they disparaged the Church of God and the priesthood.

I saw at that time at the apostolic see some of those called the Poor Men of Lyons with their leader – Bernard, I believe – who were trying to get their sect

42. *PL* 216 ep 94 col 291, ep 146 col 668 ('Dossier' ed. Meerssemann 284–6); and *PL* 216 ep 82 602A ('Dossier' 288–9).

confirmed and approved by the apostolic see. They wandered through town and country, saying that they were
imitating the life of the apostles, desiring neither possessions nor a settled home. But the Pope objected to
them because of certain peculiarities in their way of living – they cut off the tops of their shoes[43] and went
about nearly barefoot and, although they wore the caps
of religious, their hair was worn long like laymen. It
seemed scandalous, too, that the men and women
walked about together in the street, often staying in the
same houses and, it is said, sometimes sleeping in the
same bed. All of which they claim has come down from
the apostles.

Instead of them the pope confirmed some others who
had arrived, called the 'Little Poor', who repudiated
these superstitions and abuses. They went about both in
winter and in summer completely barefoot; they did not
accept money nor anything more than food unless it
happened that someone offered clothing. They never
asked for anything from anyone. But thinking that too
much profession of humility becomes boasting and that
the label of poverty, falsely assumed by so many, was
vainglorious in the sight of God, they preferred to be
called 'Little Brothers' to 'Little Poor'. They were totally
obedient to the apostolic see.[44]

.   .   .

THE FRIARS

In 1210 Francis of Assisi and his 'penitents', the 'Little
Poor', a mere twelve in number, came to ask the pope for
approval, as described above. Whereas previous applications of this kind had come from groups which had been
held to have deviated from the faith in some way, Francis
and his followers were not in that position. They had no
existing organization and they had not been challenged,
but Francis wanted papal endorsement for his desire to
preach and to live in poverty. He was, therefore, asking not

43. The sandals adopted by the Dominicans.
44. Burchard of Ursberg *Burchardi Praepositi Urspergensis Chronicon* 2nd
    edn ed. O Holder-Egger, B von Simson MGH SS (Hannover/Leip-
    zig 1916) 107–8. The translation is mine.

for confirmation of a 'rule', as no structure as yet existed, but for a general approval of his aims. Already rumours must have been abroad of Innocent's dealings with the new religious groups and perhaps of his more liberal attitude. Francis's request, however, came in conventional form. He had the support of his diocesan, the bishop of Assisi, and through him Francis obtained access to the Benedictine cardinal, John of St Paul, papal penitentiary, who had been legate to the Albigensians.[45] Through Cardinal John the request came to the pope.

In fact Innocent committed himself to nothing in 1210. But it may not be imagination to say that Innocent was impressed, for the group had not been condemned on the points of preaching and poverty as had others earlier in the pontificate. According to Thomas of Celano, what he actually said to the little group was 'Go with the Lord, brothers, and, as the Lord shall inspire you, preach repentance to all men. When the all-powerful Lord increases you in number and in grace you shall return joyfully to us and I will grant you more and establish you securely'.[46] Although Francis took what is described as a written rule to Innocent in 1210 – as is clearly stated in Franciscan sources[47] – Innocent undoubtedly gave no more than verbal encouragement. An official rule had yet to be drawn up and a *Propositum* was not appropriate. It may have been on this occasion, too, that the pope tried to persuade Francis to adopt St Benedict's Rule so as to facilitate recognition. It may also be that it was Cardinal John who persuaded Innocent not to put obstacles in the path of Francis. (The opposition within the curia was not to come to a head until the Council.) Following this dramatic meeting, it appears that the pope

45. He was created cardinal priest of St Prisca by Celestine III in 1193, and promoted cardinal bishop of Sabina by Innocent in 1204; see Maleczek *Papst und Kardinalskolleg von 1191 bis 1216. Die Kardinäle unter Coelestin. und Innocenz III.* (Vienna 1984) 114–17, esp 117, and *PL* 214 904A. He had been sent to deal with Markward of Anweiler earlier in the pontificate. It was not Cardinal John of Colonna who had been approached, as has been stated, for whom see Maleczek *Kardinalskolleg* 154–62.
46. Thomas of Celano 'Vita Prima' in *Analecta Franciscana* 10 fasc. 1, 25–7.
47. See *The Writings of Leo, Rufino and Angelo Companions of St Francis* ed. Rosalind B Brooke (Oxford 1970) 204–5 and see 59.

was on the way to acknowledging the evangelical life as an alternative way of living, not because circumstances pressed, as with the other groups, but because he was beginning to see the dynamism it might release within the established Church. At any rate Innocent did not ban a movement which in its beginnings differed very little in its aspirations from other popular movements of the time. He made only two conditions. Francis and his followers were to be tonsured, i.e. become clerks (and this was carried out by Cardinal John), and secondly Francis was to promise unconditional obedience to the pope and the other eleven to Francis. No rule was given and no order approved, but Innocent's approval of 1210 clearly allowed the Franciscans to preach.

Not only did the chronicler, Burchard, confuse the Waldenses with the Franciscans, but he also confused the Humiliati with the Dominicans who he says were recognized in 1210. Burchard continues:

There were others, namely the Preachers, who are believed to have taken the place of the Humiliati. The Humiliati, indeed, with no authority or licence from the bishop, preached to the people, putting their scythes in another's harvest, and ruled their lives, heard confessions and disparaged the ministry of priests. The pope, wishing to correct this, instituted and confirmed the order of Preachers. The former were rough and unlettered, working with their hands and preaching, receiving the necessities of life from their followers. The latter insist on the study and reading of holy scripture, writing books and hearing them expounded most diligently by their masters, as with bow and arrows and all the armour of valiant men [Song of Solomon 4: 4] they enter and stand for the defence of holy mother Church and rise from adversity and place themselves as a wall for the house of Israel [Ezekiel 13: 5]. They support the faith, teach and extol the statutes of the Church and strengthen virtues and good customs. They refute the errors and castigate the vices of men. They obey the apostolic see in all things from which they have their special authority.[48]

48. Burchard of Ursberg *Chronicon* 108 (my translation).

The origins of the Dominican Order are to be found in the south of France between 1206 and 1207 when Bishop Diego of Osma and the young sub-prior, Dominic, were engaging in disputation with heretics and those suspected of heresy. They began to live, like their targets, a more simple life, and they had considerable success in bringing back within the fold, by argument and example, disaffected members of the established Church. In fact the Dominicans, as the Franciscans, were not confirmed as an Order until Innocent's successor, Honorius III, approved them in 1216. By 1215, however, Dominic and his fellow preachers were empowered to preach in the diocese of Toulouse, with the approval of Bishop Fulk, not just against heresy but also to concentrate on faith and morals. At the beginning of September 1215 Dominic, with Bishop Fulk, left for the Lateran Council. Innocent apparently asked Fulk to grant the community a church within his diocese and he instructed Dominic to select an approved rule for the brothers to follow.[49]

. . .

HERESY

The Lateran Council, beginning in November 1215, tackled the question of what was orthodox and what heretical. Its first decree, 'Firmly we believe' ('Firmiter credimus'), was a creed or confession of the Catholic faith. It re-affirmed the doctrine of the Trinity, that God had created the universe, including all devils and demons who were not evil at the moment of their creation, the incarnation of the Son, His death, resurrection and ascension, and that only the priest might celebrate the mass in the one, true Church. It became the first chapter of the first title of Gregory IX's great canon law code. The second canon condemned the teaching of Joachim of Fiore and the third dealt with the treatment of heretics. They were to be handed over to the lay power for punishment, all leaders were to expel heretics from their lands, and preaching without the licence of the pope or the local bishop was prohibited and declared a heresy. It was clear that the

49. J-P Renard *La formation et la désignation des prédicateurs au début de l'ordre des prêcheurs (1215–1237)* (Fribourg 1977) 61–2.

framers of these decrees had the Cathars very much in mind. Decree 13 seemed a serious blow against the foundation of further congregations. In future aspirants were to enter one of the established Orders which had a stable and constant income. It looked very much as if Innocent's more liberal policy towards some of the new groups was at an end.

But what of the position of the Franciscans and of the Dominicans? Neither Francis nor Dominic was officially summoned to the Lateran Council as they were not the heads of approved Orders. They were, however, in Rome during the weeks of the Council. Perhaps word had come to them to make themselves available. They met, according to Thomas of Celano, for the first time in the house of the pope's close confidant, Cardinal Hugolinus, and it was there that Dominic apparently said to Francis, 'Let us form one society (*religio*), you and me, and live in the Church in a similar fashion (*pari forma*)'.[50] What precisely happened to the Dominicans at this point is not clear; but Franciscan sources suggest that Pope Innocent himself, overruling all other opinions, personally approved the Franciscans and informed the Council of his decision.

The satirists, the critical press of the day, found Innocent apathetic in dealing with heresy, especially charging him with neglecting the problem in Lombardy. Apathy seems to mean the pope's failure to pursue an immediate programme of repression. This criticism, from an Italian source, is possibly connected with the criticism voiced by the poet, Walter von der Vogelweide, who was outraged by the pope's efforts to collect money from German churches for the crusade against the Albigensians. For this purpose a collection box had been placed in every German church. In another song, the poet goes beyond the bounds of credibility, accusing Innocent himself of heresy and black magic. But it is the notion that money is being taken from one area to deal with the problems of another, while the area making the contribution suffers, that apparently irks. Lombardy is neglected for Languedoc. Both areas are invaded by the heretical Cathars.[51]

50. Thomas of Celano 'Vita Secunda' in *Analecta Franciscana* **10** fasc. 2, 215–17 esp. 217.
51. Schmidt '*Novus regnat Salomon*' 376; von der Vogelweide '*I saw the World*' trans. Colvin poem 28.

· · ·

THE CATHARS

'They save souls, they do not eat meat, they do not touch women,' said Alazaïs.

'Never tell my husband we have been talking about that,' Guillemette said, *'for if he found out he would kill me. He hates the heretics'.*

At the time when the heretics dominated Montaillou, Guillemette 'Benete' and Alazaïs Rives were being deloused in the sun by their daughters Alazaïs Benet and Raymonde Rives … I was passing by and heard them talking. Guillemette 'Benete' was saying to Alazaïs, 'How can people manage to bear the pain when they are burning at the stake?'

To which Alazaïs replied, 'Ignorant creature! God takes the pain upon himself, of course.'

'What sort of men are these goodmen I hear so much about?' …

'They are men like the others! Their flesh, their bones, their shape, their faces are all exactly like those of other men! But they are the only ones to walk in the ways of justice and truth which the Apostles followed. They do not lie. They do not take what belongs to others. Even if they found gold or silver lying in their path, they would not "lift" it unless someone made them a present of it. Salvation is better achieved in the faith of these men called heretics than in any other faith.'[52]

These were the words of the people of the Languedoc village of Montaillou as recorded by the fourteenth-century inquisitors. They were the descendants of the Cathars of southern France whom the Catholic Church under Innocent failed to bring back to the faith or to eradicate by more violent means.

The word Cathar comes from the Greek, meaning pure.[53] Cathars believed that the spiritual world was good and that God was essentially a spirit. The humanity of Christ was, therefore, denied. The actual world, on the

---

52. Le Roy Ladurie *Montaillou* 81, 141, 192.
53. A clear account of their beliefs is given in Runciman *Medieval Manichee* 147–62.

other hand, under an autonomous deity or Satan, head of the fallen angels, was evil. Their belief was in essence dualistic.[54] The Devil had created the terrestrial world out of envy for God's celestial world. Matter, it followed, was evil, and the creation of more matter was to be deplored because it prolonged the existence of the material world. Anything liable to create more matter was to be avoided and, for this reason, marriage was looked upon as evil, but sex was acceptable. Cathars had no belief in hell or in purgatory – hell was in this world – or in the resurrection. The sacraments and teaching of the Church were wrong and useless. The Church, by accepting lands and wealth, had compromised with both the world and the Devil. The ideal believer would be chaste, eat little, and deny him or herself physical pleasure and comfort. This would restrict the growth of matter and free the soul from the body. The Believers (or *Credentes*) were admitted in a ceremony known as the *convenientia* at which they promised to honour and serve the superior group, the Perfect. Extreme asceticism was necessary for those seeking perfection: abstinence from meat and bodily pampering, a diet of a few sparse vegetables, poverty – a hard life of preaching and wandering in which they were dependent on the Believers, whose duty it was to furnish them with food and shelter. The Perfect had received the sacrament of the *consolamentum*, a form of baptism with the laying on of hands. The Believers delayed taking the *consolamentum* until they were old and ill. A novitiate of a year (the *abstinentia*) was normally undertaken before undergoing the ceremony of the *consolamentum*. Handbooks of Cathar ritual describe the giving of the *consolamentum* which combined all the sacraments of the Catholic Church, except marriage. It was conducted by the Senior Perfect. First there was a general confession, the *servitium*, followed by the reception of the Lord's Prayer by the candidate. Next the table was prepared with a Gospel book and the book was handed to the candidate. The catechumen was addressed by name and gave the

54. There were some differences of view among them as to whether Evil would go on to eternity or end with the end of the material world, and as to whether the terrestrial world was all the Devil's work or had been created out of already existing material.

melioramentum, or promise, in which he denied the Catholic faith, renounced the Church of Rome and baptism and also the eating of flesh and eggs, lying and swearing and all luxuries and solitude. The Perfect wore a black costume and underwent three very long fasts in the year. The *endura* was the climax for the Perfect, the supreme test, when he or she starved to death; undertaken by a minority, the *endura* remained the ultimate goal for the Perfect. While the Perfects' main task was to preach and spread the Cathar doctrines, there were also Cathar bishops, who had suffragans, and deacons with administrative functions who acted as local agents, and possibly also deaconesses. In the diocese of Toulouse alone there were about fifty deacons. They recruited support from all ranks in the community – doctors, weavers, clerks, nobles, knights, artisans, men and women. The bishops, too, preached; and stories circulated that there was a black pope, who lived in Bulgaria, where the dualist heresy had originated, probably deriving from the fact that the word for priest in Slav is *pop* (papa).

The dogmatic threat of the Cathar faith lay in the denial of the priesthood, of the sacraments and of Christ as the Son of God. In many cases Cathar rituals were Catholic ones turned upside down. The questions to be asked to discover whether one was in a Cathar house with fellow Cathars are strongly reminiscent of Masonic practices. But the Cathar threat was not so much from the relatively limited number, who had become believers, and from the minority who entered the ranks of the 'Perfect', as from the vast number of sympathizers who were impressed by the example of 'the goodmen' who led lives above suspicion.

Catharism was particularly strong in the east of Europe where it had been born – in Bulgaria, the Balkan peninsula, Bosnia, Slovenia and Dragovista (on the borders of Thrace and Macedonia). The areas most affected in western Europe at the end of the twelfth century were Languedoc, Provence, and some of the great northern French and German trading towns.[55] There were also important Cathar settlements, organized as churches, in Italy, especially in

---

55. In 1143 Cathars were reported in Cologne and Bonn and there were thirty in England in 1165–6 (*Councils and Synods* I ii 920–5).

Lombardy near Milan and round Lake Garda, and two Tuscan churches at Florence and Spoleto. The 'church' of
Spoleto included Viterbo and Orvieto – two so-called papal
towns. Those in Lombardy were split into a radical group
at Desenzano on Lake Garda and milder groups at Mantua
and at Concorezzo near Milan.

Wherever Cathars were, there was an obvious political
threat. Cathars, coming from all walks of life, were in posts
of influence and responsibility in the towns. There were
Cathar 'bishops' in Lombardy at Sorano and at Vicenza,
also in Florence, and some Cathars were even in Rome itself.[56] Those towns within the Papal State that were Cathar
in sympathy were, not surprisingly, dealt with firmly.[57] A
letter of Innocent of 25 June 1198 excluded them from
local government and removed their civil rights.[58] But the
thunderings of the pope merely served to inflame. Cathars
were not even driven underground in Italy, but continued
to flaunt themselves in civic offices. In Orvieto the Cathars
in high posts put their bishop to flight. From Orvieto
Catharism spread to Viterbo. Innocent threatened action
in Viterbo in 1199, but in 1205 two Cathars were elected
consuls of the city and the chamberlain, Timiosi, was a
leading Cathar in the 'church' of Spoleto.[59] In September
1207 the pope went in person and ordered Cathar houses
to be destroyed and their goods confiscated.[60] Fierce papal
action (the same was true with Verona) was quite simply
self-defeating. During the imperial schism heresy gained a
firmer hold throughout Europe because there had been
no emperor to keep it in check.[61] After the Emperor Otto
IV's coronation in 1209, he began to apply the law against
heretics in Ferrara – it was his duty and it suited him to do

---

56. Runciman *Medieval Manichee* 126.
57. See in general Thouzellier *Catharisme* 143–6, 163–9.
58. *Reg. Inn. III* i no. 298.
59. *Reg. Inn. III* ii no. 1, 25 Mar. 1199 Innocent to the Viterbo magis-
    trates; A Dondaine 'La hierarchie cathare' in *Archivum Fratrum
    Praedicatorum* **20** (1950) 302.
60. *Gesta* ch. cxxiii and C Violante 'Hérésies urbaines et hérésies ru-
    rales en Italie du 11e au 13e siècle' in 183 *Hérésies* ed. Le Goff.
61. See e.g. Caesar of Heisterbach *Caesarius Heisterbacensis Monachi ...
    Dialogus Miraculorum* ed. J Strange (Cologne/Bonn/Brussels 1851)
    i 300 (v. 21).

so – but when war broke out against the papacy, imperial action ceased. The towns, as usual in central Italy, seized their chance of playing off rival powers, pope and emperor. The influential cities of Milan, with its Patarene past, and Bologna, the great law town – both on major routes – came out against the papacy. The pope had problems with heretics in central Italy, Lombardy and Sicily, but they were as nothing compared with those confronting him in southern France.

The pope's first actions in dealing with heresy in the Languedoc were pacific ones. He had sent legates, predominantly Cistercians. Because they were at a distance from Rome, they were given large powers. It is unlikely that the pope did not realize that the key to a successful campaign lay as much in the hands of the secular ruler as in the heavy hand of religious persuasion. He must have been encouraged by the return of the Dualist Kulin of Bosnia, and his whole court, to the Catholic Church in 1203, following overtures from the pope. Furthermore, the Kulin promised tribute to the pope and to the king of Hungary if any heretics were discovered on his lands.[62] But in the south of France political ties were complex. The count of Toulouse, the nominal lord of the region, had in fact very little control and was the vassal for territories within the area of no less than four overlords, the kings of France, England and Aragon and the German emperor, all of whom had their own particular interests to serve. The count, too, was suspected of more than sympathy towards the heretics: at any rate he had not been active in dealing with them. In 1204 Innocent wrote to the Cistercian legates in the region of Montpellier suggesting peaceful measures of persuasion and shortly after to King Philip Augustus of France. In 1206 the legate, Raoul of Castelnau, was commissioned to carry out the 'new method' and send suitable people among the heretics who, 'imitating the poverty of Christ', would win them back to the faith. The dual prongs of political action through the overlord, the king of France, and the missionising preachers might well have been successful, but the world political situation made this impossible. Philip Augustus of France was asked to

62. Thouzellier *Catharisme* 159.

intervene by the pope in 1207, but the Midi was only nominally under his lordship and he was taken up with his campaign against King John. Innocent was eager not only to settle the problem of the southern French Church but also to free the political leaders for his proposed eastern crusade.[63] Events now really took over and showed that the papacy was not in control.

. . .

THE ALBIGENSIAN CRUSADE

The murder of the papal legate, Peter of Castelnau, in Toulouse in 1208, following his excommunication of Raymond VI, the count of Toulouse, shocked the curia. It was widely supposed that Raymond was involved: he was certainly blamed for the deed. Philip Augustus permitted his barons to go to suppress the heretics. Lured by the promise of being rewarded with the heretics' lands and titles, plus the bonus of spiritual rewards as this was declared a crusade, many of the minor barons of the region set out to establish themselves. The forces of military conquest were unleashed against the heretics. The sack of Béziers was carried out with untold and mindless ferocity. Massacres took place: the main centres of heresy, Carcassonne, Pamiers, Albi, were captured. According to Caesarius of Heisterbach, the legate, Arnald Amaury, abbot of Cîteaux, encouraged the troops to what was virtually indiscriminate murder, with the cry 'Kill, kill. God will know his own.'[64] Innocent disavowed these actions but he had in fact yielded to the extremists outside the curia and in particular to the legates. While the pope was preaching moderation, his legates were in effect not echoing the words of their master. The legates claimed the title of count of Toulouse for Simon de Montfort, the successful leader of the Crusade, and proposed that he should become the nominal as well as the effective ruler of Languedoc. The question was put on the agenda for the Lateran Council's decision and Count Raymond and his son, the count of Foix, were summoned to Rome.

63. See *PL* 215 ep 76 cols 359, 360B, ep 79 cols 361–2, ep 185 cols 1024–5.
64. *Caesarius* ii 302: refuted, but indicative of the mood.

Innocent wished to leave de Montfort in possession of the old Trencavel dominions but to restore the rest of Languedoc to Raymond VI. He maintained that Simon was entitled to the possessions of proven heretics but not to those of good Catholics. If the Toulouse family were restored to the faith – and Raymond had done penance and submitted to the Church – then surely their lands should not be taken from them. The majority of the Council were for de Montfort and against the count of Toulouse and his son. The Council overcame the pope, and the few bishops who supported him, on this matter.[65] De Montfort was granted all the conquered lands. Raymond was to have a pension of 400 marks per annum and the lands that he had not lost were to be held by the Church for his son. The only winner in the contest appeared to be the king of France, who had a powerful vassal almost destroyed. Was it to substitute Simon de Montfort for Raymond of Toulouse that all this blood had been shed? So it seemed, for it was the political settlement rather than any religious one that had dominated the Council.

Within four years of Innocent's death, the heretics of the south were worshipping freely again. The Massacre of Montségur of 1244 was a repeat performance of the dreadful sack of Béziers. Four of the Perfect left the castle there with the holiest books and treasure of the Cathars to withdraw to the high Pyrenees and their stronghold of So. The Cathars were not vanquished till 1330 and the Albigensian Crusade cannot be regarded as in any sense successful.[66]

How far in this sorry tale can Innocent be blamed for the witch-hunt that led to the beginnings of the inquisition? Jonathan Sumption has pointed out that it was the fanatic Arnald Amaury, the papal legate, who has a better claim to be regarded as the father of the inquisition than

---

65. Guilhem de Tudèle *Chanson de la croisade contre les Albigeois* ed P Meyer (Soc. de l'histoire de France, Paris 1875–9) verses 3150–3665, cited S Kuttner and A Garcia y Garcia 'A new eyewitness account of the Fourth Lateran Council' *Traditio* **20** (1964) 139 n. 47. In general see also 138–43. Among the bishops present were 18 from the south of France and 12 northern bishops who had taken part in the Albigensian Crusade.

66. J R Strayer *The Albigensian Crusade* (New York 1971) i of Preface says it was successful, but this can only be seen as a very short-term success.

the relatively peaceful Dominic.[67] The persecution of the heretics during the darkest years of 1209 to 1211 bore little relation to the later judicial process. Heretics were burned in large numbers on huge funeral pyres, the normal crusading practice following every victory. Penitent and impenitent alike appear to have perished. The demand that the lay arm seek out and punish heretics in accordance with the instructions of the Church was not made until after Innocent's death. It was not until 1227 that the council of Narbonne ordered bishops to appoint 'enquirers' in each parish to report on the doings of their neighbours; and not until 1233 that Pope Gregory IX (the former Cardinal Hugolinus, protector and friend of the Friars) ordered a 'general inquisition' throughout southern France which he entrusted not to the bishops but to the Dominicans. The last Perfect to be burned by the inquisitors at Pamiers was the shepherd, William Bélibaste, from Cubières in the region of Montaillou in 1321.[68] It was ironic that the Dominicans, and to a lesser degree the Franciscans, were to take over not so much the role of the wander-preachers in this respect but of the bishops and of the Cistercians.

. . .

CONCLUSION

Thouzellier sees Innocent's actions against heretics as the continuation of the policy of the Emperor Henry VI for a uniform Christendom, 'le projet impérial'.[69] Innocent's particular achievement, however, in the wider context of the re-establishment of the power of the Church over the new society was that he adapted in a positive way to the new challenges. Le Goff is of the opinion that he was a great pope not because 'he imposed a hypothetical, legalistic feudalism'; but because he saw the value of new possibilities.[70] For Innocent had taken the broader and more humane view of the Church. He had grasped the problems and made it possible for many to return to the

67. Strayer *Albigensian Crusade* 68 and see 226–43.
68. Le Roy Ladurie *Montaillou* 364.
69. Thouzellier *Catharisme* 141.
70. J Le Goff *Birth of Purgatory* trans. A Goldhammer (1984) 210.

Church. There were no compromises on the position of the priesthood, and the laity had perhaps been offered little more than better pastoral care, but the Church had been jolted into a new era, the era of the Friars, the towns and of a popular piety that was closely associated with the friars. Innocent had, indeed, in the words of a later states-man 'brought the new world into existence to redress the balance of the old'. Less edifying is the Church's attempt to eradicate heresy not by argument and example, but by bloodshed and the sword; yet this has to be seen in the context of a warring society. The traditional treatment for heretics, and others who needed to be censured, of exile, confiscation of goods, excommunication and sentences of interdict, which merely served to harden opinion or allowed heresy to get a further hold, were not dispensed with, but at least they had been joined by preaching and reasoning. Authority had been re-imposed with the pa-pacy's insistence on proper, confirmed 'rules' and what might be described as licensing. The issues of popular devotion and personal salvation had been re-addressed. Innocent's greatest contribution was to see the opportunity that the Friars offered within the authoritative framework and in this there seems to have been a certain amount of personal action on his part, though it was left to his succes-sor to formalize and confirm the two Orders.

Chapter 5

THE PAPACY AND THE WIDER WORLD: THE FRONTIERS OF CHRISTENDOM

. . .

JERUSALEM, THE NEAR EAST AND THE CRUSADING IDEA

Innocent III, like many earlier and later popes, spent most of his life in Rome. Born in Gavignano, at school in Rome, apart from his years of study in Paris and a visit to the shrine of St Thomas at Canterbury, he had not been out of Italy. His time as pope was passed at the Lateran or St Peter's or in one of the towns of the Patrimony. Nor as a cardinal had he been sent on a legation of his own, though his talents were such as to suggest that an appointment of this kind would have followed had he not been elected pope in 1198. The legates *a latere* (literally from the side of the pope, i.e. seen as part of his body),[1] were the princes of the Church, the apostolic see's ambassadors or diplomats, representing the medieval world's greatest power, the papacy. These men, resident in the countries to which they were sent, sometimes for quite extensive periods, brought with them the official view of the Roman curia. They also observed (and in some cases absorbed) much of local conditions, regional differences and customs. Their reports to the pope and their instructions, which were carried across Europe and further by messengers over land and sea, show

---

1. Some even spoke of them as from the pope's bowels – the *inviscerati*: see N Zacour 'The cardinals' view of the papacy, 1150–1300' in *Religious Roles of the Papacy: Ideals and Realities, 1150–1300* ed. C Ryan (Pontifical Institute of Mediaeval Studies, Papers in Mediaeval Studies 8: Toronto 1989) 418.

that their power was virtually unlimited. Because of their distance from central command and the necessity at least on occasion for swift action, they were plenipotentiaries in the fullest sense. They had their own households; their powers and splendour approximated perhaps most closely to the viceroys of India during the great days of the British Empire.

Rome lay at the heart of what we may reasonably describe as the pope's empire, but at the heart of the world was Jerusalem. Medieval cartographers placed Jerusalem at the centre of their maps of the world and the Hereford cathedral *Mappa Mundi* is a fine example of this. If Jerusalem was not at the centre of the 'papal' world in fact, nevertheless it held a very central position in the pontiff's mind. The earthly Jerusalem is sometimes described as being in Christ's patrimony of the Holy Land and Christ's patrimony, like that of His vicar, had to be protected and, if necessary, regained. Although papal eyes had long since turned to the West, the significance of the East, of the Eastern Church and of Jerusalem to the Christian world could not be forgotten. The centre of papal power, Rome, might well be to the west of the Mediterranean, but the great patriarchates of Constantinople, Alexandria, Antioch and Jerusalem lay to the east: these and the Eastern Empire did not cease to influence papal policy. Relations with the East were high on any active pope's agenda.

The loss of Jerusalem and the Holy Places to the Infidel had started the great crusading movement and brought about the First Crusade undertaken at the request of Pope Urban II in 1096. The recapture of Jerusalem achieved in 1099 was of tremendous symbolic importance to Christians. In equal measure, its loss later, following the battle of Hattin in 1187, after eighty-eight years of Christian occupation, constituted a supreme catastrophe which reverberated throughout the West.[2] When Jerusalem fell, Innocent was a

---

2. In fact, as P M Holt *The Age of the Crusades. The Near East from the Eleventh Century to 1517* (1986) 61–3 has argued, things could have been worse after Hattin. Relationships between Muslims and Franks were not those of total war and the contraction of the Latin kingdom's frontiers were not of crisis proportions for the Franks still held the ports. There is no doubt, however, that the death of the great Saladin in 1193 raised Christian hopes.

young man at the outset of his career. A papal appeal for a new crusade (the Third) went out immediately the news reached the curia. But Jerusalem was not re-taken. The crusading ideal, however, was far from dead. It was, if anything, re-fired, and Innocent, no doubt imbued with the idea of a crusade from his early youth, was to devote much time and energy to the goal of recovering Jerusalem. He preached more crusades than any other pope and contributed more to the crusading movement than anyone since Pope Urban II. A large part of the pope's correspondence is concerned from the earliest years of the pontificate with the necessity of financing and undertaking a new crusade. Innocent, it has been said, was haunted by the crusading idea. Furthermore, the pope's role, as he saw it, was not merely to summon the crusade but also to lead and it was for this reason that he viewed with some misgivings Frederick II's impetuous taking the cross at Aachen in 1215 without consulting the pope. Innocent was not displeased but he chose to ignore the gesture at that point. While I do not agree with Mayer that 'a crusade was an essential means of realizing his hierarchical ideas', hierarchical ideas formed the basis of Innocent's attitude towards the conduct of a crusade.[3] And there was no doubt that it was to be a papally led enterprise, with Innocent at its head, using Christians of all ranks to spread the Christian message, extend the frontiers of Christendom and, above all, recapture Jerusalem under papal direction.

Second only to the rescue of the Holy Places in importance in the pope's mind was the unity of the Christian Church. It was scandalous that there was division and disunity among Christians themselves.[4] The schism between East and West, between the Greek and the Latin rite, which had tarnished the Church since 1054, did not seem appropriate in a more ecumenical age. Furthermore, it obscured and obfuscated the divisions between Christians and Muslims. The underlying assumption that political conquest means ecclesiastical union, that the conquered follow the religion of the conquerors, explains the policies pursued, although the reality may have been somewhat different.

3.   H E Mayer *The Crusades* trans. J Gillingham 2 edn (Oxford 1988) 217.
4.   *PL* 216 col 818.

There was no doubt of the authority of the pope as a leader of world standing. He represented a majority of Christians and there was no contradiction in medieval eyes between his role as a great religious leader and his role as a political leader, any more than there was a dichotomy between the Church's missionary activities and its crusading movement. While the task of the missionary was to preach and convert, the task of the crusader was to win and protect the Holy Places. These two roles were not seen as opposing, and medieval men did not find it difficult to reconcile fighting with conversion.[5] Missionaries and crusaders were allies in a common task, not opponents.

Innocent initiated and maintained relations not only with the kings of eastern Europe and the northern lands of the Baltic, but also with the religious and political leaders of the eastern Mediterranean. Such contacts depended mainly on legates and on letters. The kings of Armenia and of Georgia were in contact with Rome. The king of Armenia received the banner of St Peter in 1201 and his kingdom became a fief of the Roman Church, the Catholicos promising obedience to Rome. The king of Georgia was approached for help over the Latin kingdom of Jerusalem in 1211. The hierarchy of the Russian Church and the people of Russia were invited to recognize the primacy of Rome in 1206.[6] Missionizing in the Baltic brought the papacy into touch with Prussians, Lithuanians, Livs, Letts and Finns.

Religious leaders, too, were petitioned for aid. The patriarch of Jerusalem was consulted about the making of overtures to the Muslims and Patriarch Aymar apparently suggested that Jerusalem might be obtained by negotiation.[7] A peaceful arrangement on the Holy Land was sought with the Sultan of Damascus and Babylon in 1213. Captives were exchanged, and conditions for those who were not so fortunate were discussed.[8] The Fourth Lateran

5. See E Siberry 'Missionaries and Crusaders, 1095–1274: Opponents or Allies?' in *SCH* **20** (1983) 103–110.

6. J Richard *La papauté et les missions d'orient au moyen âge (xiiie–xive siècles)* Collection de l'Ecole française de Rome xxxiii (Rome 1977) 16 n. 51.

7. In general see Richard *Papauté et missions* 33, 37, 49, 53. The source for the last statement is J Bongars *Gesta Dei per Francos* (Hannover 1611) 1125–9.

8. *PL* 216 cols 509, 831–2, and see 830D.

Council was attended by the main representatives of the Eastern Church: the patriarchs of Jerusalem, Antioch and Constantinople, the patriarch of the Maronites of Lebanon and the representative of the Melkite archbishop of Alexandria.[9] Contact with the Maronites had been established in 1181 and in 1215 the patriarch, Jeremias, received the pallium from Pope Innocent.[10] There were not many areas of the known world where papal messengers were totally unknown and the pope unheard of.

The basis of the papal claim to act as a world power, indeed as a world arbiter, and to pursue a policy of interventionism on all fronts was justified in the case of Christian kingdoms 'by reason of sin'. The decretal letter 'Novit ille' spelt out the pope's power of action in the kingdom of France.[11] He has, he says, the interests of King Philip Augustus and his kingdom at heart and he has no intentions that would be harmful to the French king's jurisdictional powers. But 'No sane man would deny our right to judge and punish any Christian in matters of sin', says the pope. He has 'the duty to point out and punish sin or the blood of those who die in iniquity is on our hands'. The Scriptures are quoted to enforce the point: in particular Jeremiah 1: 10, 'I have set thee this day over the nations, and over the kingdoms, to root up and to pull down, and to waste and to destroy, and to build and to plant'; and Matthew 16: 19, 'Whatsoever thou shalt bind upon earth, it shall be bound also in heaven: and whatsoever thou shalt loose on earth, it shall be loosed also in heaven'. The pope is intervening, not to judge in feudal matters, but in a matter of sin for which he alone has authority. He has the power to judge in cases of broken oaths, imperfectly observed treaties and a breach of the peace and his legate must be obeyed.

Innocent III embraced St Augustine's theory of the 'just war' and accepted canonist development of it. Although he may not have been a pupil of the great canonist, Huguccio,

---

9. Foreville *Latran I, II, III et Latran IV* Histoire des Conciles Oecumeniques 391–5 and James M Powell *Anatomy of a Crusade* (Philadelphia 1986) 27.
10. W de Vries 'Innocenz III. (1198–1216) und der christliche Östen' in *Archivum Historiae Pontificiae* **3** (1965) 88.
11. See above and esp. the decretal letter 'Novit ille', *PL* 215 col 325.

he was an exponent of Huguccio's statement that a church-man, without necessarily having any temporal jurisdiction, had the right to wage war on behalf of the Church. Such a war would be a just war. How much more right then had the pope to correct and, if necessary, call the secular arm to his aid and the aid of Christendom? The pope, indeed, was possibly the only single authority who could proclaim a crusade. While the Church's aim was peace and the pope's traditional role that of a peacemaker, violence might be authorized in pursuit of the greater good. As we have seen in the decree 'Novit', Innocent justified papal interference in the concerns of a secular state. He also declared that violence might be answered by violence and that the Church could order princes to persecute heretics and confiscate their property. It has been argued that Innocent took a more direct control over the Albigensian Crusade because he had been virtually ignored as a voice of consequence when the crusaders in 1204 decided to attack Constantinople. It was, perhaps, easier to justify 'the just war' against heretics than against the infidel. Against the infidel it was rather 'the holy war'. But as only the papacy had the power to grant indulgences for service against both heretics and infidels, it seemed logical to assume that only the pope could declare and wage a crusade.[12]

On the frontiers of Christendom and in 'heathen' lands, the justification was that Christian persons and places should be protected and that Christianity should be spread. Against the infidel, the heathen and the heretic, the pope has powers which may be used to call in the aid of the secular arm to disseminate the faith. After the Gregorian reform canonists did not question that the royal role (both imperial and regal) was to assist the pope in certain cases. By the early thirteenth century it was well understood. Christian emperors and kings might demur about coming to the aid of the papacy in particular instances, but, on the whole, they did not contest the duty. Other reasons certainly made crusading attractive to them and caused them to embark. But the fact that they actually went

12. In general see F H Russell *The Just War in the Middle Ages* (Cambridge 1975) esp. 134–5, 180, 202–3, 294–5.

in answer to the papal summons must have made the principle seem acceptable to the majority of people.

The war *for* ideas emerged as an acceptable Christian concept following Pope Urban II's clarion call for a crusade in 1095. He had the imagination to harness the religious yearnings and latent energy of lay people for involvement in soul-saving activities in the service of a crusade. H. E. J. Cowdrey, however, has pointed out that it was Pope Gregory VII (1073–85) who, some years earlier, had made warfare a meritorious activity for the Christian.[13] Out of this notion the concept of the Christian knight was born. The crusade offered the knight remission of his sins without his having 'to drop out of society' by becoming a man of prayer, a monk. He could in future honourably pursue a military calling. As Guibert of Nogent, chronicler of the First Crusade, explained:

> In our time, God has instituted a holy manner of warfare, so that knights and the common people who, after the ancient manner of paganism, were aforetime immersed in internecine slaughter, have found a new way of winning salvation. They no longer need, as they did formerly, entirely to abandon the world by entering a monastery or by some other like commitment. They can obtain God's grace in their accustomed manner and dress, and by their accustomed way of life.[14]

There was salvation in fighting for the Cross and no apparent contradiction was seen by the authorities in winning remission of sin at the same time as searching for tangible rewards in the shape of lands and goods. Developments in the Church's penitential system made the crusade or the holy war seem one of the surest ways to gain salvation. The crusading vow rivalled the pilgrimage as the most effective means of salvation open to the majority of people. It had lost little of its attraction a century after its birth. To rally to the support of Christ, to stitch the cross on to the

13. H E J Cowdrey 'The Genesis of the Crusades: the springs of Western ideas of Holy War' in *The Holy War* ed. T P Murphy (Columbus, Ohio 1976) 19–20 – a brilliant survey.
14. Quoted Cowdrey 'Genesis of the Crusades' 23.

garment, to set out with scrip and staff – in some cases to combine the two – brought all ages and conditions of men and women, irrespective of class or nationality together in one great enterprise: the Holy War.

In adopting the crusading idea, and immediately declaring a crusade, Innocent III was acting in line with his predecessors. Following the failure of the Third Crusade ('the Crusade of the Kings') in 1192, and with the death of Saladin in the following year, Pope Celestine III published a new crusade appeal. The emperor, Henry VI, perhaps felt an obligation to fulfil his dead father Frederick I's vow. But he died at Messina on 28 September 1197 before he had been able to set out to join the crusaders, who had already re-taken Sidon and Beirut. The crusade, not surprisingly, disintegrated without its leader. A truce was made with the Muslims and most of the crusaders left for home. Celestine III survived but a few months. In August 1198, well before the end of his first year, Pope Innocent had proclaimed a new crusade and himself as leader.[15] Two legates were to go ahead to prepare the way; preachers were commissioned to enlist the faithful; indulgences were granted to crusaders and all was to be ready by the following March. The crusader army was to meet at Brindisi and Messina for a final briefing under the presidency of the pope.[16] The pope's idea of his own personal involvement as leader had a precedent, for Gregory VII had proposed to leave the Emperor Henry IV as protector of the Roman Church during his absence.[17] (Gregory had hoped, too, to worship at the Holy Sepulchre. No pope could fail to be thrilled at that prospect.) The difference, however, was that in 1198 there was no emperor. Pope Gregory had also proposed a military expedition to help Byzantium against the Turks in 1074 and had hoped to reconcile the Roman and Byzantine Churches. Some of this may have been in Innocent's mind. The lack of lay support was his most serious problem and there were delays and difficulties so that it was not until the summer of 1202 that the army began to assemble.

15. *Reg. Inn. III* i no. 336 esp. pp. 502–4.
16. Powell *Crusade* 111.
17. Cowdrey 'Genesis of Crusades' 25.

. . .

THE FOURTH CRUSADE

The Crusade, afterwards known as the Fourth Crusade, was certainly not what the pope had intended. There have been various views as to what went wrong and as to what the real intentions of the leaders of the Crusade were. But the result was an unqualified and dreadful disaster. The Crusade was deflected against fellow Christians, firstly on the Dalmatian coast, and then later against Constantinople, which fell to the crusaders in 1204. It was an ignominious and shameful outcome to what the pope had undoubtedly seen as a great crusading venture to liberate the Holy Places. Christian had fought against Christian and not surprisingly this crusade came to be labelled the 'Unholy' Crusade.

It is important to investigate what exactly had happened. In the autumn of 1201 Alexis, son of the Byzantine Emperor Isaac, who together with his father had been deposed by his uncle Alexis III, arrived in the West, doubtless to raise support for his cause. At Christmas he met with Philip of Swabia, husband of his sister the Byzantine princess Irene Angelus, at Hagenau in Germany. Boniface, marquis of Montferrat, later to become leader of the Crusade, was also present on this occasion, and there is little doubt that the question of installing Alexis on the imperial throne of the Eastern Empire was discussed. It could not but have helped the Staufen cause. The Staufen party needed support against the pope from as wide an area as possible and some historians have seen the diversion as planned by the Staufer. Their position was definitely strengthened by the choice of the pro-Staufen, Boniface of Montferrat, as leader of the Crusade. Neither the king of England nor the king of France nor the rival candidates for the imperial throne, Philip of Swabia and Otto of Brunswick, had as yet taken the cross. The most illustrious recruits were the counts Thibauld of Champagne and Louis of Blois, Count Baldwin of Flanders, Simon de Montfort and Reginald of Montmirail.

Before the diversion was made to Constantinople and plans to continue to the East were abandoned, an attack was made by the newly mobilized forces on Zara (or

Zadar) on the Dalmatian coast. This unwarranted and disgraceful piece of aggression against the Hungarians, their fellow Christians, and against King Imre, a fellow crusader, was discussed in the summer of 1202 at Venice where the crusading army was assembling. Here the doge of Venice undoubtedly made it clear to the crusading leaders that he was prepared to postpone the enforcement of the payment of money owing to him if aid was provided for him to recapture Zara, an important trading post for the Venetians. Rumour of the proposal must have reached Rome for the pope immediately wrote forbidding the attack. Whether Abbot Peter of Lucedio purposely delayed the delivery of the letter or not, we do not know – this has been suggested – but the army had already landed before the pope's letter arrived. It was too late. It is certain that the legate, Peter of Capua, was finding the Venetians difficult to deal with. All he could salvage was that some churchmen should remain with the crusading army, doubtless to give it some semblance of respectability and presumably to prevent excesses. The leader, Boniface of Montferrat, had already left for Rome, and others began to disassociate themselves from the arrangement. It was the Venetians, on whom transport depended, and who were so important to the successful start of any crusading campaign, who were the instigators of this action which augured ill for the next stage.

Zara was taken by the crusading army in November 1202. It was now too late to sail for the East and the crusaders wintered there. Sometime during this period, after they had been re-joined by Boniface of Montferrat, proposals were made by envoys arriving on behalf of Philip of Swabia that on their way to the East the crusaders should restore Alexis and his father to the Byzantine throne. In return for this aid, money would be handed over to the crusaders and they would be provisioned for another year. Furthermore, the patriarchate of Constantinople would be returned to allegiance to the pope and Alexis would join the Crusade. On hearing the news of the attack on Zara, Innocent excommunicated the Venetians, though this was not carried into effect because Boniface of Montferrat feared the dissolution of the army. The crusading fleet was in the vicinity of Constantinople when Innocent re-issued the sentence of excommunication and underlined that there should be no further attacks on fellow Christians. Did he suspect what was to follow?

Some historians have seen both the tragedy of Zara and the attack on Constantinople as accidental, implying that there was no planning or forethought for either action. The failure of a sufficient number of crusaders to arrive at Venice has been seen as the reason for the acceptance of the doge's plan. The capture of Constantinople has been explained as the end of a chapter of accidents with the unforeseeable arrival of the young Alexis in the West and his attractive proposals. Yet the accident theory is surely far too simplistic. The Venetians profited economically from both the capture of Zara – they were stone deaf to all papal orders to restore it to Hungary – and from the acquisition of Crete (in 1211) which followed the fall of Constantinople. So began for Venice a period of some sixty years of very profitable trading and even after Byzantium reconquered Constantinople in 1261 Italian merchants, and especially the Venetians, remained very influential in the eastern Mediterranean. In the second instance the desires of Alexis had been at one with the Venetians.[18]

While the arrival of the dispossessed Alexis in the West may have been accidental in the sense that he was not invited by the Staufer, his presence in Philip of Swabia's entourage, in the household of his sister's husband, must mean that he came primarily for aid. In the spring of 1201 the pope had decided in favour of Otto as the imperial candidate. The Staufen cause was at its lowest in the three years since Philip's election as king. Setton has maintained that the diversion to Constantinople represented a triumph for the Swabians over the pope and A. Carile has suggested collusion between Philip of Swabia and the leader, Boniface of Montferrat, in the revised plan. It certainly suited Staufen interests.

The suggestion that the pope himself initiated or approved the attack on Constantinople in order to restore the primacy to Rome is not borne out by the evidence.

18. See in general for this section, C M Brand 'The Fourth Crusade: some recent publications' in *Medievalia et Humanistica* n.s. **12** (1984) 33–45, and John Godfrey *1204: The Unholy Crusade* (Oxford 1980).

Innocent was not one to refuse to profit from events but that does not mean to say he countenanced the attack. On the contrary, it was condemned in the strongest language. After the second and decisive capture of Constantinople and the overthrow of the recently restored Alexis and his father, Count Baldwin of Flanders was elected as the new emperor, contrary to the expected election of Boniface of Montferrat. Innocent, without I think duplicity, now rejoiced in the possibility of closer ties with Rome, which Baldwin promised, and perhaps in the removal of Philip's allies. The re-union of the Eastern Church with Rome after 1204 was, of course, welcomed by the pope, but he made it quite clear that he would have rejoiced more at the capture of Jerusalem. The pope's joy was extremely short-lived when he heard of the subsequent sack of the city, the murder of fellow Christians and the rape of nuns.

What was clear from this sorry affair was the failure of the pope and the legates to control the Crusade. The legate and the leaders had been unable to contain the rapacity of the Venetians, and the separate and individual motives of some of the leaders, especially Boniface of Montferrat, in allowing the sack of Constantinople, were at odds with the pope's intentions. The Crusade had been diverted from its objectives by the greed of the Venetians with their superior naval force and fleet on which the crusaders depended. Innocent had not emerged as the leader nor was he listened to or consulted. Once the army was raised a multiplicity of interests began to show themselves. Innocent proved no match for the doge. Zara was not returned to Hungary. Excommunications, orders and entreaties were ignored. Nor did the Conquest of Constantinople and the setting up of the Latin empire ease the passage towards Jerusalem. Far from providing forces, money and leadership for the Crusade, the Latin empire became yet another problem for papal negotiators. Innocent can hardly be blamed personally for the failure, but it was an indicator of the weakness of papal power when secular and economic interests conflicted with his views.

Innocent's enthusiasm for a crusade had not died. Indeed it had been re-invigorated and renewed efforts were made throughout Europe to enlist crusaders (especially leaders) and to direct an army to the East. In 1211 a six-year truce had been made between the kingdom of Jerusalem and the Muslims. There would be time to launch a crusade before it expired in 1217 – indeed death came to Innocent as he reached Perugia, preaching the new crusade in the summer of 1216. The following year, 1212, saw Christian armies engaged in war on three fronts: in Spain, repelling the Muslims, in the Baltic, converting the heathen, and in the Languedoc, fighting the Albigenses. It seemed a far cry from the Christian kingdom on earth. Also in 1212 occurred the so-called Children's Crusade.

. . .

THE CHILDREN'S CRUSADE

Something of the fervour and mass hysteria which clever preachers could engender appears in the so-called Children's Crusade of 1212.[19] Research has suggested that the crusaders were not children so much as young persons on the margins of society – persons of no importance.[20] The Children's Crusade reflected the prevalent idea that simplicity and poverty might remedy all the Church's ills. Where the politicians and leaders had failed, simple Christian people might triumph. Mayer has pointed out that the cult of the Holy Innocents begins at this time. It was for this reason that little was done by the authorities to stop the crazy scheme. Both Nicholas, a young person from Cologne, and Stephen, a young French shepherd boy, claimed to have had a vision of Christ. Other 'children' joined the two and they made their way to Paris. From Paris they proceeded up the Rhine. They then crossed the Alps and entered Lombardy. They had come from parts of Europe where poverty movements were active and hence they were perhaps not so conspicuous. The ecclesiastical authorities had little chance of controlling them. Nicholas's group reached Genoa from where they were presumably hoping to sail. Another group is said to have proceeded to the pope in Rome, where they were dispensed from their vows. We do not know of the pope's reaction or involvement,

19. See Mayer *Crusades* 214–16.
20. Peter Raedts 'The Children's Crusade of 1212' in *Journal of Medieval History* **3** (1977) 279–323.

whether he knew or not of their coming, but some sane voice within the curia attempted at least a partial solution. A third party travelled to Marseilles where they are said to have embarked on ships and to have been sold as slaves in North Africa.

Much of the story of the Children's Crusade appears to be legend. It attracted later chroniclers who embroidered its importance because of the emphasis on ordinary, simple and poor people providing the answer to the ineptitude of the rich and the powerful – the kings, counts and knights who led the organized crusades. It was also in 1212 that the young Francis of Assisi decided to go on crusade. His motive was a missionary one and although he was ship-wrecked off the Dalmatian coast, he tried again in 1217 and in 1219. The motivation was linked with preaching and poverty and pursuing a good Christian life (see Chapter 4 above). Whereas the official Crusade (the Fourth), which had had little popular element had failed, the Crusade of the simple people of no importance was perhaps intended as its antidote.

We know nothing of Innocent's reaction. All we do know is that following the failure of the Fourth Crusade he was intent on proclaiming a new crusade to Jerusalem as soon as possible. The preparations indicate that the pope, possibly personally, and certainly the curia, had learnt from previous experience. The accent on the crusade as a means of salvation for the participants, in the preamble of the bull of 1213, which also summoned the Lateran Council, set the crusade in the necessary context. As a preparation for the Crusade, the pope ordered the faithful to take part in monthly processions, prayers were to be said, and after mass, men and women were to prostrate themselves while the antiphon was chanted. A special prayer was to be offered for the release of the 'land consecrated by the blood of Christ'. Priority was to be given to the Fifth Crusade and all crusading indulgences were revoked, except for the inhabitants of the Languedoc. Furthermore, at the Lateran Council on 14 December 1215 proposals concerning the Crusade were agreed that were intended to make things attractive to participants. Property was protected and priests were to enjoy their benefices while absent. Crusaders were to be immune from taxes and usury and their debts were to be frozen. Tournaments were banned for three years and trading in arms with Muslims was prohibited. The indulgence offered was liberal. A tax for three years of a twentieth on all Church income was agreed and peace was decreed in the West for the duration of the Crusade.[21] Longer and better planning is obvious and better financial arrangements were doubtless intended to prevent the situation that had arisen because of dependence on the doge for money. The Fourth Crusade had also failed because of lack of leadership and direction. The Fifth promised better with the taking of the cross by Frederick II, King John of England and King Andrew of Hungary. No pope could be a military leader, a warrior: nor could legates control a military situation. We shall never know what would have happened had Innocent survived to 'lead' a final crusade.

. . .

THE SPANISH RECONQUEST

On the fringes of Europe, crusades against the Muslims in Spain and the heathen in the Baltic had been in progress for some time. In 1189 two fleets of crusaders, bound for the East, had helped King Sancho I of Portugal to take from the Muslims Silves and Alvor, in the south of the Iberian peninsular. Celestine III had encouraged crusades against the Muslims and in 1197 had commuted to service in Spain the vows of Aquitanians who had taken the oath to go to the East. Alfonso VIII of Castile, who had been defeated by Almohad caliph Ya'qub, went on the offensive again in 1210 and in 1211 the pope appealed to the faithful to unite against the Moors.[22] In the following year, 1212, the pope proclaimed a crusade. The army mustered at Toledo, consisting of knights from France, from Léon and from Portugal, and also King Peter of Aragon and King Sancho VII of Navarre. Innocent's letter on their great victory at Las Navas de Tolosa spoke of 'the zeal of the Lord of Hosts' which had brought this about, but the pope was concerned now to direct full attention to the East

21. E Siberry *Criticism of Crusading 1095–1274* (Oxford 1985) 94; in general, J Riley-Smith *The Crusades. A Short History* (1987) is very useful, esp. 120–8.
22. *PL* 216 col 699.

and not to deflect more resources towards the Spanish Reconquest.[23] If the same spiritual benefits were available, however, the interests of Christian Iberians, kings, knights and clergy, were more easily identified with resisting Muslims, who threatened trade, profit and political stability at home, than in Palestine. At the Fourth Lateran Council the Spanish bishops petitioned for full crusading status to be restored to the Reconquest: the attraction of fighting in the East was diminished if salvation could be gained nearer home.

. . .

THE BALTIC CRUSADES

Poland was separated from the Baltic by the pagan Pomeranians and the Prussians. Its king in the early twelfth century, Boleslav III, had as his principal objectives resisting imperial pretensions and extending his frontiers against the heathen – policies which were common to many rulers on the fringe of the empire. To facilitate government he had partitioned Poland into provinces, each with its own prince. Innocent III supported one of these, Prince Conrad of Mazovia, in his conversion of the Prussians. He also found support within the Polish territories from the archbishop of Gniezno in his efforts to introduce ecclesiastical organization and discipline into the country. To maintain the conquests and the Christianization, a military brotherhood was founded and later the Teutonic knights were called in.[24]

The first northern crusade had been against the Baltic Slavs in 1147 to be followed by the crusade which Alexander III authorized against the east Baltic heathen in 1171. The Livonian crusade was inherited from Celestine III. In 1198 the bishop of the Livs was slain and Archbishop Hartwig II of Bremen appointed his nephew, Albert of Buxtehude, in his place. They proceeded between them, and with papal approval, to build up a virtual church–state, directly dependent on Rome, in the area round Riga, following

---

23. Riley-Smith *Crusades* 139–41; *PL* 216 cols 703–4, for the letters; and D W Lomax *The Reconquest of Spain* (1978) chs 5, 6, esp. 116–32.
24. See *The Cambridge Medieval History* ed. J R Tanner, C W Previté-Orton, Z N Brooke (Cambridge 1929) vi 452–6.

Innocent's summons to the Christians of north Germany in October 1199 to come to the defence of the Livonian Church. In 1204 the pope allowed priests who had vowed to go to Jerusalem and laymen who could not go to Jerusalem to serve in the Baltic instead. So began the 'perpetual crusades' of the next forty years which were much like the Scandinavian raids of the ninth century. Every summer there were campaigns. By 1208 the Livs and the Letts were settled and Albert's attention turned to Estonia. Innocent III, for his part, encouraged Valdemar II, king of the Danes, but he was busy with threatened invasion from Russia until 1219. Albert had transferred the see to Riga (1200), fostered the cult of Our Lady of Riga, argued that Livonia was 'Our Lady's dowry' and established a small military order, the Sword Brothers, his 'monastic family' in 1202. The chronicler, Henry of Livonia, a mission-priest writing in the 1220s, recorded that at the Lateran Council in 1215 to which Bishop Albert and the bishop of Estonia had gone:

> The bishop [Albert] reported the troubles, the wars, and the affairs of the Livonian Church to the supreme pontiff and to all the bishops. They all rejoiced together over the conversion of the heathen and likewise over the wars and manifold triumphs of the Christians.
>
> The bishop spoke: 'Holy Father', he said, 'as you have not ceased to cherish the Holy Land of Jerusalem, the country of the Son, with your Holiness' care, so also you ought not [to] abandon Livonia, the land of the Mother, which has hitherto been among the pagans and far from the cares of your consolation and is now again desolate. For the Son loves His Mother and, as He would not care to lose His own land, so too, He would not care to endanger His Mother's land.'
>
> The supreme pontiff replied and said: 'We shall always be careful to help with the paternal solicitude of our zeal the land of the Mother even as the land of the Son.'
>
> When the council was finished, the pope sent them back joyfully, having renewed their authority to preach and to enlist, for the remission of their sins, pilgrims who would go to Livonia with them to secure the new

Church against the assaults of the pagans. Rome makes laws, while Riga irrigates [i.e. baptizes] the nations.[25]

Establishing missions and conversion usually followed military defeat and occupation. The east Baltic was transformed by military conquest in the thirteenth century. It suited the papacy to allow bishops and monks to missionize and convert and to encourage secular leaders to lead missions of conversion which were really nothing short of military campaigns. The Danes had begun to look eastward in 1170 under Valdemar I. Innocent exhorted his son, Valdemar II (1202–41) to follow in the footsteps of his father and 'root out' paganism in the eastern Baltic.[26] Valdemar, however, was taken up with gaining control of the economically more important lands and coast between Lübeck and Gdañsk. It was not until 1216, after Innocent's death, that he turned his attention to the eastern area between Lübeck and Gdañsk. Raids into Finland were encouraged and the pope wrote to Eric X of Norway speaking of Finland as the 'land which your predecessors snatched from the pagans', while encouraging the archbishop of Lund to establish missions to convert the Finns. The military knights had been founded for the purpose of subjugating the heathen so that the missionaries might get to work. Albert's Sword-Brothers, with the Christian Letts, had gone to overcome the Estonians in 1211 in Fellin fort. Atrocities were committed and later the Sword-Brothers had to be suppressed by the Teutonic knights. The papal policy of fostering interventionism in north-east Europe brought Rome enhanced status and also money. It had been made possible under Innocent because of the weak state of the empire and it had the added attraction that it acted against the power of the Hohenstaufer. It also linked up with the struggle for power in the Mediterranean. The pope hoped that the Russians might give up their allegiance to the Eastern Church, though until 1200 the differences between the rites of the Eastern and Western

25. *The Chronicle of Henry of Livonia* trans. J A Brundage (Madison 1961) 152. See Map 3.
26. *PL* 216 col 117.

Churches were not important in north-east Europe. There was intermarriage and Latin missions were allowed in Dvina (Russia).[27]

Crusading had thus come to be employed for purposes other than the re-capture of the Holy Land. It came in fact to be used both for the defence of the boundaries of Christendom and for internal use within Christian countries. A crusade might be called to counteract heretics and also to overthrow a political settlement.[28] The crusade against the heretical Albigensians has been discussed above. In it, military might was brought to bear against the Church's enemies, but with very limited success. Such action posed a moral question. Was it permissible for a religious leader to intervene in the affairs of a state and to wage war within its boundaries? Interference with secular governments was dangerous and tended in the long term to be self-defeating because it was likely to unite people against an outside aggressor. Innocent never feared intervention. Although his acts may seem to be 'worldly', they were determined by a vision of an earthly society that was Christian and under papal leadership. Innocent condemned extreme violence, as in some of the worst excesses in the Albigensian crusade and in the sack of Constantinople, but he was prepared to accept war and bloodshed to counteract heresy and enforce papal domination.

· · ·

SICILY

In 1199, in a letter to the Sicilian people, Innocent declared a crusade against the late Emperor Henry VI's administrator, Markward of Anweiler, who had invaded Sicily and was resisting papal attempts to enforce overlordship. The pope granted to those taking part in this crusade an indulgence equal to that for those who were to set out on his crusade to the East. Markward was described by the pope as 'another Saladin'. He had allied, said the pope, with the Muslims of Sicily and thus he might jeopardize a

---

27. In general see Eric Christiansen *The Northern Crusades. The Baltic and the Catholic Frontier 1100–1525* (1980) esp. 89–127, and Riley-Smith *Crusades* 130–2.
28. Riley-Smith *Crusades* 11–17.

crusade: worse, he might upset any papal settlement of the Sicilian question.[29] The Sicilian question, on the pope's doorstep, with its ramifications for the German empire, clearly threatened the pope's interests. In the *Gesta*, Markward is accused of trying to disinherit Henry VI's heir and the pope's ward, the young Frederick. With the death of Frederick's mother, Constance, the heiress to Sicily, Markward's challenge became more serious than ever to the papacy. While Gauthier de Paléar, the bishop of Troja, and the Sicilian chancellor, stood for the national Sicilian party against both the pope and the empire, Markward on the mainland wanted to make Sicily an imperialist centre under his command.

It has been said that Innocent's strategy was much the same as Alexander III's, but unlike Alexander, Innocent had no allies. The lack of a German emperor meant that the natural opposition to the emperors in the north of Italy, the Lombard towns, were not attracted by an alliance with the papacy. Indeed, quite the contrary. While the imperial election was in dispute they had the chance of bargaining with both imperial candidates and were not interested in the pope's overtures. Nor, since Frederick was the heir to the kingdom of Sicily through his mother, was there an obvious ally in the Sicilian royal house. The pope was forced to act as feudal overlord, employing his own mercenaries in an attempt to curb Markward's aspirations. The full range of papal powers were exercised on all fronts – armies, negotiation, excommunication. But the Regno was an unruly area at any time and Markward, a slippery and treacherous character. Markward seized the abbey of Montecassino and ransomed the abbey before opening negotiations with the pope. It was a dramatic show of power. He then lured the papal legation, consisting of the cardinals, Octavian of Ostia, Guido of St Maria in Trastevere and Hugolinus of St Eustachio, who had been sent to Veroli to meet him, to an unfortified place where he hoped they would not dare to deliver any hostile

---

29. *PL* 214 cols 780–2. See Siberry, *Criticism of Crusading* 175 and E Kennan 'Innocent III and the First Political Crusade: a comment on the limitations of papal power' in *Traditio* **27** (1971) 231–49.

message from the pope. Gauthier de Paléar supported the pope against Markward, but he did not wish to see either the Germans or the Romans triumphant. On Markward's death in 1203, another German, William Capparone, seized the palace of Palermo and the custody of Frederick. The crusade which had been called against Markward had never materialized. The heel of Italy was Innocent's Achilles heel, ever sensitive, rendering the papacy vulnerable. Nothing was achieved by the threatened crusade, but Innocent had been driven to use the crusade to destroy a political enemy and had been forced into a position where he appeared more as a partisan than the overlord of Sicily, the guardian of Frederick and the arbiter of Europe.

. . .

ENGLAND

There is no convincing evidence that the pope sanctioned a crusade against England, but this is the story in one English chronicle, that of Roger of Wendover. Innocent had, however, in his dealings elsewhere provided some fuel for this rumour. King John could not stay excommunicate and obdurate forever, and the next step for the pope to take would logically be to depose the king or to free his subjects from allegiance. Prince Louis of France had been persuaded by his father, the French king, to abandon his proposed joining the Albigensian Crusade, for which he had taken the cross, in favour of invading England. With John's surrender of his kingdoms to the pope, however, in 1213, the French 'crusade' against an excommunicate became an attack on a papal vassal.

Innocent's interests, if they ever had been, were no longer in favour of a crusade against England. On Ash Wednesday 1215 King John took the cross and this provoked Innocent to write a few months later, describing the English baronage in their revolt against their crusading overlord as 'worse than the Saracens [i.e. Muslims]', since 'they are trying to depose a king who, it was particularly hoped, would succour the Holy Land'. The same theme is expressed in a letter to the archbishop of Bourges and his suffragans, where the barons are again described as 'worse than Saracens' for they have 'rebelled treacherously and wickedly against their Lord and Christ's soldier, the king of

England' and 'having taken the Cross, they now seem renegades working to fulfil the pagans' hopes by hindering such a magnificent Crusade'.[30]

. . .

THE GREEK CHURCH

Innocent's dealings with the Greek Church in the Latin Empire of Constantinople demands some attention.[31] After the restoration of Alexis and his father, Isaac, to the Byzantine throne in 1203, the Church of Constantinople came more under the direct influence of Rome as Alexis had promised. The overthrow of the Emperors Comnenus in 1204 and the installation of Baldwin of Flanders as the first Latin emperor brought even closer contact. Although Innocent had opposed the attack on the Greeks (and, indeed, this was never forgiven), he had welcomed the prospect of re-union of the Greek and Latin Churches which had been in a state of schism since 1054. Innocent insisted on the claims of the Holy See and the primacy of Rome. A Latin patriarch, the Venetian Thomas Morosini, was appointed. The patriarch was to request the pallium from the apostolic see 'without which he cannot validly exercise the patriarchal office'. Innocent's aim seems to have been to get obedience to Rome – all else would follow. The prelates of the Greek Church were to take an oath of obedience to the Holy See – in fact few did. Most of them retired to Nicaea or parts of the Byzantine empire outside Latin rule.

Innocent's chance came in 1206 when, after the death of the Greek patriarch, John Camaterus (the Latin patriarch, Morosini, had been quite uncanonically appointed), the moderate party sought union, under the overriding authority of Rome, provided they could have a patriarch who shared their language, customs and traditions. Innocent was not visionary enough, however, to accept this nor the repeated call for a general council, the Greek way of settling disputes. He had once cancelled Morosini's

---

30. *SLI* nos 80 and 87, esp. pp. 208, 226, 227.
31. See in general J Gill 'Innocent III and the Greeks: Aggressor or Apostle?' in *Relations between East and West in the Middle Ages* ed. Derek Baker (Edinburgh 1973) 95–108. I have differed from him on several points. More important, see Steven Runciman *The Eastern Schism* (Oxford 1955) ch vii.

appointment and then re-appointed him. The underlying difficulty was that if there were two patriarchs the Latin patriarch would inevitably be seen as the interloper. The Greeks returned – many had removed themselves to remote parts of the Empire – and elected their own patriarch, and the ruler of Nicaea, Theodore Lascaris, now began to be recognized as the lawful emperor. Innocent sent legates – Benedict, cardinal of St Susanna, and Pelagius, cardinal bishop of Albano – to Constantinople to discuss theological matters with the Greeks, with a view to working towards unity. Doubtless the *filioque* clause, which had been a major element in the split between East and West, was included in the discussion, for the Eastern Church had never accepted the addition to the creed of the words claiming that the Holy Ghost came from the Son as well as from the Father. The papal representatives worked through an interpreter, the Greek abbot of Otranto. Innocent did not interfere with the customs and rites of the Greek Church (and these were confirmed at the Lateran Council in canon 4), but he did decree that new bishops and abbots should be anointed in accordance with the Latin custom and in the Lateran Council he legislated against those Greeks who re-baptize and wash altars on which Latin priests have celebrated.

Innocent could not accept the ancient traditions of the Greek Church. The Greek and Latin Churches were as far apart as they had been before 1204. Conquest had not brought acceptance of a foreign Church and a foreign language. Possibly it was difficult for the pope, after the initial shock of the fall of Constantinople, not to see the hand of God in the conquest – and the choice of a piece of the True Cross, brought out for veneration at the final mass of the Lateran Council, may have symbolized for the pope the union of the two Churches. Though there were other relics of the True Cross in Rome it was this one, a new relic from Constantinople, that was chosen to encourage the projected crusade.[32] It was perhaps not forgotten that a relic of the True Cross had been lost at the ill-fated battle of Hattin in 1187. Latin Constantinople survived until 1261, but it cannot be said that there was religious unity.

32. S Kuttner and A Garcia y Garcia. 'A new eyewitness account of the Fourth Lateran Council' *Traditio* **20** (1964), 165.

. . .

CONCLUSION

After Innocent's death the decline of the old crusading ideal – of the voyage to the Holy Land and of becoming the soldier of Christ for the remission of sins – started to become apparent. Innocent had, perhaps unwittingly, introduced or furthered trends that led to this decline. Pilgrimages were made nearer home to relieve guilt and win the remission of sins. The purpose of the pilgrimage to Jerusalem was frustrated if the Holy Places were in the hands of the Infidel. The crusade to the Holy Land to win back the Holy Places was joined by other crusades at no such distance which had new attractions for the participants. Crusades were now waged within Europe for political purposes and against political settlements. The papacy's political crusades, which originated in Sicily under Innocent, reached their climax in the wars fought against the Emperor Frederick II under Innocent's two successors, Popes Gregory IX and Innocent IV. Not only were crusading wars sanctioned against political enemies but also approved against heretics in predominantly Catholic countries – 'the enemies within'. The Albigensian War weakened the papacy's message. The forces of reaction and alarm prevailed against the voices of reason and persuasion and from 1208 brought civil war to the south of France. Christianity became more and more militant and muscular and associated with armies and war. By the 1220s the idea of a continuing or 'perpetual' crusade was justified as a defensive measure to aid the missions on the frontiers in the Baltic north, where armies and missionizing had always been closely associated. Christians used as papal mercenaries were paid by crusading privileges. Innocent was not the first pope to grant indulgences to crusaders who fought heretics at home equal to those granted to crusaders who fought in the Holy Land. Such concessions had been made by Alexander III in the Third Lateran Council; but it was Innocent who exploited these redemptions which it could be argued led to the brisk trade in pardons of later years. He allowed that a vow to take the cross might be commuted for a money payment. Redemption seemed more and more to be associated with the payment of money. Finally, he was the first pope to tax the Church for crusading purposes. In the beginning the pope asked for a subsidy, following the example of Celestine III, but at the end of 1199 he imposed a clerical income tax of a fortieth. The Lateran Council approved a tax on all church income and so established the right that the pope might tax the clergy. It also made it possible for monarchs to take the cross, levy the tax and then postpone their departure.[33] By the end of the thirteenth century it had brought the papacy into disrepute.

33. On taxation see Siberry *Criticism of Crusading* 126–30, 146, and Riley-Smith *Crusades* 143–5.

FINAL ASSESSMENT

If Innocent III had been simply a secular ruler posterity would probably have accorded him the epithet 'the great'. The papacy after Innocent's pontificate was a force with which lay powers and secular rulers would have to reckon. It was to continue to attempt to direct secular governments, control the emperor and spread Christianity. On the one hand, it could be argued that the immense moral force wielded by the papacy was strengthened by Innocent III; on the other, that it was precisely that moral force that was weakened by an interference in political dealings and in the affairs of Mammon that should have concerned lay rulers only.

The conflict is inherent in the long history of the papacy and the problem is perhaps insoluble. We cannot make an absolute distinction between moral reasoning and practical politics, nor between good and evil. How should we and how can we judge a medieval pope?

During the Second World War, Pope Pius XII tried to act as an arbiter, to maintain a position of neutrality. For this he was mainly condemned by both sides. Negotiations for peace having failed, the Vatican was left as a tiny, separate state within a fascist city of Rome and the fascist Italian state. Dependent on a fascist state for its electricity, gas and water supplies, it might be said without undue cynicism that it had to compromise to some degree to exist at all. It also had to look to the future, both to the future of Christianity and to its future within the Europe that was likely to emerge. It was obsessed with the threat of Russia and, more specifically, with atheistic Communism.

There is a sense in which later events and behaviour may illuminate and help us to understand the past. If Innocent had an obsession it was with the threat from the Staufen emperors if central Europe, Germany, merging over into the Imperial lands and cities of northern Italy, were to be joined with the Sicilian territories to the south of Rome and the island. For this reason his earliest moves were to act as arbiter between the claimants to the imperial throne. Dislike of the Staufer for their aims of imperial aggrandizement convinced the popes that they needed to control the emperor and this Innocent endeavoured to do. In fact Innocent died before the news could reach him that Frederick II had undertaken on 1 July 1216 that after the imperial coronation he would make his young son Henry a ward of the Roman Church, as king of Sicily, and had promised that the two kingdoms should not be united. Innocent also needed a territorial base to control the Romans and the city of Rome. This was a practical consideration. The papacy could not function successfully as a homeless, wandering power at the mercy of some secular ruler. It needed freedom from secular control and power enough to enforce its message.

A power of such immense moral stature as the papacy acts on a different plane from most secular states. In a despatch to the British government during the Second World War the British representative to the Vatican, Sir d'Arcy Osborne, wrote:

Not only is the atmosphere of the Vatican supranational and universal, at any rate to an extent sufficient to affect political judgement and decision, but it is also fourth-dimensional and, so to speak, outside of time. That is to say that the Pope and his advisers do not consider and resolve a problem solely in the light of its temporary and obviously apparent elements. Their approach and survey are by habit and tradition unlimited in space and in time so that, for example, they can regard the Savoy dynasty as an interlude, and the Fascist era as an incident, in the history of Rome and of Italy. They reckon in centuries and plan for eternity and this inevitably renders their policy inscrutable, confusing, and on occasion reprehensible to practical and time-conditioned minds.[1]

For the Vatican, one could well read the Lateran. Not only are we dealing with a long-term institution but one that is steeped in tradition. Pius XII was, perhaps, linked not totally nebulously with the events of seven and a half centuries previously. When the pope justified himself for not condemning Nazi aggression in Poland, he said that he had been reading St Catherine of Siena and knew when it was incumbent on a pope to speak out, but that such action would make matters worse for the Poles.[2] The past cast its shadow. Innocent, too, looked to the past. There is little in his policy that was not traditional. Government meant finding sources for action in the past and re-interpreting them. It was a search of previous authorities for action. Of course, tradition changes, and some of it may be relatively new, but it must be fitted into a background of precedent and justified by appeal to previous texts, especially biblical ones. Government did not demand new ideas. To be acceptable it had to be based on tradition. The sources for Innocent's actions are to be found in the past.

Advisers often push their leaders further than they would otherwise go. The picture we get of Innocent's curia is very imperfect, shadowy; but the old guard among the cardinals continued in positions of authority. There was, however, an immense legal interest (and the law itself had to have roots in the past, to be texts that were re-interpreted). The source of the law, as of government, was transcendental. It came from above – not from the people below. The pope was its mouthpiece. There was an interest in codification and declaration, above all an interest that saw the great university of Bologna approach its apogee, an

---

1. Owen Chadwick *Britain and the Vatican during the Second World War* (Cambridge 1986) 315–16. Harold Macmillan had already remarked '... a sense of timelessness – time means nothing here. Centuries come and go, but this is like living in a sort of fourth dimension. And at the centre of it all, past the papal guards, and the noble guards, and the Monsignori and the bishops and the cardinals and all the show of ages – sits the little saintly man, rather worried, obviously quite selfless and holy – at once a pathetic and a tremendous figure' quoted 302, from *The Blast of War 1939–1945* (1967) 556 and *War Diaries The Mediterranean 1943–1945* (1984) 587.
2. Chadwick *Britain and the Vatican* 111–12.

interest, too, that put the authority of approval firmly in the hands of the pope. The relationship between the canon law and the natural law and between the natural law and the divine law could not be questioned.

Most of Innocent's theories had their sources in the past. The idea of the vicariate of Christ originated with St Bernard. It was used by Pope Adrian IV to describe the pope's powers; it was employed increasingly by Innocent and especially by his chancery. The Petrine commission was thus extended but it had an ancient root. We know of Melchizedek, the king and the priest, from the Bible.

Basic tenets of policy were also to be found in the past. To Gregory I, in the distant past, was due the theory of the *moral* role of the papacy. In the eleventh century to Gregory VII, more than any other pope, belongs an emphasis on active government and interventionism, and to Urban II the First Crusade. With Innocent II there emerges something of the idea of the papal court as the judicial tribunal of Christendom. From Adrian IV's pontificate the pope may have come to see the importance of a territorial base, for Adrian had paid much attention to the Papal State to control relations with the emperor. Finally, there is a debt to Alexander III, who, if not a great jurist himself, presided over a period of unprecedented legal activity and a great council at the Lateran.

All this might have been as nothing, but there is always the imponderable side of politics – chance. And politics is a game of opportunities. With the temporary collapse of imperial authority, Innocent had the chance to attempt to shape the future. There was the opportunity to apply what had been denied before – papal overlordship and papal dominion – and from this stand came the possibility of more active intervention in the separate and emerging kingdoms and over the higher officers of the Church.

Stability and a clear policy is another great advantage in politics. Innocent's reign was the longest of the thirteenth-century popes – eighteen years. This compared favourably with the reign of Alexander III – twenty-two years – which was probably the most significant pontificate of the twelfth century. Innocent left what may be called a 'political' testament, a papacy committed to controlling imperial ambitions, to launching another crusade and to active leadership of Christ's earthly kingdom. The power over the crusade came to the pope through the weakness of the empire. The northern crusades gave the popes the opportunity to contain the Hohenstaufer and also were quite profitable to the papacy. Alexander III had authorized a crusade against the Eastern Baltic heathen in 1171; Innocent concentrated on Livonia. And from its commencement in 1198 papal activities in the Baltic lasted till 1268, Clement IV's pontificate. By the 1220s the idea of a 'perpetual' crusade had come into being.

What then was Innocent's achievement? And what is his place in the long history of the papacy and in the development of the medieval Church? Innocent, like other great historical figures, has suffered from being judged in the light of later events and on different terms from his own. In the nineteenth century historians made judgments in his favour for establishing the Papal State. He became a cult figure for those who believed in the legitimacy of papal temporal power and it is of little surprise that it was Pope Leo XIII (1878–1903) who brought his mortal remains back to the Lateran to rest in an elaborate memorial, balanced in the opposite transept by a monument to himself. Few can doubt the importance of the Papal State to Innocent. A pope from the Campagna knew about feudal lordship, fortified towns and the necessity of controlling routes and was aware of the pope's weakness if he could not control the emperor and the area surrounding Rome (and of course Rome itself). Innocent's policy of *Recuperatio* was to remain important as long as the papacy was a power with secular dimensions.

Innocent, too, in terms of later history, was seen very much as the representative of a 'governmental' party. This can be seen in two ways: first within the Church, in bureaucratizing offices and in the legal system, and secondly outside in relation to the separate kingdoms. Active government of this kind could not take place easily without a settled base. He had gone as far as was possible to provide this in 1216. The problem of the emperorship continued for as long as an emperor existed. For the thirteenth century Innocent had laid down a strategic plan.

Innocent had set the pope above the emperor and the lay answer was some while in coming. Some nationalist historians have therefore seen Innocent as the villain of the piece. He had interfered in the running of kingdoms. In the long term this may have affected the growth of nationalism, but the nation state was not a concept that was meaningful in the thirteenth century.

Above all Innocent had given leadership – on this all historians seem to be agreed – and with that leadership went a certain amount of unity, unity of purpose, and unity of Europe (i.e. Western Christendom). Innocent had shown political leadership. It was for the papacy to direct and lead crusades. It was for the pope to advise and counsel kings, to settle questions of the leadership of states. This had been shown at the Fourth Lateran Council. In many ways the Lateran Council saw the pope at his most powerful, considering the problems of the empire and of the separate kingdoms. It also showed him as the reformer and clarifier. Though most of the work of implementation followed his death, he had in effect provided the basis for Catholic Christian behaviour. He had tidied up the marriage law, prohibited ordeals, outlined the Church's position on the sacraments and particularly confession. Above all he had attempted to revivify the aims of the priesthood.

Any recent analysis of Innocent III's influence would have to take into account the legal aspect of the pontificate. In the chain of events there was nothing sensational here. Official compilations of canons came to triumph over private ones and the papacy therefore came to be seen as the fount of the declaration of what was to be the corpus of the Canon Law. Innocent's successor, Honorius III (1216–27), continued the policy of approving an official collection, but it was Honorius's successor, Gregory IX, who commissioned the second part of the *Corpus Iuris Canonici*, the 'Decretales' of 1234, incorporating many of Innocent's decisions. All of this could have come about without Innocent, but he undoubtedly came to be seen later as an important contributor to legal declaration, to which, of course, the Fourth Lateran Council contributed. In the realm of the law, Innocent played his part, but Gregory IX's activity in ordering codification, the glosses and commentaries of Innocent IV (1243–54) and the Sext or additional book of decrees (to the five of the 'Decretales') of Boniface VIII (1294–1303) could have taken place without him. His emphasis, on the other hand, on the pope's part in making the law and in using this as a tool for the reformation of society is important, as is his activity in the papal court and in the extension of the judge-delegate system. This network of courts reached perhaps its apogee under Innocent IV. Innocent III's court and his personality seem to have impressed contemporaries, the new Solomon, the third Solomon, as they called him. Even allowing for the remark having been made with the tongue in the cheek, there seems to be expressed a favourable acclamation here.

While an interest in politics was perhaps responsible for most of the judgments on Innocent in the early years of the present century, within the last generation the emphasis has been on practical politics and how far triumphal papal intentions could be and actually were carried out.

The modern interest in Innocent, and hence the criteria on which he is most likely to be judged, has been mainly in his pastoral legacy, in the new Church, in the new Orders and to some degree in the crusading idea. As part of interventionism in the reform of the Church, Innocent (or at least his advisers, but probably Innocent personally) must be given the credit of foresight in the approval of the Franciscans. Later popes were left the task of dealing with the constitutions of the Orders – in particular Honorius III and Gregory IX. By 1250 both the Franciscans and Dominicans were well established, entrusted with preaching and collecting for crusades and also with moral reform, taking over from the Cistercians as the most influential religious group both on the papacy itself and in the Christian world at large.

But it is dangerous to look to the future and then go back to seek the sources and origins. Innocent has been charged with introducing the Inquisition. This rests on the activities of Dominic in southern France, but there was no papal approval of the inquisition until Gregory IX's reign, a generation after Innocent. Innocent's record in dealing with heresy was not particularly successful. He has again been stigmatized as the first pope to grant indulgences and to introduce the first direct taxation. But indulgences had been issued by earlier popes and taxation was to be much extended by later popes, and there is no continuous pattern of development from this pontificate onwards. Active policies, in particular crusades, demanded money and this was another massive problem for the papacy. Similarly, the maintenance of administrators, the growing edifice of the 'Roman' curia had to be supported. Innocent attempted to address this problem. Innocent has also been held responsible for introducing the notion that the pope was infallible and could not err.[3] All these charges stem from interpretations made in the light of later events.

In considering Innocent's place in the history of the medieval papacy we have to bear in mind that there was not an inevitable linear or progressive development from pontificate to pontificate. The Papal State was later to be lost – or at least partially reclaimed – and had to be regained. Emperors were to revive and press their rights. The papacy was again to be subject to lay powers and influence and to the intrigues of secular rulers and in 1303 Pope Boniface VIII was to be publicly humiliated by a king of France. Innocent had ruled autocratically, sometimes consulting his cardinals. By the fourteenth century the notion had grown that general councils should control the pope: any pretensions towards papal infallibility were halted if councils could overrule popes. But power did not stay with the councils and in the mid-fifteenth century papal autocracy was re-established. From 1309 to 1376 the papacy was exiled from Rome for the longest period ever during the 'Babylonish Captivity'. Schism, which had been banished from the Church by the thirteenth century, reoccurred in the fourteenth century, and in 1409 two popes were deposed by the Council of Pisa. There was no unhindered development from one pontificate to the next.

Within the Church there has always been conflict between the ascetic and retiring spiritual leader, the contemplative, and the forceful Christian, regulating society towards more acceptable behaviour and attitudes,

---

3. The argument stemmed from Brian Tierney's statement that the doctrine of infallibility was unknown in the Church between 1150 and 1250. David d'Avray claimed to find it with Innocent III, but, in a rejoinder to Tierney, he admitted that Innocent's claim in the text cited was one from which the doctrine *could* develop. See *Catholic Historical Review* **66** (1980) 17–21, 700–1; **67** (1981) 60–4, 275–7.

actively missionizing. The struggle between the spiritual Franciscans and the conventuals, between religious ideal and successful organization, between simple faith and scholarly argument, are all part of the same tension. Had the pope become the successor of the Emperor Constantine, indeed of Caesar, rather than of the apostle Peter? The election of Pope Celestine V, a dazed hermit, to the throne of St Peter, represented the opposite extreme to the active government of a pope such as Innocent III. To Innocent, popes must be magisterial within this world. Their office was to lead and direct and to lead and direct through institutions and the law. Where he elaborated curial thought, it was to place the pope firmly above emperor, kings and bishops as the leader of Europe. 'Just as the moon derives its light from the sun ... so, too, the royal power derives the splendour of its dignity from the pontifical authority'.[4] To form his 'cosmology', Innocent drew on his own experience, on earlier papal thought and on the circle of Peter the Chanter at Paris.[5] With far-reaching effects, he followed previous papal initiatives and exploited the opportunities that arose to command the leadership of Europe between 1198 and 1216. Innocent had succeeded at least temporarily in liberating the papacy from the empire and in controlling kings.

4. *PL* 214 col 377.
5. The particularly apt description is Kenneth Pennington's.

APPENDIX: CHRONOLOGY OF INNOCENT III'S PONTIFICATE

1160 or 1161	Innocent born Lothar dei Conti, probably at Gavignano near Segni, Italy. Educated at school in Rome; Paris before mid-1187; Bologna (?)1187–9
1187	Made papal subdeacon
1189	Created cardinal deacon of SS. Sergio and Bacco by his uncle, Pope Clement III. Writes 'De Contemptu Mundi'
1197	September. Emperor Henry VI dies; his heir Frederick aged 2 years and nine months
1198	January. Pope Celestine III dies. ELECTION of Lothar dei Conti of Segni as POPE INNOCENT III February. Enthronement as POPE INNOCENT III March 8. Philip of Swabia, brother of Henry VI (from the Hohenstaufen family) elected king of Germany June 8. Otto of Brunswick, youngest son of Henry the Lion (a Welf), elected as king of Germany DISPUTE for CROWN OF GERMANY and IMPERIAL TITLE begins July 12. Archbishop of Cologne anoints and crowns Otto in Cologne September 8. Archbishop of Tarentaise anoints and crowns Philip in Mainz November 27. Empress Constance, mother of Frederick, dies
1199	April 6. King Richard I of England dies. Accession of King John

1200	'Proposita' of the Humiliati
	Christmastide. SECRET CONSISTORY of POPE AND CARDINALS to decide the Imperial Schism
1201	March. Pope decides in favour of OTTO
	May. King Philip Augustus of France takes back Ingeborg of Denmark as his lawful wife
	June. Papal bull for the HUMILIATI
	August. Pope legitimizes children of Philip Augustus and Agnes of Meran
1202	FOURTH CRUSADE commences
1203	August (?). Pope falls ill; rumours of his death
1204	CONSTANTINOPLE taken by Christian crusaders
	King Peter of ARAGON becomes a papal vassal
1205	Pope threatens excommunication and deposition of Archbishop Adolf of Cologne for changing sides in the imperial dispute
	Count Palatine and other princes desert Otto's cause
	July. Archbishop Hubert Walter of Canterbury dies
1205–6	Disputed CANTERBURY election
1207	June 17. Pope consecrates Stephen Langton as archbishop of Canterbury after election in the papal curia
1207–8	PEACE NEGOTIATIONS between STAUFER AND WELFS arranged by pope
1208	January. Murder of papal legate in Toulouse
	ALBIGENSIAN CRUSADE against heretics in southern France begins
	March 23. Papal INTERDICT pronounced on ENGLAND; bishops leave
	June 21. MURDER of PHILIP OF SWABIA
1209	January 12. King John excommunicated
	March 22. DECLARATION OF SPEYER. Otto recognizes right of pope over Sicily
	October 4. CORONATION OF OTTO (IV) as EMPEROR at ROME
1210	Pope verbally approves Francis of Assisi's Rule for the Friars Minor
	Otto invades SICILY.
	November 18. Otto excommunicated by the pope

	December 28. Pope publishes official law collection addressed to Masters and Scholars of BOLOGNA
1212	Children's Crusade
	July. Battle of Las Navas de Tolosa: frontiers of Christian kingdoms extended against Muslims in southern Spain
1213	April 19. Summons of General Council of Church for November 1215
	May 13. King John becomes VASSAL OF THE POPE and holds ENGLAND as a PAPAL FIEF
	July. GOLDEN BULL OF EGER
1214	Battle of BOUVINES. King Philip Augustus of France defeats King John and the Emperor Otto IV
1215	November 11. Meeting of the General COUNCIL at the Lateran (known as the FOURTH LATERAN COUNCIL)
1216	July 16. INNOCENT dies at Perugia

GENERAL BIBLIOGRAPHY

Commensurate with Innocent's influence over Europe, there is an immense bibliography in every European language for the pontificate. I have tried to keep this book based, so far as is possible, on original sources, most of them not translated from the Latin. In compiling this general bibliography I have had to be highly selective. Readers should note that the place of publication is London unless otherwise stated.

. . .

CHAPTER 1

Helena Tillmann, *Pope Innocent III* originally published in German (Göttingen 1954) now translated by W Sax (Amsterdam 1980); I S Robinson *The Papacy 1073–1198. Continuity and Innovation* (Cambridge 1990) for some of the background; W Ullmann *A Short History of the Papacy in the Middle Ages* (1972; 1974); W Ullmann *The Growth of Papal Government in the Middle Ages* (1955); W Ullmann *A History of Political Thought: the Middle Ages* (1965); M Maccarone 'Innocenzo III prima del pontificato' in *Archivio della Deputazione Romana* **66** (1943); M Maccarone *Studi su Innocenzo III* (Padua 1972); K Pennington 'The legal education of Pope Innocent III' in *Bulletin of Medieval Canon Law* **4** (1974); W Imkamp *Das Kirchenbild Innocenz' III (1198–1216)* (Stuttgart 1983); W Maleczek *Papst und Kardinalskolleg von 1191 bis 1216. Die Kardinäle unter Coelestin. und Innocenz III.* (Publikationen des Historischen Instituts beim Österreichischen Akademie der Wissenschaften, Vienna 1984); R Krautheimer *Rome, Profile of a City, 312–1308* (Princeton 1980); F Gregorovius *History of the City of Rome* *in the Middle Ages* trans. A Hamilton esp. V pt 1 (1897); R Brentano *Rome before Avignon. A Social History of Thirteenth Century Rome* (1991); *Master Gregorius: the Marvels of Rome* ed. and trans. John Osborne (Toronto 1987); Jonathan Sumption *Pilgrimage* (1975); R W Southern *Western Society and the Church in the Middle Ages* (Pelican history of the Church 2, 1970); *The Religious Roles of the Papacy: Ideals and Realities, 1150–1300* ed. Christoper Ryan (Toronto 1989) esp. ch. 1: K Froehlich 'St Peter, papal primacy, and the exegetical tradition, 1150–1300'; K Pennington *Pope and Bishops: the Papal Monarchy in the Twelfth and Thirteenth Centuries* (Philadelphia 1984); C Morris *The Papal Monarchy* (Oxford 1989); J A Watt 'The theory of papal monarchy in the thirteenth century' *Traditio* **20** (1964); B Tierney 'The continuity of papal political theory in the thirteenth century. Some methodological considerations' *Mediaeval Studies* **27** (1965).

. . .

CHAPTER 2

H Fuhrmann *Germany in the High Middle Ages c.1050–1200* trans. T Reuter (Cambridge 1986); O Hageneder 'Zur Entstehung des Thronstreitregisters Papst Innocenz' III und dessen Eingreifen in den deutschen Thronstreit' in *Römische Kurie. Kirchliche Finanzen. Vatikanisches Archiv. Studien zu Ehren von Hermann Hoberg* ed. E Gatz (Miscellanea Historiae Pontificiae 45, Rome 1979) 275–80; F Kempf *Papsttum und Kaisertum bei Innocenz. III* (Rome 1954); T F X Noble *The Republic of St Peter. The Birth of the Papal State 680–825* (Philadelphia 1984); P Toubert *Les structures du Latium médiévale ... du ixe à la fin du xiie siècle* 2 vols (Rome 1973); D Waley *The Papal State in the Thirteenth Century* (1961); P Partner *The Lands of St Peter* (1972); M Laufs *Politik und Recht bei Innocenz. III* (Cologne 1980); Robert L Benson *The Bishop-Elect* (Princeton 1968); John W Baldwin *The Government of Philip Augustus* (Berkeley 1986); W E Lunt *Papal Revenues in the Middle Ages* 2 vols (New York 1934); T C van Cleve *The Emperor Frederick II of Hohenstaufen* (Oxford 1972); K J Leyser 'The Emperor Frederick II' – a review of van Cleve in *The Listener* 16 August 1973 reprinted in *Medieval Germany and its Neighbours 900–1250* (1982) 269–76; J R Sweeney 'Innocent III, Hungary and the Bulgarian

Coronation: a study in medieval papal diplomacy' *Church History* **42** (1973) 320–34; J C Moore 'Count Baldwin IX of Flanders, Philip Augustus, and the papal power' *Speculum* **37** (1962) 79–89.

. . .

CHAPTER 3

S Kuttner 'The Revival of Jurisprudence' in *Renaissance and Renewal in the Twelfth Century* ed. R L Benson and G Constable (Oxford paperback 1985) 299–323 and K W Nörr 'Institutional Foundations of the New Jurisprudence' in *Renaissance and Renewal in the Twelfth Century* 324–38; *The Cambridge History of Medieval Political Thought c. 350–c.1450* ed. J H Burns (Cambridge 1988); Fourth Lateran Council decrees in *English Historical Documents* vol 3 1189–1327 ed. H Rothwell (1975); R Foreville *Latran I, II, III et Latran IV* Histoire des Conciles Oecumeniques vi (Paris 1965); S Kuttner and A Garcia y Garcia 'A new eyewitness account of the Fourth Lateran Council' *Traditio* **20** (1964); Christopher Brooke *The Medieval Idea of Marriage* (Oxford 1989); E Rathbone 'Roman Law in the Anglo-Norman Realm', *Studia Gratiana* **11** (1967) 255–71; S Kuttner and E Rathbone 'Anglo-Norman Canonists of the Twelfth Century', *Traditio* **7** (1949–51) 279–358.

. . .

CHAPTER 4

Sophie Menache *The Vox Dei. Communication in the Middle Ages* (Oxford 1990); E Delaruelle 'Dévotion populaire et hérésie au môyen âge', and C Thouzellier 'Tradition et résurgence dans l'hérésie médiévale' in *Hérésies et sociétés dans l'Europe pré-industrielle 11e–18e siècles* ed. Jacques Le Goff (Paris 1968); C Violante 'La pauvrété dans les hérésies du xie siècle en occident' in *Etudes sur l'histoire de la pauvrété* ed. Michel Mollat (Paris 1974) 347–69; C Thouzellier 'Hérésie et pauvrété à la fin du xiie et au début du xiiie siècle' also in *Etudes sur l'histoire de la pauvrété* 371–88; C Thouzellier *Catharisme et Valdéisme en Languedoc* (Louvain/Paris 1969); R I Moore *The Origins of European Dissent* (London 1977); B Bolton 'Innocent III's treatment of the *Humiliati*' *Studies in Church History* **8** (1971) 73–82; B Bolton 'Sources for the early history of the *Humiliati*' *Studies in Church History* **11**

(1975) 125–33; Diana M Webb 'The pope and the cities: anti-clericalism and heresy in Innocent III's Italy' *Studies in Church History:* Subsidia **9** (1991); R Brooke 'Recent work on St Francis of Assisi' *Analecta Bollandiana* **100** (1982); A Dondaine 'La hierarchie cathare' *Archivum Fratrum Praedicatorum* **20** (1950); Steven Runciman *The Medieval Manichee* (Cambridge 1955); J R Strayer *The Albigensian Crusade* (New York 1971).

. . .

CHAPTER 5

J Riley-Smith *The Crusades A Short History* (London 1987); H E Mayer *The Crusades* trans. J Gillingham 2nd edn (Oxford 1988); J Richard *La papauté et les missions d'orient au moyen âge (xiiie–xive siècles)* Collection de l'Ecole française de Rome xxxiii (Rome 1977); E Siberry *Criticism of Crusading 1095–1274* (Oxford 1985); H E J Cowdrey in *The Holy War* ed. Thomas P Murphy (Columbus, Ohio 1976); E Siberry 'Missionaries and crusaders, 1095–1274: opponents or allies?' in *Studies in Church History* **20** (1983) 103–110; Eric Christiansen *The Northern Crusades. The Baltic and the Catholic Frontier 1100–1525* (1980); D W Lomax *The Reconquest of Spain* (1978); E Kennan 'Innocent III and the first political crusade' *Traditio* **27** (1971); C R Cheney *Pope Innocent III and England* (Päpste und Papsttum 9, Stuttgart 1976); John Godfrey *1204: The Unholy Crusade* (Oxford 1980); C M Brand 'The Fourth crusade: some recent interpretations' *Medievalia et Humanistica* n.s. **12** (1984) 33–45; Peter Raedts 'The Children's Crusade of 1212' *Journal of Medieval History* **3** (1977) 279–323; Jonathan Sumption *The Albigensian Crusade* (1978); J M Powell *Anatomy of a Crusade 1213–21* (Philadelphia 1986); S Runciman *The Eastern Schism* (Oxford 1955).

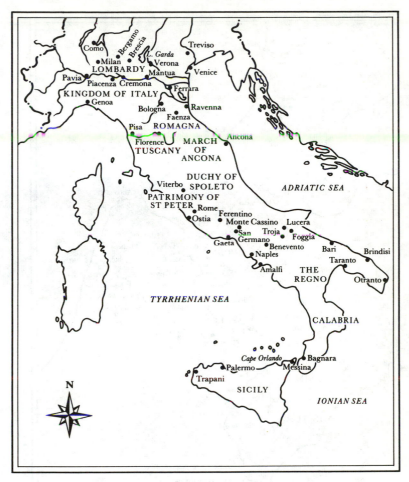

Map 1: Italy

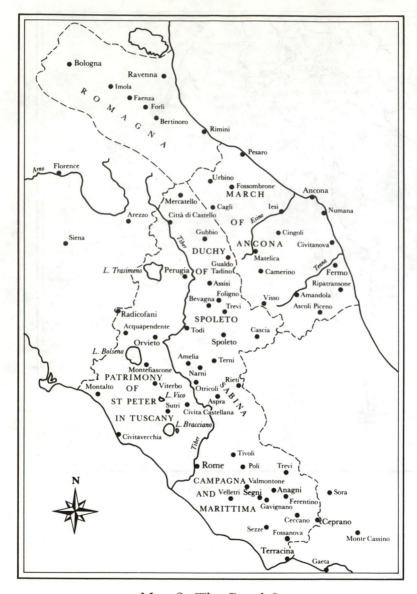

Map 2: The Papal State

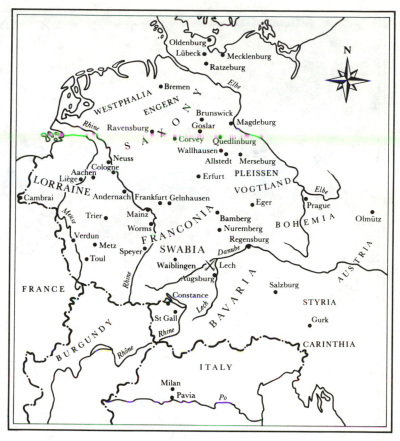

Map 3: Germany

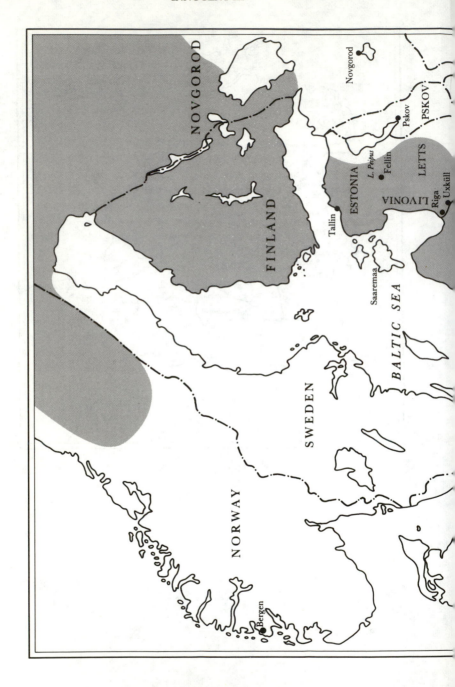

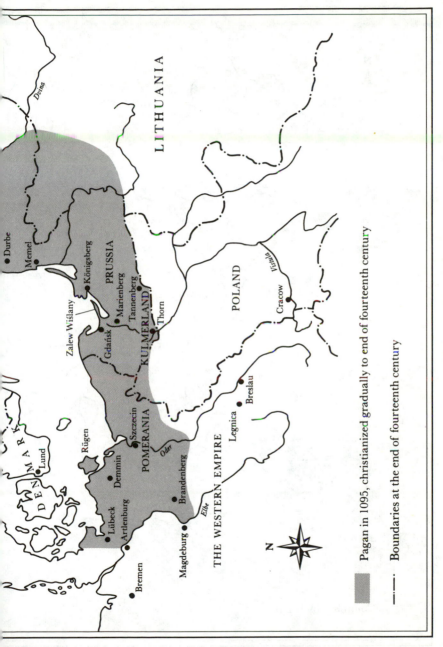

Map 4: The Baltic region

Pagan in 1095, christianized gradually to end of fourteenth century

Boundaries at the end of fourteenth century

Map 5: Europe and the Near East

INDEX

The following abbreviations have been used: abp = archbishop; bp = bishop; cdnl, bp, pst, dcn = cardinal, bishop, priest, deacon; *Comp.* = *Compilatio;* ct = count; emp. = emperor; k. = king; patr. = patriarch, patriarchate; qu. = queen